The Swing Book

DEGEN PENER

The Swing Book

Foreword by **Scotty Morris**

Little, Brown and Company ► Boston, New York, London

First Edition

Book design by Lisa Diercks
Drawings by Jason Schneider
Step chart on page 74 by Mary Reilly

Library of Congress Cataloging-in-Publication Data
Pener, Degen.
   The swing book / Degen Pener ; foreword by Scotty Morris.
      p. cm.
   Includes bibliographical references.
   ISBN 0-316-69802-4
      1. Big band music — History and criticism. 2. Swing (Music) — History
   and criticism. I. Title.
ML3518.P46 1999
781.65'421 — dc21   99-042126

10 9 8 7 6 5 4 3 2 1

MV-NY

Printed in the United States of America

To the memory of my own Louis,
my grandfather Herman Louis Dammerman,
and for Richard Anderson

CONTENTS

FOREWORD

W hat do I love about swing? I love the music, the history, and the legacy the legends have left for us to learn from. It's romantic, it's powerful, and no other music I know of can move so many people. The bottom line is that it's American music and it's our heritage. It's not hype or a fashion statement, it's jazz music. It's as much Satchmo, Duke, and Krupa as it is Dizzy, Bird, and Miles, and all I know is that when it's done right, IT SWINGS.

With the rebirth of, or newfound interest in, swing music, you have a new batch of lions trying to make their mark on this music. I know my influences range from the aforementioned, but also everything since, from the Beatles to Black Flag. In my opinion, no great musical experience repeats itself, it moves on. It's about the music and the moment. Everything else is secondary.

What's exciting about this moment right now is that all types of people are being turned on to this music. Bands like us, and a handful of others, did it the old-fashioned way, by building a nationwide following from the grassroots level. We decided we would go out and win over every person, one at a time. We put on high-energy shows and toured relentlessly: the fans, they appreciate that. They also know these bands aren't a bunch of prefabbed groups that have been put together by some entertainment company creating the next best thing.

Because the music is connected to dancing, each city has its own interesting scene. I love to watch the dancers from night to night wherever we go; they are incredible. In some cities swing has just gotten going and it's wild, there's so much new uninhibited energy. In cities that have been doing it for a while, you see some of the best, most intense dancing anywhere. That is one thing that this music has brought back. Couples are dancing together and actually working off each other again. It's been over twenty-five years since people have gotten together like this.

I also like to see that people are now dressing up for these events. Women are wearing beautiful dresses, and guys are taking pride in what they are wearing. It's very romantic, and it's all just a part of the show. If you come to dance, you'll be swinging to some of the best live music that's out there today. If you come to be entertained, it's one hundred percent. Watch the dancers and they will blow your mind. Watch the band and you'll be tapping your toes and singing along for a week.

When Big Bad Voodoo Daddy emerged almost a decade ago, people didn't know what to think of us. All they knew was they were having a great time and the music was exciting and fun. Well, not much has changed since then, and in the next couple of years the new bands are going to prove what they are really made of. I think people will fall in love with this music more now than ever before.

— SCOTTY MORRIS, lead singer, songwriter, and founder of Big Bad Voodoo Daddy

The Swing Book

*A*t a remarkable event held on May 26, 1999, thousands of dancers, musicians, and lovers of all things swing gathered at New York's Roseland Ballroom to celebrate the birthday of a living legend. On that night, Frankie Manning — the original choreographer of the most famous and thrilling troupe of swing dancers of all time, Whitey's Lindy Hoppers — turned eighty-five years old. Friends and strangers from around the world partnered up and hopped and spun to the music of the veteran Count Basie Orchestra and the neoswing George Gee Orchestra. Brilliant zoot suits, sharp fedoras, classy rayon dresses, and sweet gardenias dotted the crowd. From teenage Lindy Hoppers to longtime fans such as Bette Midler, they all came to fete Manning, the man who invented the Lindy Hop's outrageous air steps all the way back in the thirties. The dancer who blew away the room night after night at Harlem's famous Savoy Ballroom. And an entertainer who once traveled the world turning people on to the Lindy. Manning — whose dance card was filled that night (eighty-five women danced with him, one for every year of his life) — seemed more vibrant and alive than many people half his age as he soft-shoed the night away. For a few magical hours, it felt as though the swing era had never ended.

Of course, it had. After most of the big bands disbanded in the late forties and partner dancing later fell by the wayside, Manning's career faded too. For thirty years he worked at the post office in New York. But Manning, like swing, was merely dormant. In the 1980s and 1990s, dancers and musicians discovered swing all over again. People from Sweden to London and from New York to California, caught up in an inexplicable wave of synchronicity, began learning how to dance the Lindy as it was done back at the Savoy. Musicians started reviving the sounds of Louis Jordan, Louis Prima, and Basie. And these new swing lovers tracked down Manning and gave him a beautiful gift: a second career as a dancer. Now he travels nonstop once again, teaching the Lindy Hop, inspiring crowds wherever he goes, and living and breathing the music that keeps him so young.

Today, whether it's a party as grand as Manning's birthday do or a dance at the local club, swing nights are back everywhere. Classes at dance studios are filled beyond capacity. Longing for a dash of glamour in their lives, people are dressing up in the timeless looks of the forties. Guys and dolls are touching each other on the dance floor. Most important, swing music is once again what it was created for: songs to dance to and not just listen to.

This book is meant as an introduction to the world of swing and its incredible rebirth. Inside you'll discover how the music and dance originally came to be and who the people were that brought it back. You'll learn all about the Lindy, from its moves to what makes it so much fun. You'll meet the singers and musicians, both old and new, who swing the smoothest, croon the sweetest, and even rock the hardest, plus find out what each artist's best albums are. There's an extensive guide to shopping for the most stylin' fashions of the thirties and forties. Finally, there's a city-by-city listing of the top dance spots, the best dance instructors, and the most up-to-date on-line events calendars across the country and even abroad. Whether you've always loved this music and dance but felt you didn't quite fit in or you're finding out about swing for the first time, you'll find that there are now hundreds of places to enjoy it and meet like-minded fans, from Singapore to Dayton and from Saskatchewan to Dallas.

While writing this book, the question I was constantly asked was why did swing come back? The answer is quite simple. Swing ended prematurely. The peak years of the original era lasted from 1935 to 1945, just ten years. As a friend of mine, musician Michael Kroll, observed recently, there have been so many musical movements in the twentieth century, and we've moved on so quickly from one to another, that not all of them have been completely explored. "Did swing really have its full chance to expand upon itself before rock 'n' roll took it somewhere else? Maybe it just wasn't finished," says Max Young, co-owner of San Francisco's Hi-Ball Lounge. After years of being considered old-fashioned, even schmaltzy, swing has been rescued from the nostalgia dustbin. "It's about affirming what has come before," says Rob Gibson, executive director of Jazz at Lincoln Center. "We're saying that was good, let's build on that."

With the swing revival, the music and the dance that have been called America's most important contributions to the world are taking their proper place in our culture. We are owning our heritage. In the process, we are also discovering that the real roots of swing are as fresh and compelling and full of life as ever, and that the music and dance can grow and inspire new artistic creation. "The question isn't why did it come back. The anomaly is that it ever went away," says Bill Elliott, founder of the neoswing Bill Elliott Orchestra. But that's the beauty of swing. It's always capable of swinging back.

CHAPTER 1

The Golden Era of Swing

*T*rying to define the term *swing* is as difficult as attempting to do an air step at your first dance class. Even the great Louis Armstrong was silent on the subject. "They asked him, 'What is swing?' and he thought for a while and said, 'If you don't know, don't mess with it,'" recalls jazz legend Lionel Hampton, who first played with Armstrong back in 1930. Another swing innovator, Benny Goodman, the so-called King of Swing, admitted that describing the music left him just as flummoxed. Swing, he once said, "is as difficult to explain as the Mona Lisa's smile or the nutty hats women wear — but just as stimulating. It remains something you take 5,000 words to explain then leaves you wondering what it is." Now, more than fifty years after the movement first started, swing is more of a muddled concept than ever. Does swing equal jazz? Is swing the same as big band music? Is swing exclusively a dance music? And is there any such thing as pure swing? Contrary to many people's assumptions, the most accurate answer to each of those questions is no.

In true technical terms, swing isn't a particular type of music at all. It's a way of playing music, the manner in which a beat moves, something you can hear and feel and, best of all, do. As bandleader Artie Shaw has said, "Swing is a verb, not an adjective. . . . All jazz music swings. It has to. If it doesn't swing, it's nothing." Unlike the finality expressed in a pounding rock beat, each pulse of truly swinging music contains in it an open, joyous space of possibility, even if the song is a hard-luck blues tune. "Jazz or swing — it's all the same as long as it has that beat," Ella Fitzgerald once said. "Just about any kind of music can swing," says Johnny Coppola, a trumpeter once in the bands of swingers Charlie Barnet, Woody Herman, and Stan Kenton. "A good marching band can swing. Bach played right can swing."

FACING PAGE: *The marquee of the elegant Savoy Ballroom, also known as the "Home of Happy Feet."* (ARCHIVE PHOTOS)

Now let's swing this all up a bit. Swing, of course, is hardly just a musical concept. It was also a sweeping, complex movement that enchanted and entertained America during two of the country's periods of greatest trial, the Depression and World War II. Looked at historically, swing *was* jazz music played by big bands primarily for dancing. At its peak in the late thirties, it was a readily identifiable kind of music, with such glorious standards as Count Basie's "One O'Clock Jump," Duke Ellington's "Take the 'A' Train," and Goodman's "Sing, Sing, Sing" coming as close as possible to a pure concept of swing. It was at once some of the hottest, most amazing jazz ever created and also the first and only form of jazz to be embraced by a mass audience. At the heart of it was the close relationship between the music and the dancing. This wasn't music played in a concert hall to be passively appreciated. Every night, from coast to coast, thousands of deliriously transported couples swung and jitterbugged and swayed the evening away.

The phenomenon of swing took on deeper meanings as well. Swing was as important for its cultural resonance as it was for its musical achievement. In a time of brutal racism, swing was a model, if never perfect in practice, of harmony and equality between black and white musicians. To some observers, it was the melting pot in action; to others, it was America's singular contribution to world culture. While it soared to artistic heights, it also remained profoundly populist. The average Jack and Jill felt included in its expansive energy. The Lindy Hop, the dance that went hand in partner's hand with the music, was proclaimed an American folk dance. A product of the New Deal years, it was even seen as a model of the pluralistic democratic ideas of the decade. When America went to war, the already strong symbolism of swing became magnified; it came to be seen as representative of the best things the country had to offer. For the boys overseas, it was a major force in defining what they were fighting for.

So how did a bunch of three-minute songs end up with so much cultural weight attached to them? To find out, you need to start all the way at the beginning. The roots of swing go back to the very birth of jazz.

STIRRING THE POT IN NEW ORLEANS

Although early innovator Jelly Roll Morton once claimed to have created jazz, no one person can take credit for inventing this music. But one city, New Orleans, does deserve that distinction. During the 1800s, this overheated city on the Mississippi was by all accounts a sort of mosh pit of cultures, from French and Spanish to African and Caribbean to English and Irish. And in the midst of this modern-day Babel, the city's black population began to forge a new language that would unite two great musical traditions. At the time, the sounds of Africa and of Europe couldn't have seemed more antithetical. But the child of the two — at first a bastard in the eyes of white America, but later, during the swing era, a favorite son — would grow up to be many times the sum of its parts.

According to Ted Gioia's insightful *History of Jazz*, African music, though itself varied, is built on a number of shared characteristics, all of which would shape jazz and in turn swing. These include call-and-response patterns, in which a leader sings or plays a line and is answered back by the group; the playing of instruments in a style that resembles the sound of human voices; emphasis on improvisation; and most important, an astonishing array of complex rhythm patterns that were often layered one on top of another. To this mix were added strong European elements. Blacks in America began composing and writing down music that had only been played by ear. They began fitting their music into the Western form of the short popular song and taking inspiration from the rich melodic heritage of Europe.

How these two forms of music actually came together in

nineteenth-century New Orleans isn't documented. There are no written and certainly no recorded examples of their creations. What is known is that New Orleans, unlike the rest of America, took a much more tolerant attitude toward African music. In most other places, it wasn't allowed to be played at all, but in pre–Civil War New Orleans slaves regularly held dances in the city's Congo Square. These were "an actual transfer of totally African ritual," writes Gioia, "to the native soil of the New World."

When Congo Square met Giuseppe Verdi (New Orleans had the first opera house in America), the results were potent. As Lionel Hampton concludes, "The plantation bosses would bring musicians over to perform from England and France, and the slaves would listen to what they played from outside the window. They changed it from the opera. When you hear a famous song like 'High Society,' it's a good copy of *Rigoletto*. Black workers heard these songs and they were putting it in swing time. And it came from the plantations up through the streets of New Orleans to the cafés of New Orleans."

By the turn of the century, jazz — even if it wasn't yet called jazz — had coalesced into a distinct sound in the Big Easy. Inventing outside of musical academies, the small New Orleans combos celebrated freedom of expression and spontaneous creativity. Taking a cue from the new and closely related music of ragtime, the rhythm of jazz became "ragged" or syncopated, giving emphasis to beats that were not traditionally stressed. Even the way that such early jazz musicians as Buddy Bolden, Kid Ory, King Oliver, Nick LaRocca, and Jelly Roll Morton played their instruments was original. They put an emotionalism and edge into the very sound of the notes themselves. Classical European musicians had generally attempted to produce the purest tones possible with their instruments. Instead, as musician Richard Hadlock remembered, New Orleans clarinetist and sax giant Sidney Bechet exhorted him to play one note in as many ways as he could. Bechet, according to Hadlock, told him to "growl it, smear it, flat it, sharp it, do anything you want to it. That's how you express your feelings in this music. It's like talking."

In turn, jazz inspired people to sing differently. Like instruments, voices also began to sound more like they were talking. Instead of vocalizing right on the beat, singers got hep to the new rhythmic devices of jazz and started to play around with how they phrased lyrics.

And then there was the blues. Developing around the same time as jazz and reaching an early popular peak in the twenties with such singers as Ma Rainey and Bessie Smith, this powerful music exerted an immeasurable influence on jazz. Named for the music's blue notes, which don't fit into the more precise European conceptions of do-re-mi, the blues contributed its wonderfully nuanced tone and distinctive attitude of strength in the face of adversity to jazz. Meanwhile, jazz provided a new avenue for the blues, working it into more complex and up-tempo arrangements. These myriad influences and developments first came to national attention after 1917, when the Original Dixieland Jazz Band, a group of white musicians, made the first jazz recording. They were soon followed by influential records from the King Oliver Creole Jazz Band, which introduced the man who would effect a cataclysmic change in jazz, **Louis Armstrong**. (For more detailed biographical information on Armstrong and other major jazz artists whose names are in bold print, see chapter 4.)

THE SOLO STEPS FORWARD

Before Armstrong, the New Orleans bands were small groups that sought to hone a collective sound. As Ted Gioia writes, "The New Orleans pioneers created a music in which the group was primary, in which each instrument was expected to play a certain role, not assert its independence." But as anyone who's ever heard Armstrong knows, keeping a lid on this individual would have been impossible. With his hugely resonant warm voice, clarion trumpet calls, and larger-than-life personality, Armstrong was poised to dominate the American musical landscape as perhaps the most important singer and musician of the twentieth century.

While he was never a major bandleader, Armstrong deserves to be called the true father of swing music. After leaving New Orleans for Chicago in 1922 — his journey was part of a great migration of musicians and blacks in general who left the South for better job opportunities in the North — Armstrong began to assert a new role for jazz musicians. On a series of legendary recordings begun in 1925 with groups known as the Hot Fives and Hot Sevens, he overthrew the ensemble ethos of New Orleans by blowing and improvising the hottest solos ever. These records, considered the most historically significant in jazz, show Armstrong at his most wildly inventive. On such songs as "Potato Head Blues" and "Wild Man Blues" he broke free of jazz conventions, letting loose a panoply of new melodies and rhythmic ideas. But his genius wasn't only at creating breathtakingly elaborate riffs. There was logic and strength and structure behind his every flight. On one song, "Heebie Jeebies," recorded in 1926, Armstrong scats for the first time on record, giving to voice the same improvisational space enjoyed by a musical instrument.

None of this is to say that Armstrong was the only one making the solo supreme. Such jazz greats as cornetist Bix Biederbecke, clarinetists Frank Teschemacher and Pee Wee Russell, and trombonist Jack Teagarden were also working magic in Chicago at the same time. But Armstrong's influence on swing would prove the most decisive. Every solo you'll ever hear, on anything from Benny Goodman to Count Basie to Louis Jordan, owes a debt to the man that music writer Albert Murray has called the Prometheus of jazz.

Once the solo had come into its own, all that needed to happen was for it to find a home. The final step in the birth of swing was the creation of the big band.

THE BIGGER, BETTER BAND

Fletcher Henderson, the man credited with putting together the first swing big band, got his first gig in 1923 at a spot in New York called the Club Alabam, and within a year he had hired Armstrong. While the New Orleans trumpeter wasn't a favorite of Henderson's, Armstrong and his already magnificent solo skills had a profound effect on others in the band, most notably saxophonist **Coleman Hawkins** (who would turn the then-lowly sax into a star player) and arranger Don Redman. Where Redman excelled was in adapting the call-and-response of jazz to a full orchestra. He would set entire sections against each other, a regiment of reeds giving a shout-out and a platoon of brass answering back. The band music became richer, denser, and more textured, a sea of sound that was no mere backdrop for the new hot solo. Redman, living in New York, was also attuned to the popular music of the Big Apple, bringing in more influences from Broadway and Tin Pan Alley than had previously been present in jazz. (However, it should be noted that recent scholarship is challenging Henderson's primacy in this area. Richard Sudhalter in his 1999 book *Lost Chords: White Musicians and Their Contributions to Jazz 1915–1945* argues that the Henderson band was only one of a number of bands effecting these changes during the twenties. White bands such as those of Jean Goldkette, which included Bix Biederbecke as a soloist, and Ben Pollack, which had Benny Goodman, were evolving in similar ways.)

Whoever deserves the most honor, one thing is clear: the melding of the improvised solo with the richly orchestrated dance band was the key to making swing happen. And not only did the sound surpass anything that had come before it but also the new swing bands began to be seen as a representation of the country's political ideals. Hot soloists within big bands: here was an artistic model for individual freedom of expression within the context of a larger group. As Goodman once said, swing "has the spirit of American democracy in it."

THE SWING OF HARLEM

While this late-twenties jazz sounded like what we now recognize as swing, it still wasn't called swing. It was jazz, plain and simple. In fact, the swing era itself had yet to be ushered in. During the early thirties, before swing reached its mass mainstream level, it flourished in smaller pockets around the country while the so-called sweeter and less musically challenging bands like those of Guy Lombardo and Wayne King were tops nationwide. Important bands keeping the flame of hot jazz alive included the **Earl Hines** Orchestra in Chicago; the **Casa Loma Orchestra,** a collective of white musicians that built a following on college campuses; and Kansas City's Bennie Moten band (Count Basie's early home), which recorded the seminal tune "Moten Swing" in 1932.

But the hardest-swinging jazz bands were concentrated in one place above all others. Harlem at this time was a hothouse of creative activity and musical one-upmanship. **Chick Webb** held court at the Savoy, where he first introduced **Ella Fitzgerald** to the world as a professional singer. His competition included the outrageous **Cab Calloway** and the powerful ensembles of **Jimmie Lunceford** and McKinney's Cotton Pickers, featuring the arrangements of Don Redman. In tandem with the intellectual and literary movement known as the Harlem Renaissance, jazz in Harlem was evolving fast and furiously. This was where the showy piano playing known as Harlem stride had flowered in the early twenties, with innovators such as James P. Johnson and the larger-than-life **Fats Waller** creating a bridge from the more jagged ragtime piano into the more fluid keyboard style of swing. It was a place of rent parties (music shindigs held near the end of the month to help pay the rent), all-night cutting contests (in which musicians would go at it for hours trying to top each other), and the achievement of a new level of sophistication both in the music and in the presentation of jazz.

No one put jazz in a tuxedo, both literally and figuratively, quite like **Duke Ellington**. Urbane, brilliant, the poet laureate of

Duke Ellington mixes it up with Lionel Hampton. (ARCHIVE PHOTOS/
METRONOME)

swing, Ellington rose to prominence after securing a long-term
gig at the segregated Cotton Club in 1927. "Black people entertained at the Cotton Club, but you could not go into the Cotton
Club. It was in the heart of Harlem and we couldn't go in," says
Lindy Hop pioneer Norma Miller. At the club, however, Ellington
was one part of an amazing floor show, complete with tap dancing, burlesque-style dancing (one move was called the Harlem
River Quiver), and vaudeville numbers. Ellington's exotic music
—known as "jungle music" at the time—fit perfectly into the
high-energy environment. But in addition to honing his skills as
a great entertainer, Ellington was also creating some of his most
enduring classics, songs like "Creole Love Call," "Black and Tan
Fantasy," "Mood Indigo," "Sophisticated Lady," "Solitude," and "In
a Sentimental Mood," which reached the soul through new and

unexpected ways. In these early days, Ellington began creating jazz that could be appreciated as high art. Oh, and he also created a little number during this period called "It Don't Mean a Thing (If It Ain't Got That Swing)." The movement never had an anthem that said it so well.

THE BIRTH OF THE LINDY HOP

In addition to the Cotton Club, Harlem in the early thirties was literally crawling with raging night spots. There was the Apollo, with its hard-fought amateur contests; Minton's, an after-hours joint; and Connie's Inn, where Waller first staged his famous *Hot Chocolates* show featuring the song "Ain't Misbehavin'." But no place compared to the one and only Savoy Ballroom. What was said of New York City was doubly true at the Savoy: If you could make it there, you could make it anywhere.

Opened on March 12, 1926, and situated just a block from the Cotton Club, the Savoy will go down in history for making the Lindy Hop the most famous, cherished, wildest, and enjoyable dance in America. Those who were there at the time still get deliriously misty remembering it. What was the Savoy like? Enormous and elegant, it took up an entire city block on Lenox Avenue between 140th and 141st Streets in Harlem. There were two bandstands set up, so when the house band took a break, a visiting orchestra was ready to start blowing—that way the dancing never let up. Decorated in gold and blue with multicolored spotlights, it had an enormous 50-by-250-foot hardwood dance floor that had to be replaced every three years because of sheer wear and tear. Significantly, it was also perhaps the first integrated dance hall in the country. "The Savoy was practically half white and half black," recalls premier Savoy Lindy Hopper Frankie Manning. "The only thing they wanted to do at the Savoy was dance. They didn't care what color you were, all they wanted to know was, 'Can you dance?'"

The Lindy, of course, wasn't discovered at the Savoy. It was danced throughout Harlem in the twenties and soon began spreading around the country—despite overwrought concerns that the dance was too sexual. But fueled by the sounds of the Savoy's fast and furious Chick Webb band, the dancers there engaged in all-out competitions that pushed the Lindy to ever greater heights of creativity and energy. The dance developed out of several other popular dances, such as the Charleston, the two-step, and the Texas Tommy. The Lindy's innovation, however, was the swingout, or breakaway, in which dance partners would temporarily drop arm contact and create their own moves. The breakaway gave the dancers as much room to improvise as the musicians now had. No other previous dance had provided such space for personal expression. And early Lindy fanatics at the Savoy took the new style and ran with it. Led by such dancers as Shorty George Snowden, Big Bea, Leroy "Stretch" Jones, Little Bea, and George "Twistmouth" Ganaway, they began both refining and pushing the limits of the Lindy. The five-foot two-inch Snowden invented a bent-knee, low-to-the-ground move that became so famous that Count Basie immortalized it in the song "Shorty George." Jones created the twist steps for followers as the alternative to the Lindy's back step. And the dance began to take on its characteristic African-American style. Loose in the legs and knees, the Lindy Hoppers flowed across the floor with an unstoppable horizontal momentum.

It was also at the Savoy that the dance was christened, in fittingly improvised fashion. Not long after Charles Lindbergh completed his inspiring solo flight across the Atlantic in 1927—making the once formidable distance seem just a hop over the ocean in the popular imagination—a reporter at the ballroom asked Snowden what he was doing. Not having a name for the dance yet, Snowden made one up, dubbing it "the Lindy Hop." One reason the name stuck was that a new generation of dancers was on the rise. This younger group, soon to be dubbed Whitey's

Lindy Hoppers, would take their brand of Lindy out of the Savoy and around the world.

The youngsters, who took over as the club's premier dancers in the early thirties, drew their inspiration, and a fair share of moves, from the older innovators. "We copied what we saw them do," recalls Norma Miller, who started her dancing career at the Savoy. Miller was one of a group, reaching eighty people at its peak, who were scouted, hand-picked, and pushed to excel by Herbert White, known as Whitey for the streak in his hair. A former bouncer at the Savoy, White started choosing the best dancers he saw on the floor — the pros congregated in a part of the club called the Cat's Corner — and forming them into a troupe. Today the names of these swing-dance pioneers — Frankie Manning, Willamae and Billy Ricker, Naomi Wallace, Leon James, Al Minns, and Norma Miller, among others — are repeated from dancer to dancer with awed reverence. But back then, Whitey's Lindy Hoppers were just a bunch of kids out to make their names, have a ball, and simply see what they had in 'em. "Those were the beginning days of the Lindy Hop, everything that was created was new. There were no rules. We made it up. The only rule was: If it looks good, do it. If it don't, throw it out," says Manning. (For the story of Manning's rediscovery by swing revivalists, see chapter 2.)

Back in the thirties, Manning was the chief choreographer of the group, and the smoothest cat at the Savoy. "When he's just standing still, Frankie is swinging. He doesn't have to do one thing with his muscles and you know he's feeling it," says jazz singer Ann Hampton Callaway, star of the new musical *The Original Broadway Swing*. But Frankie's contribution involved much more than just standing around. He was the first to choreograph ensemble Lindy numbers. And sometime around 1936 he made his lasting mark on the dance, creating the aerial, the move that turned the Lindy Hop into a showstopper. Never before had anyone thought to throw his partner in the air, twirl her around, and catch her again. And on top of that do it all in time to the music as a true dance step. "The idea came to me because of a famous step that Shorty Snowden and his partner Big Bea used to do," recalls Manning. "Now, she was six feet tall and she would take Shorty on her back and walk off the stage, and it always tore the house up. So I got the idea that I wanted to make a step out of it, not just a lift. I went to my partner Frieda Washington and told her. And she said, 'I ain't picking you up on my back. Forget that!' And I said, 'That's not what I want. What I want to do is pick you up on my back, and not just for you to lay there, but to roll over and come down in front of me. We'll do it to the music.' Just picture this: something you've never seen, you don't know how to do, your partner doesn't know how to do it either. She said, 'Yeah, OK.'"

With Manning leading the way, Whitey's Lindy Hoppers brought the dance and their wildly distinctive way of doing it to an ever expanding and thoroughly wowed public. White, according to Norma Miller, "wanted to be the man to make the Lindy Hop a famous and accepted art form." The first step on the road to the Lindy's greatness began in 1935 when White entered his dancers in New York's first annual Harvest Moon Championship, a city-wide competition that put the Lindy side by side with such traditional dances as the fox trot, rhumba, waltz, and tango. "It was the biggest dance contest ever held in America and of course it was important to us," wrote Miller in her memoir, *Swingin' at the Savoy*. "It was the first time the Lindy Hop was in a dance competition. It was the only black entry in the contest and we were very proud of that." The Savoy dancers took first, second, and third prizes in the Lindy section. "When we got up on the dance floor, we kicked ass and it became such a popular dance it couldn't be denied," recalled Miller. From there, Whitey's troupe traveled around the world, touring Europe and South America, performing at the New York World's Fair and on Broadway, at the Cotton Club and the Moulin Rouge. They even met the queen of England. Most important, they were in movies, an important record of the dance that would live to inspire a new generation of dancers in the eighties and nineties. Even to this day, people say that the troupe's performance in the film *Hellzapoppin'* has never been topped.

In 1943 the Lindy was honored by its own cover story in *Life* magazine, which called it "a true national folk dance." But if Frankie Manning, Norma Miller, and the rest of Whitey's Lindy Hoppers had ever been given the full acknowledgment they deserve for helping make that happen, they'd be as famous today as Fred Astaire and Ginger Rogers. Unfortunately, at the spot where the Savoy once stood (it closed in 1958), there's not even a plaque mentioning the wellspring of dancing genius that was unleashed there.

THE ARRIVAL OF THE SWING ERA

While you wouldn't know it from all the activity in Harlem in the early thirties, jazz enthusiasts at the time were terribly worried that the music was in decline. With the Depression gripping the nation, record sales fell from precrash totals of 104 million a year to just 6 million 78s sold in 1932. According to David Erenberg's incisive *Swingin' the Dream,* sales of record players plummeted 90 percent after 1929. The cash-strapped public also began to feel that the music itself was perhaps too decadent during such a period of nationwide want. As one critic wrote at the time, "The public was in no mood for the reckless promptings of jazz." In late 1934 Fletcher Henderson went bankrupt. Saxophonist Sidney Bechet opened a dry-cleaning establishment to help ride out the dry spell. It was sweet crooners like Bing Crosby who ruled the airwaves.

As the country's economic prospects began to rise under the policies of the New Deal, though, the stage was set for swing's breakthrough into the mainstream of America. And the man who would bring it to mass popularity was **Benny Goodman**.

In some ways, Goodman was an unlikely man for the role. He

wasn't a showman. He looked like a square. As portrayed in *The Benny Goodman Story* by Steve Allen, he was always fumbling for words. But even before his rise to fame, Goodman played the clarinet with a passionate excitement and clear brightness that marked him as a one-of-a-kind talent. Born to a poor Jewish family in Chicago, and developing an early love of jazz, Goodman toured with the prominent Ben Pollack band during the late 1920s. But despite some early success after moving to New York, by 1933 he was reduced to one low-paying radio gig. According to Erenberg, Goodman no longer saw a "future for jazz and contemplated forming a society orchestra." What drew Goodman back to playing real jazz? Credit the influence of his good friend and supporter John Hammond, an Upper East Side political leftist who was the most influential behind-the-scenes man in swing. In addition to promoting the careers of **Count Basie, Billie Holiday,** saxophonist **Benny Carter,** and **Lionel Hampton,** among others, Hammond pushed Goodman to work with black musicians and singers, a step that helped reinvigorate the clarinetist. Beginning in 1933 Goodman recorded with Bessie Smith (it was her last studio session), Holiday (it was her first), and pianist Teddy Wilson, who would soon join Goodman's path-breaking trio, the first high-profile integrated group in jazz. Said Goodman singer **Helen Ward** of these early years: "They were playing a brand of music nobody else had attempted with a white band at that time."

Goodman's break came when he was hired in 1934 to be one of three house bands on the NBC Saturday-night radio show *Let's Dance.* The steady paycheck allowed him to purchase scores of hot arrangements by Fletcher Henderson; the show exposed him to a nationwide audience. While the radio program was heard late at night on the East Coast, listeners in California heard Goodman's band swinging like crazy during peak evening hours. But Goodman himself wasn't aware of this and, in fact, didn't see his fortunes improving much. *Let's Dance* was canceled after just one season. Goodman then set out on a national tour

Benny Goodman and drummer Gene Krupa get their licks in. (CORBIS-
BETTMANN)

that was at first nowhere near a smash. At a gig in Michigan, only
thirty people showed up. In Denver the manager of the local ballroom threatened to cancel their contract after the first night.

When the Benny Goodman Orchestra arrived in California,

however, it was a different story. On August 21, 1935, Goodman and his exemplary sidemen, including drummer **Gene Krupa** and trumpeter Bunny Berrigan, wrote the book on overnight success. Opening at the Palomar Ballroom in Los Angeles, the band started by playing its safer, sweet material. When that failed to excite the crowd, Goodman decided, as he later wrote in his autobiography, *The Kingdom of Swing,* "The hell with it, if we're going to sink we may as well go down swinging." The band pulled out its most charged Harlem-style arrangements and let themselves go, improvising and blowing with a passion. The dancers, many of whom had been turned on to hotter swing music by listening to the *Let's Dance* show, went wild beyond expectation. (Californians would later be the ones responsible for reviving swing too — see the next chapter.) The next day, the engagement at the Palomar was the talk of the music world. The entertainment paper *Variety* soon began a column titled "Swing Stuff." And Goodman started calling his orchestra a swing band. At the tender age of twenty-six, Goodman could rightfully lay claim to the title the King of Swing.

THE GLORY DAYS

Goodman's triumph in California was the catalyst for a revolution in music and dance in America. During the late thirties, hundreds of new swing bands formed all across the country. In response to the demand, at least five of Goodman's own sidemen — Krupa, Berrigan, Wilson, Lionel Hampton, and **Harry James** — were able to go out and start their own orchestras. Established bands such as those led by **Jimmy** and **Tommy Dorsey,** Jimmie Lunceford, and **Charlie Barnet** rode the groundswell of enthusiasm, while Bing's brother **Bob Crosby; Woody Herman,** with his hit song "Woodchopper's Ball"; and **Artie Shaw,** with "Begin the Beguine," became household names. Swing fans eagerly awaited each issue of *Downbeat* and *Metronome* magazines to see how their favorite band rated in the latest readers poll, or which star soloist had been snatched up by another band. As pianist Ralph Burns put it, "If you were a jazz musician playing with Woody Herman, you were almost like a movie star." Ellington, as quoted in David W. Stowe's *Swing Changes,* noticed a huge increase in attention from fans. "Audiences, today, invariably crowd around the bandstand, eager to grasp every solo note and orchestral trick." Enormous new ballrooms were constructed across the country—breathtaking dance palaces like the Hollywood Palladium that could hold thousands of couples. The bandleaders even had the gumption to start a practice known as swinging the classics. Tommy Dorsey jazzed up Rimsky-Korsakov's "Song of India," while Maxine Sullivan had a hit with a tweaked version of the Scottish folk tune "Loch Lomond." Opponents argued that Ravel, Strauss, Mozart, and Debussy were rolling in their graves from receiving similar treatment.

Swing was boffo business. According to Stowe, the recording industry, which had grossed just $2.5 million in 1932, was hauling in $36 million by 1939. Bands fought for lucrative hotel contracts, a slice of the exploding jukebox market, the attention of bookers who controlled national tours, and commercially sponsored radio programs. The relatively new radio business, in fact, was one of the most important factors in promoting swing. Fans would listen to live recordings from such famous ballrooms as the Pennsylvania Hotel in New York and the Meadowbrook Club in New Jersey. Even Hollywood fell hard for swing, producing scores of movies featuring bandleaders (see "Swing on Film" in the appendix for a list of great swing flicks). How popular was swing? One Saturday in March 1937, the Goodman orchestra played at 8:30 A.M. before the showing of a movie at the Paramount Theater in New York. According to awestruck accounts, hundreds of kids showed up before sunrise to wait in line. Three thousand swingers in all turned out, many of them jumping out of their seats and dancing in the aisles during the performance. Suddenly jazz was being played everywhere, from the big city to the small town, all under the guise of a new name, swing. As blues popularizer W. C. Handy, writer of "St. Louis Blues," once said: "Swing is the latest term for ragtime, jazz, and blues. You white folks just have a new word for our old-fashioned hot music."

More than just popular music, swing became an entire lifestyle. Indeed, it was considered the first real youth culture in American entertainment, the beginning of a series of musical uprisings that would continue from rock in the fifties through grunge in the nineties. "It was like when the Beatles came along. The kids were listening to what they considered their music and theirs alone," says trumpeter Tommy Smith, who played with bandleader Ray Anthony. Swing had its own slang, popularized by Calloway in his *Hepster's Dictionary,* and its own styles of dress—just think of the bobby-soxers and zoot-suiters. (For more on swing's fashion and lingo, see chapter 6.) What really propelled swing, however, was jitterbugging, the new name that the Lindy Hop acquired as it was embraced by an increasing number of white dancers. Back in the thirties, the jitterbug could scare the establishment just as much as Elvis's pelvis did two decades later. Newspaper accounts used words such as *frenzy, pandemonium,* and *ecstasy* to describe the phenomenon. And one psychologist ominously warned of the "dangerously hypnotic influence of swing, cunningly devised to a tempo faster than seventy-two bars to the minute—faster than the human pulse." In 1938 the swing era even had its own Woodstock, a swing jamboree in Chicago featuring Jimmy Dorsey and Earl Hines that drew 100,000 fans. It was described by the *Chicago Daily Times* as "the most hysterical orgy of joyous emotions by multitudes ever witnessed on the American continent." But let the observers make their pronouncements. For the dancers themselves, there was an unparalleled connection being made between themselves and their fave bands. "Really, as a musician you did it as much for the dancing as you did for the music," said Count Basie singer **Joe Williams** in

Norma Miller's *Swingin' at the Savoy.* "All of that was together at one time, it was one great communication . . . ; the dancers inspired the musicians and vice versa."

Swing also began to be taken much more seriously as an art form. In the twenties Paul Whiteman, the leader of one of the most popular dance bands, attempted to put jazz on the same level as European classical music, labeling his endeavor "symphonic jazz." Yet even in the thirties, jazz still was considered a more lowly form of music. "In those days people thought if you were playing jazz, you were stepping down," Artie Shaw told writer Fred Hall in *Dialogues in Swing.* But the pioneers of swing demanded to be accepted on their own terms. And the pinnacle of this push occurred on January 16, 1938, when Goodman's orchestra made a landmark appearance at Carnegie Hall. On that historic night, tension was high. The band members were a bit overawed by the grand symphony space and got off to a tepid start. But soon they began to play in the same way they would let loose in the most informal dance hall. Drummer Gene Krupa beat the drums like a dervish, his hair flying, sweat dripping. Members of the Count Basie and Duke Ellington orchestras made guest appearances. And Goodman's integrated quartet played the most well-received numbers of the night, with Lionel Hampton's rhythmic masterpieces on the vibraphones thrilling the crowd. By the time the band went into its closing number, "Sing, Sing, Sing," the crowd was crying out and applauding in a state of near delirium. It was an epochal success. "Carnegie Hall was always known as the holy of the holiest," recalls Hampton. "No jazz had ever come near there."

That concert was only the first half of what was easily the most magical night ever witnessed in swing. As soon as the Carnegie Hall show ended, members of the Goodman band raced uptown to Harlem to catch another singular event. Count Basie, the newcomer from Kansas City, was taking on Chick Webb, the king of the Savoy, in a battle of the bands. Basie's sound represented a new approach to swing. Injecting the blues of the Southwest into the big band format and perfecting a propulsive four-beats-to-the-bar rhythm that moved the music along like never before, Basie's band was a direct challenge to the sounds of Harlem. Compared with the complex arrangements of bands like Webb's, Basie's songs were stripped to their essential elements, touching the simple beating heart as much as the head. The crowd—which included Ellington; vibraphonist Red Norvo and his wife, singer Mildred Bailey; and Goodman—was relishing the face-off. If that wasn't enough, Ella Fitzgerald, Webb's singer, and Billie Holiday, Basie's vocalist, also squared off against each other that night. According to electrified accounts of the evening, the bands blew so hard at each other, it seemed as if the walls of the Savoy were about to fall down. While battles of the bands weren't actually judged competitions, the audience would often clearly clap more for one orchestra than another. But the crowd's reactions to Webb and Basie were so close that the debate over who had triumphed lasted long after the night was over.

Despite these scenes of black and white musicians playing and socializing together at the Savoy and Carnegie Hall, there were still serious inequities that even the most famous African-American bandleaders suffered because of their color. White bands enjoyed a number of advantages, getting lucrative hotel bookings and radio shows that few black bands could nail down. If a white group and a black group recorded the same song, as with Goodman's and Basie's versions of "One O'Clock Jump," the white band's version stood a much greater chance of being a hit. And without long-term hotel contracts, black bands were forced to take endless tours made up mostly of one-night gigs. Traveling, especially in the South, was often a series of painful humiliations and difficulties. Black musicians couldn't stay at most hotels, even the ones at which they were performing. In some cities they sometimes couldn't even find a restaurant that would serve them. Cab Calloway was beaten in Kansas City when he tried to enter

the Pla-Mor Ballroom, where his friend Lionel Hampton was playing. In another unconscionable incident, a theater manager in
Detroit forced Billie Holiday to wear greasepaint onstage during
an appearance of the Count Basie Orchestra. His reasoning? He
worried that the light-skinned Holiday might look white under
the stage lighting and that the audience would be offended. As
Holiday once said about the racism she encountered as an entertainer, "You can be up to your boobies in white satin, with gardenias in your hair and no sugar cane for miles, but you can still be
working on a plantation."

In other ways, however, the swing movement was a model of
pluralism and racial equality. Many bands, arguing that they
wanted to play the best music possible, fought for integration. In
addition to Goodman's quartet, other breakthroughs included
white bandleader Artie Shaw's hiring of Billie Holiday, and black
trumpeter Roy Eldridge's addition to Gene Krupa's orchestra. A
number of black bands, including those of Lucky Millinder and
Earl Hines, began to include white members as well. "The arts led
the way in breaking down the discrimination against our people,"
says Norma Miller. "It was the arts that opened the door for black
people to go through." The sentiment expressed at the time was
that song (and also dance at places like the Savoy) was a common
meeting ground. "Audiences don't draw color lines when they're
listening to music," said Goodman pianist Teddy Wilson. (Women,
on the other hand, were pointedly not given equal status in the
swing world. While most bands had female singers, few orchestras, white or black, would consider hiring anything but male
instrumentalists.)

Was it this newfound harmony that fueled the success of
swing? The late thirties, a moment when cross-fertilization
between black and white musicians was at its greatest peak, is
often considered the high point of the swing era. Duke Ellington
was then moving into a period of enormously inspired activity.
Spurred by the arrival of composer Billy Strayhorn, bassist Jimmy

Blanton, and saxophonist Ben Webster to the band, Ellington began creating such classics as "Take the 'A' Train" and "Cotton Tail." The integrated nightclub Café Society opened in 1938 in Greenwich Village. The boogie-woogie piano style of Kansas City caught on as a national craze. From Basie to Goodman, from Lunceford to Barnet, swing brought together blacks and whites as never before. It was a golden age in American music. As James Lincoln Collier wrote in his biography, *Benny Goodman and the Swing Era,* "Swing was better—more sophisticated, more genuinely musical—than virtually any popular music before or since." No wonder that today, when pop music is dumbed down to such desultory levels, the swing era is drawing us back.

THE RISE AND FALL OF SWING

During World War II, swing became even more popular than ever, but did it still really swing? That's the question that arises with the arrival of **Glenn Miller** in jazz. Miller was the most famous bandleader of the early forties. On a mainstream level, his songs, including "In the Mood" and "Pennsylvania 6-5000," are still the most well-remembered tunes of the swing era. But Miller's rise to prominence signaled a new development in swing. His music, more catchy than ambitious, got further and further away from its roots in jazz and its ties to African-Americans. While swing's lyrics had previously reflected the urban experience, Miller's subject matter tended more toward nostalgic images of small-town America. The "Chattanooga Choo-Choo" didn't stop in Harlem.

As Americans fought the war, however, Miller's music took on a deep meaning for both civilians and soldiers. In 1942 Miller gave up his money-making orchestra, enlisted in the army, and started his own military band. A model patriot, he boosted morale playing for the troops throughout Europe. Swing, in general, began to be seen as a representation of the values that America was defending. As President Franklin Roosevelt said at the time, music could "inspire a fervor for the spiritual values in our way of life and . . . strengthen democracy." Betty Grable and Rita Hayworth (both of whom married bandleaders, Harry James and Artie Shaw, respectively) and swing singer **Lena Horne** became the most popular pinups. The **Andrews Sisters** had a hit with "Boogie Woogie Bugle Boy." After the Nazis labeled jazz "nigger-jew" music, swing (as later depicted in the movie *Swing Kids*) became an anti-Fascist symbol. During the war, as American soldiers moved into Europe, they turned Europeans on to the music as never before. However, the war years also added a new conservatism to swing. The boys overseas generally wanted to hear the songs that they already knew from home, not new tunes. When Miller died in an airplane crash in 1944, he was justly hailed as a hero. But many saw his music as the harbinger of things to come. "I think that band was like the beginning of the end. It was a mechanized version of what they called jazz music," said Artie Shaw in *Dialogues in Swing.*

Soon after the end of the war, and seemingly out of nowhere, the swing business started to collapse. By late 1946 Woody Herman, Harry James, Tommy Dorsey, Benny Carter, and **Les Brown** had all disbanded their orchestras. Soon after, Cab Calloway, Charlie Barnet, and Artie Shaw called it quits too. The Basie band held on until 1950. But an era had clearly passed. Trumpeter Johnny Coppola recalls playing a late-forties date with bandleader Stan Kenton in Oakland. "The crowds weren't there," he says. "Kenton was in shock. He looked around and said, 'Where is everybody?' They were home watching TV."

Actually, television was just one of many reasons that the big bands fell by the wayside. A 30 percent cabaret tax instituted in 1944 raised the price of going out. GIs returning from the war, once the young fans of swing, were older and looking to start families. The war effort had also put a major strain on the bands. They were hampered from touring by the rationing of gasoline and rubber, while losing huge numbers of musicians to conscription. "The war took all the men out of there," says Norma Miller. The manufacture of jukeboxes was temporarily stopped, and the production of records was cut 30 percent. Meanwhile, a standoff between the American Federation of Musicians union and the music industry, which created a ban on recordings by orchestras, crippled swing as well. Begun in late 1942, the union strike lasted more than a year. While some big bands held on after the war, their cultural dominance had ended.

Despite the effect of all these social changes, however, music was simply evolving on its own, the way it always does, decade after decade. In jazz, in the forties, a New Orleans Dixieland revival took off. This interest in earlier jazz was itself a roots revival, reflecting a feeling that swing had become empty and inauthentic. At the same time, bop, many of whose proponents had been swing band players (the foremost being Dizzy Gillespie), ushered in an exciting new sound that, unfortunately, with its emphasis on dissonance and its relative lack of melody, wasn't danceable. "When I came out of the army we got a gig working with Dizzy Gillespie's band and afterward I said, 'Dizzy what is this stuff? What the f— is that?' I did not understand that music at all. So this is one thing that killed swing," recalls Frankie Manning.

Just as jazz and dance split apart, so did jazz and popular music. Vocalists, not orchestras, began to dominate the charts. Previously, during the height of the big band era, singers had been no more important than musicians. Often they felt like mere accessories. "The bandleader never wanted to be outshone by anybody. So most of the male vocalists had to stand there, ramrod stiff, sing a chorus, go sit down, get up, sing the last chorus, and sit down again," recalls Frankie Laine, one of the biggest new solo singers of the late forties and early fifties. **Peggy Lee,** Patti Page, **Nat King Cole,** and others benefited from the change, but the one man to kick it all off was **Frank Sinatra.** After quitting Tommy Dorsey's band and creating a sensation at New York's Paramount

Theater in the early forties, Sinatra made the momentous decision to strike out on his own. "One could see the writing on the
wall: the focus now was going to be on an individual instead of
on 16 men," said jazz singer **Mel Tormé** in *Dialogues in Swing*. In
a huge reversal, the band was now mere backup to the singer.
While many of these singers still performed music that swung,
they were more likely to be doing it at a lounge than in a dance
hall. Jazz still enjoyed periods of popular upswing—among the
most famous were Ellington's 1956 appearance at the Newport
Jazz Festival and Ella Fitzgerald's songbook recordings. A handful
of reconstituted bands, such as those of Count Basie and Les
Brown, enjoyed success too. But according to David W. Stowe's
Swing Changes, "None of these ensembles . . . sought to connect
with the dancers swing had reached."

While the big bands were effectively over, however, swing
wasn't totally in eclipse. Driven by the influence of Count Basie's
fast-moving blues sound, a new musical form grew out of swing.
You could catch a glimpse of it in 1942 when Illinois Jacquet
honked and wailed his way through his sax solo on the Lionel
Hampton tune "Flying Home." By the end of the forties, it even
had its own name, jump blues, a powerful, hard-rocking mix of
jazz arrangements and solos with the deep soul of the blues. The
saxes blasted and the horns keened like never before. The singers
shouted the lyrics, and a strong backbeat pushed the music. And
it was all firmly rooted in swing. Jump blues' most famous artist,
Louis Jordan, who sold millions of records after the war, had
been a saxophonist with Chick Webb. The trumpeter **Louis
Prima** had written "Sing, Sing, Sing" for Goodman. And singer
Wynonie Harris had performed for Lucky Millinder's swing
band. "Whether you are stompin' or you're jumpin' or you're
swingin' . . . , you're talking about the same type of beat, the
same type of groove, and the same type of tempo," says Albert
Murray in the documentary *Bluesland*. But Jordan—whose
smash hits included "Caldonia" and "Choo Choo Ch'Boogie"—

led the way in paring down the size of the orchestras, finding a big sound with his new seven-piece combo.

In doing so, he was a decisive catalyst in the creation of both rock 'n' roll and R&B. Back in the day, promoters began using the terms *swing* and *rock* fairly interchangeably to describe jump blues bands like Jordan's. Recalls Claude Trenier, leader of the jump band the **Treniers,** who sang with the Jimmie Lunceford Orchestra: "We went to the Blue Note in Chicago and the owner said what kind of music was that and we said we're just having fun. It's swinging. But he put on the marquee 'The rock and rollin' Treniers.' They just changed the name." Once the rock era exploded in the mid-fifties, Jordan's influence was still pervasive. Rock legend Chuck Berry has said, "I identify myself with Louis Jordan more than any other artist." "He was everything," James Brown once said, as quoted in John Chilton's Jordan biography *Let the Good Times Roll.* And while rocker Bill Haley never acknowledged Jordan's influence on his music, Jordan himself claimed, "When Bill Haley came along in 1953 he was doing the same shuffle boogie I was." Indeed, in the last few years there's been a major reevaluation of rock's pioneers afoot. It's clear that as much as Haley and even Elvis were rocking, they were swinging too. Adds bandleader Bill Elliott, "What people forget is that all through the fifties, even though there was rock and roll, the dancing was still essentially swing dancing." By now, everyone knows the story of how white musicians and record labels repackaged black R&B and created rock in the fifties. But it's possible to trace a line from rock back to R&B and then further back to swing. And that's exactly the path that today's neoswingers took to find their musical roots.

CHAPTER 2

The Rebirth of Swing

*L*et's get one thing perfectly clear: swing wasn't brought back by a Gap ad. The origins of the swing revival date back at least two decades. It began on a grassroots level and has slowly, steadily, and within the last several years, furiously grown and deepened into the full-fledged movement it is today. A true rediscovery of the dance, music, and style of the original era, the resurgence first sprang up among small pockets of like-minded but isolated people scattered in cities all across the world. Dancers from Stockholm and London to New York and Los Angeles began learning and falling in love with the real Savoy-style Lindy Hop, the crazed jitterbugging and dangerous aerials that once had social critics in apoplexy. Musicians up and down the West Coast searched for and embraced the hotter facets of swing, the screaming improvisational jazz riffs and licks that back in the day had shocked the establishment. And also out in California, scenesters started once again wearing the most defiant and colorful fashions of the forties: the zoot suit, an outfit that had once incited riots (see chapter 6). Who are the people who brought back swing? In the best of ways, they're a motley crew of jazz aficionados, former punk rockers, rockabilly and ska fanatics; hard-edged greasers and squeaky clean nostalgics; street-kid dancers and ballroom refugees; history buffs; and best of all, some of the era's original musicians and Lindy Hoppers. What they all had in common was a desire to go back to the roots of swing, and what they found was that it could have a freshness and power all over again.

Fresh was not what you would call the swing that was hanging around before the revival happened. Swing, of course, had never really died out. For years it was kept alive by society dance bands across the country who trotted out old chestnuts like "In the Mood" over and over again at weddings, charity benefits, and golden anniversary parties. The average kid growing up in the

FACING PAGE: *Big Bad Voodoo Daddy.* (MARK JORDAN)

seventies couldn't be blamed for equating swing with a graying Guy Lombardo trying to liven up New Year's Eve on television. Or, even worse, with the bubbly schmaltz of *The Lawrence Welk Show*. By the eighties and nineties, however, even those saccharine reminders of big band's glory days had exited the stage. No less a person than Duke Ellington's foremost modern-day champion, Wynton Marsalis, artistic director of New York's Jazz at Lincoln Center, has said that when he was young the name Ellington called to mind "old people and Geritol." Adds Jack Vaughn, president of the neoswing label Slimstyle Records, "The swing music of old was marginalized by movie soundtracks and car commercials. It became background music." And the dance was in even worse shape. Most ballroom studios around the country, while still teaching swing, promulgated a watered-down, lifeless version of the dance that was short on improvisation and big on routine. "It was often just a basic six-count East Coast," says dance teacher and historian Margaret Batiuchok, one of the people most responsible for bringing back the Lindy.

Over the years, a number of new singers, from Bette Midler to Harry Connick Jr., have helped popularize the era's standards, though often the choice of material has focused on the sweeter, more conservative songs. Think of Midler's rousing cover of the Andrews Sisters' "Boogie Woogie Bugle Boy" in 1971; Midler also sang with the Lionel Hampton band on Broadway in 1976. Around the same time, the Manhattan Transfer's jazzy vocals brought back hits such as the Glenn Miller classic "Tuxedo Junction." In the mid-eighties Linda Ronstadt recorded a slew of old-fashioned tunes on a trio of albums produced by famous Sinatra arranger Nelson Riddle. And in 1989 swing got an enormous boost with the release of the hit soundtrack from *When Harry Met Sally*, featuring a then-twenty-two-year-old Harry Connick Jr. crooning in full Sinatra mode. Starting in the mid-eighties, a traditionalist revival, led by Marsalis, also began making its mark on the jazz world.

What made the swing scene take off as a certified cultural movement, however, was when musicians began looking back to swing's hardest-driving music. In London in the early eighties, swing, or more correctly, swingin' jump blues, experienced its first modern-day comeback. **Ray Gelato,** as part of the Chevalier Brothers, and Joe Jackson, who released a before-its-time album of Louis Jordan and Cab Calloway material called *Jumpin' Jive* in 1981, started to bring back the best of the jump blues sound. London's scene was a harbinger of today's swing craze. "There were swing dance nights and a lot of bands playing the music over in England, and they used to wear the zoot suits and the two-toned shoes. I think there was a big cross-pollination with American people coming over and seeing the thing here," says Gelato. (For more information on Gelato and other neoswing musicians highlighted in bold print in this chapter, see individual entries in chapter 5.)

While swing's popularity in London eventually died down, the Brits were certainly out there before anyone else. But can they or any handful of people really be credited with reviving swing? Today everyone and his daddy-o likes to lay claim to that distinction. Almost every band points out how long they've been around (1989, 1991, or even 1993 are considered far-back years in the history of the revival). Answering the question, however, is as tough and controversial as saying who invented jazz in the first place. No one owns the music and the dance. Nevertheless, the musicians like to think they made it popular and new again, while the dancers believe that they get short shrift from the music side, which wouldn't have become so big without them. The Europeans, meanwhile, feel overlooked by the Americans for their contribution. And in many ways all of them are right. But two people truly do stand out as the greatest modern-day, Goodman-style popularizers of swing. Appropriately, one of them, the **Royal Crown Revue**'s Eddie Nichols, is from the music world, while the other, Frankie Manning, hails from the dance side. The pair couldn't be any more different.

A MUSICAL REDISCOVERY

The founder of the influential band Royal Crown Revue, Eddie Nichols is one of the few neoswingers who can use old-time lingo and be taken seriously. "That guy's got a thousand-yard stare" he says of one hard-luck friend. Nichols himself could have ended up the same way. A singer and percussionist who grew up in New York City, Nichols moved out to Los Angeles in 1984 and quickly fell into the city's thriving hard-core punk rock scene. At one point he was unemployed and lived on the streets. He did find a job, cleaning toilets at a filthy punk club called the Cathay de Grande. In the late eighties he started playing in a rockabilly band, but he also started abusing heroin around the same time, a habit he didn't kick for almost a decade. All in all, he was one of the most unlikely people you'd ever imagine being drawn to "Geritol" music. "I was truly ignorant of the whole thing when I started doing it," says Nichols, who claims he stumbled onto the sound by just jamming and playing around with chord changes. Suddenly he realized the music sounded retro, really retro.

Nichols and the other founding members of the group—who also included the Stern brothers from the punk band Youth Brigade—began listening to the jump blues of Louis Prima and Louis Jordan, just like the Brits had done. "You couldn't go out and buy the complete works of Louis Prima on Rhino back then," says RCR's guitarist James Achor. "I would buy 78s from this Goodwill for a nickel apiece. I would buy them one hundred, two hundred at a time and I'd go home and listen to them. It wasn't like I went to the record store. I had to get the shovel out and dig for it. It was archaeology of all this American music. For some reason it had been lost. As a kid you didn't hear about Louis Jordan or Louis Prima."

For them and for other early swing musicians—part of a generation that had been raised solely on rock—it was as if they were hearing this music for the first time. By the late eighties, the great pioneer Louis Jordan was far from a household name. In fact, he'd almost been forgotten. Many of these musicians were newcomers to jazz and refugees from the raw, aggressive punk scene (Scotty Morris, founder of **Big Bad Voodoo Daddy,** and Vise Grip of San Francisco's Ambassadors of Swing were both ex-punkers). They were, however, becoming increasingly disenchanted with rock, with both the late-eighties hair-metal-guitar bands like Guns n' Roses and the developing grunge movement. Remarkably, they found something in swing that spoke to their punk sensibilities. "Here was this music and it rocks just as much but with a little more refined energy," says RCR trumpeter Scott Steen. **Eddie Reed,** a member of the LA rockabilly scene and later the founder of the popular Eddie Reed Big Band, remembers being bowled over the first time he listened to Artie Shaw. "I heard an eighteen-year-old Buddy Rich slamming the drums at breakneck speed and shouting like some punk rocker in the background exhorting Artie Shaw into this pyrotechnic clarinet solo," he says. The music that really turned on the scene, adds Steve Lucky of the neoswing **Steve Lucky and the Rhumba Bums,** was "the really hard-swinging, gut-punching, jumping stuff." If your main exposure to the big band era was a song like "Stardust," then the fact that this ferociously spontaneous music existed at all was a revelation.

The wild showman Cab Calloway, the bluesy Count Basie, and, of course, Prima and Jordan became the guiding inspirations of the new scene. By contrast, at this point in the revival the more traditional big band leaders, such as Benny Goodman, Tommy Dorsey, and, pointedly, Glenn Miller, were not. Looking back, it's easy to see why. For ears attuned to rock but yearning to get back in touch with America's musical roots, jump blues was the natural entry point. "The late forties is the most entertaining period to me," says Nichols. "It was like a crossroads where there are aspects of jazz and rock and rhythm and blues. It's when there were still a lot of interesting chord changes but the beat started rocking too."

These revivalists, while searching for the roots of rock, found swing unexpectedly. And in the process they began to question whether the supposed great divide between the two genres is really as enormous as most of us have been taught, the idea that before rock came on the scene nothing else cool ever existed. They began to discover that not only did jazz have an influence on early rock but also swing music could be just as wild and energetic. Instead of focusing on the differences between swing and rock, they began to hear similarities and see progressions. To today's ears, bands like Bill Haley and the Comets have begun to sound very swing. The distance between Lionel Hampton's 1946 hit "Hey! Ba-Ba-Re-Bop" and Gene Vincent's 1956 hit "Be-Bop-A-Lula" doesn't really seem so far. "To me, swing encompasses band, jump blues, and the beginnings of rock and roll. The current term *swing* has become a convention for talking about retro dance music in general," says Carmen Getit, vocalist and guitarist with Steve Lucky and the Rhumba Bums.

Intriguingly, the rockabilly revival of the late seventies and eighties had taken modern musicians back to the sound of the fifties and tantalizingly close to the brink of jump blues. Inspired by such rebellious rockin' fifties singers as Jerry Lee Lewis, Gene Vincent, and Eddie Cochran, early eighties bands like the Blasters and Brian Setzer's Stray Cats made hits of such songs as Little Richard's "Keep A-Knockin'" and "Rock This Town," respectively. The rockabilly rebirth helped bring back partner dancing too. "That's when kids started couples dancing. They were doing the jitterbug, which is like a fifties mishmash. I called it sling dancing. It was just grab your girl and spin her around," says Reed.

By the late eighties and on into the early nineties, the rockabilly scene in Los Angeles had become a vibrant "roots" music movement. Centered around such clubs as the King King and the Palomino, the roots scene included musicians looking back toward traditional country, western swing, and even Louis Jordan. "It was a great crossroads moment. It was very diverse," says Royal Crown Revue guitarist James Achor, who recalls going to performances by Chris Isaak, Dwight Yoakum, the rockabilly and Western swing band Big Sandy and his Fly-Rite Boys, and a ska-type band fronted by Joey Altruda. "They were the first band I really saw do a Jordan song," says Achor. Exploring the musical past was suddenly hip. "Once kids started getting into vintage Americana," says Nichols, "there was more of a tendency to enjoy other styles like swing and rhythm and blues."

From all this inspirational ferment, Royal Crown Revue — which officially formed in 1989 — created a sound they call "hard-boiled swing," or "gangster bop." The Stern brothers and Achor brought their punk attitude to the music. Nichols brought in his experiences in both punk and rockabilly, while the band's saxophonist, Mando Dorame, had grown up listening to the doo-wop and blues albums of his sax-playing father. They tracked down and met Sam Butera, Prima's colorful saxophonist and arranger. The band members were all watching old film noir movies and reading gangster novels. Everything went into the jazz and rock stew, purists be damned. "What would happen if Duke Ellington had had James Brown and the Sex Pistols to listen to? Who knows what he would have sounded like," says RCR trumpet player Scott Steen. Adds Nichols, "I thought, let's try to put something a little newer, a different energy into it and make the lyrics a little darker. When I started the band though, I thought, Well, maybe we'll just play for grandmas. I didn't know who the hell was going to go to our shows. And all of a sudden there were these young kids getting into it."

Granted, Royal Crown Revue wasn't the only band exploring the swing and jump blues era at this time. Groups such as the **Cherry Poppin' Daddies** in Oregon, the **Senders** in Minneapolis, and Beat Positive, an early incarnation of New York's **Jet Set Six,** were starting to jump too. Steve Lucky even had a jump blues band back in Ann Arbor, Michigan, in the early eighties. The Roomful of Blues, an influential Rhode Island band that started playing jump material in the early seventies, was perhaps the ear-

Royal Crown Revue's film noir–influenced CD cover art. (WARNER BROS. RECORDS)

liest harbinger of the swing revival. Clearly this was in the air — everywhere. "A lot of bands, mostly within the same age group, started around the same time, and none of them had any idea that anybody else besides themselves was trying this kind of music," says Michael Moss, the publisher of San Francisco's *Swing Time* magazine, the first periodical devoted to neoswing. "Something was going on in the culture where hundreds of young musicians started gravitating toward this swing idea."

What made Royal Crown Revue stand out? Their sound was

undeniably new. Instead of just covering past hits, they were writing original material such as "Hey Pachuco!" a tribute to early Hispanic zoot-suiters, and the explosive "Zip Gun Bop." "Royal Crown was the first band to give it a punk edge and give it a raw energy that could translate into a new younger generation," says Max Young, co-owner of San Francisco's swing club the Hi-Ball Lounge. "They said, 'This isn't the swing that your grandfather listened to. This is stuff that's gonna hit you in the head.'" Nichols began wearing zoots early too. "Walking around in LA in a zoot suit would get my ass kicked almost as much as being a punk rocker would," says Nichols. The band's look became a striking mix of gangster, greaser, and Hispanic cholo styles; their album art played up the film noir attitude.

But most important, Royal Crown Revue got themselves seen and heard. From the beginning they toured relentlessly. "They'd head out across the country in this broken-down Winnebago that they called the Death Wagon," says Eddie Reed, who has known Nichols since the pair were part of LA's rockabilly scene. On the road, the band made a conscious decision to pursue gigs at rock clubs, not jazz spots. "We invented this kind of music for ourselves and we wanted to play it for our peers," says Achor. "We wanted to go where people our age go and hang out. So we played with grunge bands. Or we'd play punk clubs. Or heavy metal places." RCR began priming a whole new audience to connect with jazz in a different way. Later other bands—like Big Bad Voodoo Daddy, which formed in Ventura, California, in the early nineties and had a similar rock-meets-swing approach to the music—also sought to get their music heard on the traditional rock circuit. "We started to create a place to make it happen. There weren't any swing clubs then. We would play anywhere," recalls trumpeter Glen Marhevka of BBVD. Adds Achor, "If somebody hadn't done that, there would have been no other reason for it to become a part of popular culture." Along the way, Royal Crown Revue began inspiring other musicians to start their own groups. Their fired-up jump blues sound defined the direction of the early neo-swing movement. The band struck a nerve with the kind of people—you may have been one yourself—who've always loved swing music but who somehow felt they were born in the wrong half of the century. "People just resigned themselves," says Achor, "saying, 'There's just never going to be anybody like-minded at all ever anywhere like me. I'm the loneliest guy in the world with my Frank Sinatra records.'"

But there was one town that got turned on by Royal Crown Revue like no other. The city was San Francisco, and when the band first played there, they helped take the swing renaissance to a whole new level.

SCENESTER CENTRAL

What the Royal Crown Revue happened upon in the Bay Area was a nascent and wildly enthusiastic retro scene congregating in the most surprising of places. Housed in a one-time gay bar right near the corner of former hippie central, Haight and Ashbury, the Club Deluxe opened in 1989, coincidentally the same year that RCR came together. The art deco–style bar was populated with a cast of characters right out of an old-time variety show. The colorfully named Vise Grip was the doorman. Lounge acts like Mr. Lucky—who had an act called the Mr. Lucky Experience that performed Martin Denny-esque covers of Tears for Fears songs and disco versions of "The Girl from Ipanema"—and Connie Champagne and Her Tiny Bubbles would sing there regularly. Another former punk named Timmie Hesla, who had started a Basie-and-Ellington-influenced swing band back in 1985, played gigs there as well. And a twenty-one-year-old Morty Okin, the short but irrepressible trumpet player who would go on to form the rockin' swing band the **New Morty Show,** showed up at the club soon after moving away from Michigan. "It was very, very underground," says Okin. "There was basically a suit-and-tie dress code.

It was like walking into a time warp. And everyone was basically drinking like fish and having a great time."

On the club's tiny stage, in front of the spot's even tinier dance floor, a small group of jazz musicians played standards on open-mike Sundays. Vise and Morty used to sit in with them, and in 1991 Vise started his own swing band, inspired mostly by Cab Calloway, called St. Vitus Dance. Pretty soon retro music shows began happening elsewhere around town. In 1991 **Lavay Smith,** a more straight-ahead jazz singer who's now a star of the swing movement, became a regular performer at the new Café du Nord. And the historic Bimbo's 365, a grand art deco nightclub from the thirties that had once hosted such greats as Prima, Ellington, and Buddy Rich, reopened and started holding semiregular swing nights too. There were also a series of after-hours garage parties. Modeled after speakeasies, the events occasionally had invites that were just matchbooks with location information printed on the inside. "They'd start around midnight and go until about seven in the morning in a big warehouse space. There wasn't as much of a division as there is now between swing and rockabilly. It was all one big crowd," says Nancy Myers, who threw many of them.

San Francisco differed from Los Angeles, however, in that from the start the clothing was almost as important as the music. The Bay Area went mad for retro threads. Forties straight-skirt dresses, double-breasted pinstripe suits, fedoras, and wide ties began making appearances, alongside fifties rockabilly jeans and ducktails and sixties sharkskin jackets. "People used to show up in real vintage clothes because that's what they could afford. It was cheap. It didn't matter if there was a stain on it," says Myers. "I have a great photograph that to me describes the whole scene at the time. It has a woman in the background with a mohawk and a big pin on her jacket that says 'Bitch,' and a couple of girls on the other side that look more rockabilly that are swing dancing, and then there's a couple of other people dressed in their forties suits."

Wearing retro clothes, however, also became a form of rebellion for the group, no matter how oxymoronic the concept seems. As the edges of modern fashion swung ever more extreme — to multiple piercings and tattoos — wearing a swing-era outfit was a way of being surprisingly different. And the more the Club Deluxe crowd learned about the old clothes, the more they fell in love with their style, their quality, and their timelessness. Aficionados soon became experts, knowing, for instance, to look for "Union Made" labels and figuring out what distinguishes a 1942 suit from a 1947 piece. "It started off as a culture that was based around this concept of America," says *Swing Time* publisher Michael Moss. "A lot of people were gathering together and sharing these Americana discoveries, be it music or salt and pepper shakers from the thirties or old cars or movies or books or old clothes. It formed this retro community that wasn't defined. It was just as much a forties thing as a fifties rockabilly thing as a sixties lounge thing. All these different subcultures were forming around the Deluxe around 1991."

Into this retro crowd stumbled the Royal Crown Revue. "It was surprising. Here was this bunch of people who were into the music and had all the clothes, who were living it real hard-core, and yet they didn't have a band in the scene," remembers RCR's Achor. The band's first shows in San Francisco galvanized, electrified, and inspired the Deluxe crowd. "Seeing the Royal Crown was definitely my most memorable night. They really had everything down, from the music to the suits to the matching guitars. They were just awesome," recalls Okin. Adds Johnny Boyd, lead singer of the hugely popular band **Indigo Swing,** "The whole thing started for me when I saw them at the Deluxe."

"That was the moment when it started to be a swing culture," says *Swing Time*'s Moss. "Suddenly there was a band that fit the scene perfectly." Overnight, San Francisco became the epicenter of the swing revival, eventually becoming the city with the best vintage stores, the home of *Swing Time,* and the place where the first book on swing, V. Vale's jam-packed *Swing! The New Retro Renaissance,* was published. All the pieces of the revival were in place, except one: the dancing.

BEGINNING THE BEGUINE — AGAIN

In the early eighties the original spirit of the Savoy was a distant memory. The dance that had swept the country in the thirties with its originality and exuberance had by the fifties become a white-bread mishmash of Lindy moves known only as the jitter-bug. "The Lindy Hop was an extinct word. Nobody said that word," says Erin Stevens of the Pasadena Ballroom Dance Association. And by the latter part of the century, that American Bandstand–style swing had been diluted even further, the dance taught in the majority of ballrooms a pale shadow of the original Lindy Hop. "There was no kind of understanding that black people had any involvement in it," says Ryan Francois, a champion dancer and teacher who began Lindy Hopping in London in the early eighties. "Media culture had taught me that all this stuff happened in the fifties with white bobby-soxers and in the forties with the GIs." A black man himself, Francois, like many who rediscovered the Lindy, first glimpsed the dance's African-American origins watching old movies like *Hellzapoppin'* and *A Day at the Races,* which had scenes of Whitey's Lindy Hoppers in action. "I remember thinking not only did black people do this stuff, I had never seen it done that well," he adds. Another now-world-famous teacher, Jonathan Bixby, remembers staying up late on the phone with his partner Sylvia Sykes to watch the movie *Buck Privates,* an Abbott and Costello movie with one dance sequence in it. "This was before VCRs and we'd be up at three in the morning to catch this one snippet of dancing. It was brilliant. And I'd be like, 'Okay, you watch their feet. I'll watch the top. Okay. Bye,'" he says. But ultimately, watching flicks wasn't enough. "After a while," says Bixby, "we knew we had to find some people."

And just as the musicians would soon do themselves, a handful of dancers from a score of different cities searched for the roots of swing. Their quest led them all back to the same place, the original city where the dance was created, New York. While swing music had been recorded on thousands of vinyl records, the Savoy-style Lindy was preserved in only a handful of old movies. Yet it still lived in a far more vibrant, if less accessible, way. A loose network of former Savoy dancers, including some members of Whitey's Lindy Hoppers, was spread across New York, and these new swing enthusiasts were about to find them. "New York was where the history was, that's where you could research it," says Francois.

In 1982 a country-western bar in Greenwich Village called City Limits started booking a swing band occasionally, which attracted a group of dancers who went on to form the New York Swing Dance Society. "It became this real hub of activity," says Teddy Kern, who was part of the scene at the time and is now co-owner of New York's Dance Manhattan studio. "And some of the black dancers who had been Savoy dancers found out about it and started showing up there." Among them was George Lloyd, a former Savoy regular and master aerialist (he'd competed in the Harvest Moon Ball back in the day). "He wasn't a show person. He was just an awesome social dancer," says Kern, who recalls the respect and excitement the old-time dancers generated. "We had never seen them before. And we just had this love affair on the dance floor, all of us. They became celebrities to our little group.

"Then they began to tell us about this place uptown," she continues, "an old club that had been revived called Small's Paradise on 135th Street and Seventh Avenue. The Al Cobb Big Band was playing there in the back room, the Queen of Sheba room, which was fabulous. It had pink sconces and gold curlicues on the walls and a dance floor like butter. Like *butter*. You just couldn't sit down. And all of us from City Limits migrated uptown every Monday night. It was like a religion. And they welcomed us. We were white kids from downtown, most of whom didn't know diddley-squat about swing dancing."

More luminaries from the Savoy days began making appearances at Small's Paradise by 1983. There was Al Minns, one of the original members of Whitey's performance troupe. Norma Miller, another dancer in the group and the only one to go on to a lifetime career in show business, showed up full of stories and her trademark saucy humor. On the scene too was Ernie Smith, who wasn't a dancer but who had done important research on the dance, which included tracking down hard-to-find movies with Lindy scenes. Seemingly out of nowhere, a group of surprisingly accomplished Lindy Hoppers from Sweden, who had formed the Swedish Swing Society in 1978, also showed up in New York. And eventually a reluctant Frankie Manning, the former head choreographer for Whitey's Lindy Hoppers and the man who would go on to promote the revival of the dance like no one else, set foot inside the club. "Norma brought Frankie there. And from what she said she had to drag him there," says Kern. While Manning would occasionally turn up at the club and dance, it was Minns—already a teacher at the downtown Sandra Cameron Dance Center—who was the real deacon of the scene at that time. "Everyone idolized Al. He was the hero," says Teddy Kern. Soon the Swedes had brought Minns over to Stockholm to teach them the dance. Norma Miller, meanwhile, was choreographing a Lindy show at the downtown jazz club, the Village Gate. The Lindy was coming back to life.

Sadly, Minns died suddenly in 1984. And Small's Paradise soon shut its doors too. But the dancing didn't end. In 1985 twelve swingers banded together and formed the New York Swing Dance Society in Minns's memory, convincing a now-defunct downtown venue called the Cat Club to host a swing dance once every two weeks. "We got the idea from the Swedes to have our own swing dance society," says NYSDS cofounder Margaret Batiuchok. Dawn Hampton, a terrific social dancer and a former member of the swing band Duke Hampton and His Family Band, remembers how skeptical she was when she first heard about the club. "My neighbor kept telling me, 'They are dancing over there.' I thought that meant disco dancing, which I didn't go for. I didn't think anybody was swing dancing any more."

It was at these swing nights that Manning—in Minns's stead—took on the role of mentor to the dancers. The nightclub soon became the nexus for several extraordinarily fortuitous meetings between swing dancers from around the world. "We pretty much all descended there almost at the same time," recalls Ryan Francois, who showed up at the Cat Club one night as part of a British group called the Jiving Lindy Hoppers. There he encountered not only the New York dancers and the Savoy originators (more veterans, such as Charlie Mead, Sonny Allen, and Willamae Ricker, were surfacing at the club) but also two pairs of ultimately influential dancers from California. The four—partners Bixby and Sykes from Santa Barbara and Erin Stevens and Steven Mitchell from the Pasadena Ballroom Dance Association—have been credited more than anyone else with reintroducing swing dancing to the West Coast. "We all had gone looking for Frankie Manning and the original Whitey's Lindy Hoppers. We went and found him and said, 'Teach us. Show us stuff,'" says Francois. "But what was amazing was that we all pretty much descended on the Cat Club at the same time. For some reason, we had the same idea at the same moment and none of us knew each other. That was the providence of it. For three straight nights we jammed and got to know each other. It was the wildest event that ever truly happened. All these people from different places met each other with the same objective, and we just gave each other respect. There was no plan for it. And I think that's what kept us going for the next ten years. That was the beginning of the nucleus and it just grew out from there." Adds Erin Stevens, "We knew we had to go to New York to find the roots of swing. And so did all these people from other parts of the world. It was like *Close Encounters of the Third Kind.*"

Soon Stevens and Mitchell convinced Manning, who had worked at the post office for the last three decades, to begin teaching professionally. Suddenly Manning had a new life, traveling to Sweden, Los Angeles, Washington, and countless other places. With his infectiously warm spirit, his authority, his simply wonderful dancing, and his longevity (the idea soon gained currency that a lifetime of swing dancing will keep you as agile, healthy, and good-natured as the octagenarian Manning is), Manning spread the gospel of Lindy well. Once the music began to take off a few years later, the groundwork had already been laid for the dance to join in.

IT ALL COMES TOGETHER

That the dance and music revivals both happened independently of each other is odd (swing is, after all, a dance-based music) but also understandable (bebop had severed the link between the Lindy and jazz music in the forties). "Just three years ago," promoter Lee Sobel recalls of the early swing music scene in New York, "I saw the Blues Jumpers play at Louisiana Bar and Grill and there was not one person dancing. There was not even a place to dance. The dance floor was all tables." At early swing music concerts in California, people danced, but it would have been a stretch to call it the Lindy. "It was like a cross between a mosh pit and dancing," says Nancy Myers of the speakeasy parties that took place around 1991 and 1992.

By 1993 that all began to change. While clubs with swing nights had opened in San Francisco, Los Angeles still didn't have a spot of its own. That April a new club opened that would become the most famous swing place of all. Located in a gorgeous building once occupied by the famous Brown Derby club, the Derby was a nostalgia lovers' dream. It still had its original domed ceiling with an art deco–style wood diamond pattern on it, constructed in 1929 by Cecil B. DeMille. "It was a huge hang-

out for stars like Clark Gable, Errol Flynn, Carole Lombard, and Buster Keaton. It had a beautiful oval bar that had been used in the movie *Mildred Pierce* in 1945," says the club's co-owner Tammi Gower, who restored the club and opened it with the idea of promoting both swing music and dancing. "It was really in decline and had become a pretty downscale steak and Italian place," she says. "The great ceiling had been covered with a nine-foot drop ceiling. But I walked in and thought, This would make an incredible club. Believe me, everybody tried to talk me out of it." For the first two years the Derby booked the Royal Crown Revue every Wednesday night. The club also made a point of bringing in swing dance instructors to give lessons. "By about the third month, men started coming in in zoot suits and women in rayon dresses. It was pretty much a hit from there on out," says Gower.

Also in 1993, two more dance-oriented and increasingly popular bands, the **Bill Elliott Orchestra** and the Eddie Reed Big Band, played their first gigs in the Los Angeles area. Influenced little by rock, both musicians had consciously modeled their groups after big band leader Artie Shaw's more traditional swing orchestra of the late 1930s. Elliott soon began performing regularly for swing dances at Erin Stevens's Pasadena Ballroom Dance Association. Dancing also began to take off in San Francisco around this time; the local Lindy group Work That Skirt came together in 1994. And dancers began to meet up with musicians in even more out-of-the-way places like Ventura, California. Terri and Lee Moore (who had learned swing dancing at the Pasadena Ballroom), of the now world-renowned aerials troupe the Flyin' Lindy Hoppers, moved to Ventura in 1994 and heard some jumping swing music in a small local club called Nicholby's. "Here was Big Bad Voodoo Daddy on this stage and everyone was sitting and watching. No one was dancing and they were like 'This is freakin' wrong,'" says Terri's twin sister, Flyin' Lindy Hopper Tammy Finocchiaro. "They came out and Lee just pointed at me," says BBVD's Scotty Morris. "They lit the house on fire and we were like, Where did you learn that? We had never seen swing dancers before."

The scene had now fully formed, with the style, music, and dance all together. But even by then, it was still relatively underground. "For the first four or five years, it was only San Francisco and Los Angeles. Both cities had a ton of bands and we'd just send them back and forth," says Michael Moss. The original scene at the Deluxe had been thirty or forty people. Each time the crowds grew, from two hundred people to six hundred people to more than a thousand, the pioneers of the swing revival would end up slack-jawed at its rising popularity. At the Derby, where Big Bad

Voodoo Daddy eventually took over the Wednesday slot from Royal Crown Revue, lines soon snaked around the block. "There was a line starting at 7:00 P.M. and it was there until one in the morning," says BBVD's Glen Marhevka. "People would order pizza in line and have it delivered." The more swing grew, the more wonderfully unbelievable it was to the people at its core. But even this popularity turned out to be just the tip of the iceberg. Swing was about to be discovered nationally and picked up by the media. It would never be the same.

NATIONAL SUCCESS

The mainstream swing snowball—fueled also by the popularity of the revived cocktail culture—began rolling with the release of the Jim Carrey movie *The Mask* in 1994. Featuring a zoot-suited Carrey dancing with Cameron Diaz to the Royal Crown Revue's "Hey Pachuco!" at a forties-style nightclub, the movie was the first to demonstrate neoswing's crossover appeal. Soon newspaper and magazine stories began to cover the phenomenon, usually taking an incredulous approach to the fact that swing had returned and treating it like just the latest pop culture novelty trend. Some fad. In 1996 the hot indie film *Swingers* premiered, starring Jon Favreau and Vince Vaughn. It featured Big Bad Voodoo Daddy performing their original song "You and Me and the Bottle Makes Three Tonight (Baby)," a snazzy collection of retro clothes, and some scenes of spot-on dancing. A year later the **Squirrel Nut Zippers**—a band that's been lumped in with the swing revival though their sound is more of a twenties hot jazz vibe—saw their 1996 single "Hell" become a hit on alternative rock stations, a surprising development that was credited with opening the radio waves to even more retro music. Benefiting from that entrée in 1998 were "Jump, Jive, an' Wail"—a cover of Louis Prima's classic by the **Brian Setzer Orchestra** (which the former Stray Cat had put together in Los Angeles in 1993)—and

Ten Years of Swing: A Timeline

1989
- ► Royal Crown Revue, the pioneer band of neoswing, forms in Los Angeles
- ► The Club Deluxe, ground zero for the retro scene in San Francisco, opens
- ► Midsummer Night Swing, a month of outdoor dance nights, debuts at Lincoln Center in New York
- ► *When Harry Met Sally,* with its Harry Connick Jr. soundtrack, is released

1990
- ► *Five Guys Named Moe,* the musical based on the life and music of Louis Jordan, has its world premiere in London's West End. The show plays 445 hit performances in New York when it opens there two years later

1991
- ► Café du Nord opens in San Francisco, becoming the weekly home of singer Lavay Smith
- ► Royal Crown Revue plays its first shows in SF at warehouse speakeasy parties, then at the Deluxe
- ► Big Bad Voodoo Daddy forms in Ventura, California
- ► Nathalie Cole releases "Unforgettable," her "duet" with her father, Nat

1992
- ► Spike Lee's *Malcolm X* premieres, boasting some of the best swing dance scenes on film. No wonder: Savoy originals Norma Miller and Frankie Manning assisted with the choreography
- ► Debbie Allen's *Stompin' at the Savoy* TV movie debuts
- ► St. Vitus Dance, early neoswing band formed by Vise Grip, plays its first live show at the Deluxe

the Cherry Poppin' Daddies' original song "Zoot Suit Riot." Both singles not only became huge radio hits, but also had videos in heavy rotation on MTV. "This is the most awesome thing I've ever been in front of," said Setzer at the time. In particular, Setzer's video, which featured such hard-core dancers as LA's Sylvia Skylar and San Francisco's Cari Seiss, slickly captured the style, dancing, and music of the scene all in three minutes. Ska bands, who with their emphasis on horns were another early influence on the revival, now started morphing into swing bands. "Kids that drove Vespas and wore porkpie hats are now putting on zoot suits and playing Benny Goodman," says Jay Siegan, a manager of such swing bands as the New Morty Show and Blue Plate Special. Venues like the Lawrence Welk Resort Center in Branson, Missouri, started jumping on the swing bandwagon, promoting their forties-revue shows as part of the new craze. Vintage prices went through the roof. Pretty soon Setzer's third album, *The Dirty Boogie,* had sold two million copies, and Big Bad Voodoo Daddy (even without a radio hit) and the Cherry Poppin' Daddies each sold a million records. Within the course of six months, swing, the music that people started doing again simply because they loved it, was big business. "It was an impossible dream. Who would ever have thought that a band could make money playing swing music on MTV? No way. Forget about it," says Michael Moss.

And then there was that Gap commercial, the eight-hundred-pound gorilla that finally propelled swing into the stratosphere. Featuring Louis Prima's original "Jump, Jive, an' Wail" and a new stop-motion cinematography that brought the Lindy's aerials into breathtaking relief, the Gap's "Khakis Swing" commercial was as much a hit as any song when it premiered in April of 1998. After the ad was taken off the air three months later, customers screamed for more. "You can't believe the responses we got. We got letters and calls saying, 'Why did you take it off so soon? I've only seen it three times and I love that ad.' The public wasn't ready to give it up yet. So we put it back on the air," the Gap's

1993

▸ The Derby, LA's first all-swing nightclub, opens in the soon-to-revive Los Feliz neighborhood
▸ Also in Los Angeles, Brian Setzer, Bill Elliott, and Eddie Reed all play their first big band gigs
▸ It's official. Lounge music is back: Frank Sinatra's chart-topping *Duets* is released
▸ The movie *Swing Kids,* about jitterbug fans in Germany just before the war, premieres. While not a hit, it's credited for giving juice to the dance scene

1994

▸ Decked out in zoot suits, Jim Carrey hams it up and Royal Crown Revue plays it up in *The Mask*
▸ MTV produces "Tony Bennett Unplugged"
▸ On November 18 the great Cab Calloway dies

1995

▸ *Swing Time* magazine, the first magazine dedicated to the swing scene, is published
▸ The Hi-Ball Lounge, San Francisco's first all-swing nightclub, opens in the space once occupied by the legendary Jazz Workshop

1996

▸ Jon Favreau's *Swingers* puts the swing scene on the map, showcasing Big Bad Voodoo Daddy playing at the Derby
▸ Slimstyle, the first swing independent record label, sets up shop in Tucson

1997

▸ The Squirrel Nut Zippers' "Hell" becomes a radio hit. While the sound is more twenties hot jazz than swing, the success of the song creates an opening for other retro-style tunes

Michael McCadden told *Entertainment Weekly*. And despite the fact that it used hardly a single real Lindy dancer (the dancers in the ad were almost all models) and it promoted khakis (a plain, unisex look that was in fact antithetical to the dressed-up atmosphere of the swing movement), it brought droves of eager novices into dance studios, wanting to have as much fun as the people in the ad seemed to be having. "The ad put it over the top," says Diane Lachtrupp, co-owner of New York's Stepping Out, which like every dance studio around the country was soon scrambling to keep up with the demand for classes. Just as in the thirties, jazz had once again gone mainstream under the label swing. No one in the movement was going to be singing the blues.

POST BLOW-UP SWING

Or so it seemed. While the success of swing in 1998 was unexpectedly huge, the growth was just as unexpectedly double-edged. The expectations put on what was still in many ways a grassroots scene ratcheted up about 1,000 percent. "Everybody got big dollar signs in their eyes," says Moss. Club owners who weren't part of the scene rushed to start swing nights, often not realizing that most dancers don't drink much except water. When some of these events inevitably folded, the word started spreading, truthfully or not, that the swing fad had peaked. You know the old saying that they like to build you up just to tear you down? Many swingers felt that the media was doing just that in early 1999. What it had trumpeted only six to twelve months before was already being written off as just another trend. *Time* and the *New York Times* both predicted that the clock was running out on the revival. There's even been a Sprite ad slamming swing as a passing fad.

The truth isn't anywhere near so bleak, though the swing scene has been experiencing its fair share of growing pains as it matures. While the new rock-oriented bands were what sparked

1998

- ▶ It's the year of "Jump, Jive, an' Wail" as the Gap ad revives Louis Prima's original cut, and Brian Setzer's cover debuts accompanied by a killer-diller video
- ▶ The legend passes on. Frank Sinatra dies at age eighty-two
- ▶ Swing sells: Fans snap up 2 million copies of Setzer's *Dirty Boogie* album, while Big Bad Voodoo Daddy and the Cherry Poppin' Daddies each surpass 1 million in sales

1999

- ▶ The hundredth anniversary of Duke Ellington's birth shines the spotlight on one of the greatest composers of all time
- ▶ Big Bad Voodoo Daddy plays the Super Bowl
- ▶ The Grammys reward the Brian Setzer Orchestra
- ▶ Lindy innovator Frankie Manning's eighty-fifth birthday is celebrated with coast-to-coast parties

the revival, in the past couple of years the dancing has come to really dominate the movement. In turn, as the Lindy Hoppers become more experienced, they've been gravitating toward bands that play more dancer-friendly midtempo songs. "I definitely was affected and influenced by what dancers were interested in and looking for," says bandleader Bill Elliott. "On our first CD everything is fast and slow. By the time of our second I was including several midtempo numbers." Adds Eddie Reed, "I do songs that are tailor-made for Lindy Hop." But while the newer fave bands, such as Indigo Swing, Seattle's **Casey MacGill,** Elliott, and Reed, favor a more traditional sound over rock influences, that makes them less likely to cross over to MTV. The classic big bands are as much an inspiration to them as jump blues. Reed's band replicates the Artie Shaw Orchestra of the late thirties. Elliott cites Tommy Dorsey as an inspiration. According to Chris Siebert of

Lavay Smith's band, audiences are getting more sophisticated and are starting to appreciate the more complex but equally thrilling arrangements of the big band era. "They've had a little taste of it and they get hungry and they want to find out more," he says. Others in the scene, however, worry that without the rock element, neoswing is losing its edge. Says *Swing Time*'s Moss, "This breakthrough in modern pop music doesn't really have to do with Glenn Miller or Benny Goodman."

No matter what style of music they play, all of the bands still encounter some friction with the dancers, and vice versa. "We joke about it because the dancers and the bands are really like people in a dysfunctional marriage," says Elliott. "Each needs the other but can't really get from the other what it wants. What the dancers want from the bands is exactly the tempos that they want to dance to all night long. But each dancer has a different idea of what that is. What the bands want from the dancers that they don't get enough of is applause and admiration and appreciation." Conflict has also arisen among the dancers themselves. In the last few years, a different type of Lindy Hop—dubbed Hollywood style by its popularizers, LA dance teachers Sylvia Skylar and Erik Robison—has been revived. A smoother way of swing dancing, it's best seen in such movies as *Buck Privates* and the hard-to-find short *Groovy Movie*. Savoy-style aficionados and Hollywood fans don't always get along. When the new revival first started in Los Angeles, "they would throw salvos at each other," says Santa Barbara teacher Sylvia Sykes.

Despite these occasional lapses of perspective, the swing scene is in fact opening up to more influences than ever before. Neoswingers are embracing rockabilly again. Some bands are trying to hybridize rap and swing (such as the **Yalloppin' Hounds**) and soul and swing (such as **Vargas Swing**). Realizing that back in the day, people would dance waltzes, tangos, cha-chas, and foxtrots as well as swing all in one night, Lindy Hoppers are starting to add everything from hip-hop to salsa to their repertoire. Swing and the jazz community, completely estranged during most of the revival, have begun to find common cause also (see page 157 in chapter 5).

In 1999 swing continued to hit new peaks. Big Bad Voodoo Daddy performed at the Super Bowl. In February Brian Setzer won two Grammy's and the *New York Times* announced, "Over half a century since its heyday, swing is officially pop music again." Bill Elliott and **George Gee** have revived the tradition of the great battles of the bands, playing an enormous July 4, 1999, weekend show at the historic Hollywood Palladium. Instead of relying on club owners, dancers are starting to create and run their own events, such as the swing nights at LA's Satin Ballroom, where more than a thousand Lindy Hoppers crowd the hall's enormous floor once a month. Everywhere you look there are new swing magazines—such as *Atomic* and *Modern Lounge*— and movies, including *Swing,* with Lisa Stansfield, and an in-the-works HBO biopic of Frankie Manning. Lincoln Center's month-long Midsummer Night's Swing concert program draws thousands of dancing couples every night. Colleges across the country now boast swing clubs. And new bands are forming all the time. "I get ten to twenty demos a week," says Tammi Gower of the Derby. Keeping it all together is a hopping Internet community, made up of hundreds of swing Web sites, through which fans of the music and dance keep in touch.

Many people are relieved that swing may no longer be the fad of the moment. To those people who are passionately attached to the music, dance, and style of the swing era, it feels like it's theirs once again, not the province of the latest marketing hype. Swing's grass roots are as strong as ever.

TEN REASONS SWING CAME BACK

There are as many theories about why swing has returned as there are moves you can do on the dance floor. Some feel the swing movement is a backlash against the musical styles and social mores (or lack thereof) that have emerged over the past several decades. Others believe the renaissance of swing is simply the next logical progression in the nostalgia cycle, in which everything old is repackaged for a new, younger audience. Here, in no particular order, are a few theories (besides the fact that swing's just great) that swingers themselves have put forth about why swing came back:

1. Safe Sex. Swing provides a way of enjoying physical intimacy without the dangers of sex. "I think of partner dancing as safe sex," says bandleader Bill Elliott. "You can very closely correlate the rise and fall of couples dancing sort of opposite the sexual revolution. In the sixties and seventies, it was fine for people to be dancing ten feet apart if they were going to go to bed an hour later. In the nineties, when there's much more sexual reticence and carefulness, it plays a part in courtship." (Interestingly, the word *swing* has made a corresponding journey. It began as a purely dance and music term, later became a reference to casual sex, and is now reverting to its original, more innocent meaning.)

2. Respect for Our Elders. Swing's fans are young and old— from teenagers just learning how to Lindy Hop to their grandparents, who danced to Basie and Goodman. What a contrast to the musical landscape of the nineties, where the latest nineteen-year-old pop sensation comes and goes in a flash. Swing music, on the other hand, brings generations together. Its newest fans are giving long-overdue recognition to the creators of our musical heritage who are still with us, such names as Frankie Manning, Anita O'Day, Keely Smith, Sam Butera, Lionel Hampton, and Illinois Jacquet. The younger generation recognizes that these "old-timers" have something invaluable to teach us, and the elders are eager to share their passion for the music and dance that has kept them young at heart.

3. Grunge. "People were killing themselves over that music," says singer Ann Hampton Callaway of grunge. "People don't kill themselves over swing."

4. The Blurring of Gender Roles. Since the sexual revolution of the 1960s, gender roles have become increasingly ill defined. Women were told they should ask men on dates, pay their own way, and be the sexual aggressors. Men, meanwhile, worried they could be threatened with a sexual harassment suit if they so much as looked twice at a woman. The swing movement reembraces certain established conventions: men hold doors, buy drinks, and ask women to dance. In the dance, they tend to be the leaders, the women the followers. No one wants to go back to the days of ingrained sexism, but everyone is clearly searching for a new and better balance in the relationship between guys and dolls.

5. The Gap-ification of America. In fashion, androgyny is the norm. Clothing is unisex and drab—both boys and girls wear jeans or khakis, baggy sweatshirts, and baseball caps—and people have lost all sense of style. The swing scene marks a return to glamour. The women wear elaborate hairdos, full makeup, and feminine frocks, whereas the men are clean-cut, sporting tailor-made suits and such "manly" accessories as fedoras, suspenders, and ties.

6. The Internet. The Internet has helped support swing in two ways. On the one hand, the Net has allowed music and dance lovers to find one another and spread the good news of swing across the globe. Yet at the same time, people are searching for a release from their cyberlives. Now more than ever, they want to get out and touch each other, to meet face-to-face after interacting all day through their computer screens. Swing provides a safe forum in which to meet, mingle, and have fun.

7. America's Retro Obsession. The renaissance of swing comes on the heels of the neolounge movement, which was all about clothes and style, drinks and cigars, and bachelor pad music by the likes of Esquivel, Bennett, and Sinatra. Swing adds the element of dance and expands the musical repertoire back in time to include big band and jump blues. Moreover, both the swing and lounge movements reflect modern society's wholesale turn-of-the-millenium obsession with all things retro, including the revival of seventies and eighties music and fashions.

8. CDs and VCRs. CD and VCR technology has made the great music and movies of a bygone era available to the masses. Many dancers learned their first moves watching classic films such as *Buck Privates* or *Hellzapoppin'* on late-night television. Now they can not only buy these films for relatively little money but also purchase instructional videos from some of the top dancers in the world. Similarly, whereas swing lovers once had to rely on their grandparents' old vinyl records, now major labels have released collector's series on CD. Featuring the greatest hits of Jordan, Prima, Dorsey, Ellington, and dozens of others, these new compilations have helped to further the swing movement.

9. Gym Burn-Out. After twenty years of step aerobics and pumping iron, many fitness fanatics have grown tired of the routine. Swing offers a way to stay in shape while also having fun. "You are killing two birds with one stone," says Tammy Finocchiaro of the Flyin' Lindy Hoppers. "You are being social, you are dressing up, and you are exercising."

10. Seinfeld. There is simply too much jadedness in our lives. People are open once again to sweetness, romanticism, and sentimentality. There's even a new term for it: postironic sincerity. Says San Francisco entertainer Mr. Lucky, "I think we have to give 'corny' a little more breathing room in order to preserve that little germ of naïveté that I have inside of me."

CHAPTER 3

What Makes the Lindy Really Hop

S wing dancing. Jitterbugging. The Lindy Hop. They're all pretty much the same words for one of the most exciting, playful, and joyous dances ever invented. At its best, swing dancing is an electric communication between two partners, an unspoken dialogue of individual impulses moving into harmony. It's a world of difference from the dancing that most of us now do in nightclubs. You know, the formless booty-shaking freestyle dancing that can sometimes feel like you're in your own lonely bubble. In the Lindy, you're going to have fun relating to another person instead of just to the music. You'll find a certain comfort in the fact that everyone does several of the same basic patterns. On top of all that, you get to touch another person. "People want to get back together again, they're tired of being apart," says Lindy legend Frankie Manning, explaining the resurgence of swing dancing. Adds Teddy Kern, cofounder of New York's Dance Manhattan studio, "My whole theory is to touch a stranger. You can touch somebody you've never met before and dance with them. That's what's magic about partner dancing."

Don't worry, however, that swing dancing is going to feel rigid because it has a few set rules. Unlike some ballroom dances, the Lindy Hop offers lots of space for improvisation. Because of its signature swingout, or breakaway, move, in which the two partners can briefly separate and do their own steps, the dance allows for inspired moments of spontaneous creativity. "It's like visual jazz," says San Francisco teacher and American Lindy Hop champion Paul Overton. "There are a thousand things you can do. There's no end to it. The Lindy Hop just has a very loose base to it and people make up new moves all the time." Just like in any good relationship, the aim is for the dancing couple to achieve the perfect balance between structure and freedom. As Savoy veteran Norma Miller puts it, "The Lindy is the complete coordination of two bodies."

PREVIOUS PAGE: *King of the aerials Frankie Manning sends partner Ann Johnson through the air at the Savoy.* (W. EUGENE SMITH/BLACK STAR)

Classic Lindy Hop is known as Savoy style. Rooted in African movements and danced very low to the ground with a bend in the torso, it's based on the Lindy as it was popularized and refined at the Savoy Ballroom in the late twenties and early thirties. It's exuberant and sometimes very wild, with its Charleston kicks, gravity-defying aerials, rhythmic finesse, and a swinging bounce in the knees. The weight is forward on the balls of your feet. The hands are up, waving and expressive. Most important, the knees are kept bent and elastic, letting your body swing down and up again along with the music. That swing you feel when you hear Count Basie? That's the swing you want to let your body give in to.

Of course, Savoy style isn't the only form of swing dancing. The Lindy's close cousin is the jitterbug, a less Afro-centric version of the dance that became popular once swing crossed over to the white mainstream in the late 1930s. There are also more smooth and upright styles of the Lindy called Dean Collins and Hollywood style that are gaining in popularity in recent years. (For more information on different styles see page 88.)

While each type of swing dance has its own distinct look, they are all basically variations of the Lindy, one of the most interesting-to-watch social dances in the world. Check out an experienced couple Lindy Hopping. Together, they are a whirl of kicks and turns. Changing positions and stances, their hands connect and reconnect, trailing around each other with stunning precision. To the outside observer, they look as though they've been rehearsing their dance for days beforehand. In fact, it's something the pair is improvising right before your eyes on the dance floor.

Watching skilled Lindy Hoppers can be both thrilling and intimidating. Sure, it looks great, you're thinking, but how will I ever be able to do *all that stuff?* Well, don't be fooled by all the tricks and variations. The complicated moves, of course, are what attracts new dancers to the Lindy. Everybody wants to look as good as those dancers in the Gap TV commercial. Indeed, today's most accomplished dancers and teachers first got into it to learn the Lindy's bells and whistles. Recalls Erin Stevens of the Pasadena Ballroom Dance Association of her first meetings with Frankie Manning, "We were like, 'Give us the tricks. Give us the show items.' It was always about what new moves did you get." Swing dancing's resurgence was initially fueled by new dancers trying to match the unbelievably wild moves that Whitey's Lindy Hoppers pulled in old movies like *Hellzapoppin'*. "The kids saw *A Day at the Races* and they thought that all those kicks and air steps is swing dancing," says veteran New York dancer and former swing band member Dawn Hampton.

In the last few years, however, there's come a realization that most of those showy moves are just that—they were choreographed for professional dancers to be done in performance. "We were really creating a spectator sport," says Norma Miller. One secret of the famous Savoy dancers, however, wasn't caught on film. In addition to appearing on Broadway and in films, they always remained social dancers also. Interacting with regular dancers in ballrooms kept their dancing authentic.

Today's swingers didn't catch on to this at first. Manning, the mentor of the Lindy Hop movement, wasn't interested in passing along all the tricks it turns out. "From the start, he was trying to give us the heart and soul of the dance. It took a while for us to listen," says Stevens. Recently there's been a new emphasis on the basics. "It was a real backward process for everyone the world over," adds Stevens. "The Lindy is getting away from the choreographed tricks. There's this big push away from aerials and tricks toward working with your partner, listening to the music, creating some connection, adding more jazz."

That's great news for beginners. Even hard-core veteran swing dancers are now focusing more on the basics, which are easy to get a grip on quickly but take years and years to perfect. Lindy Hoppers are realizing that in many cases less is more. "You can really lose yourself much more easily if you are doing four variations and not forty. You're less worried about what you're doing next. You can go out and see eighty-year-old couples who are happy doing five or six variations all night," says New York dancer and teacher Fredda Seidenbaum.

So what is the heart and soul of the Lindy? It's having a great sense of play, a desire to explore what your body can do, and the ability to share that with a partner. "Jumping around is fun. You get into it because it's fun. You don't get into it because it's a science project," says Debra Sternberg, a Washington, D.C., teacher. While learning the dance requires a lot of time and energy, the Lindy Hop also asks that you not take it too-too seriously. So keep that in mind. In the movie *Swing Time,* Ginger Rogers asks Fred Astaire, "Are you as scared as I am?" Astaire replies: "Don't be nervous. It's only a dance we have to do. It's nothing to worry about."

LEARNING TO DANCE

To become a righteous Lindy Hopper, you'll want to take a series of classes with an experienced teacher. Getting hep to the Lindy requires patience and a certain amount of—let it be said—commitment. That can be frustrating at first for dancers who are accustomed to just going to a club and doing whatever they like. Lindy isn't do your own thing. "This is a skill. This is like a sport. If I gave you a tennis racket would you believe me if I said you could go play Chris Evert after one class?" asks Seidenbaum. Although you can be assured that your first class will be instantly gratifying—you'll be smiling and swinging before you know it— you'll want to keep coming back and learning more.

To get even better, you'll also want to watch out for workshops that studios hold with celebrated visiting dancers such as Manning; Ryan Francois, the choreographer of *Swing Kids* and his partner, Jenny Thomas, both of whom are appearing in the Broadway musical *Swing;* Charleston expert Louise Thwaite; the hip-hop-influenced Steven Mitchell; Singapore's Sing Lim; and

Sweden's spectacular performance troupe the Rhythm Hot Shots. Many nightclubs offer free lessons in the evenings before the nightclub starts really hopping. You'll also want to watch great old movies like *Hellzapoppin'* and *Buck Privates* for inspiration. Also, there are on-line instructions (see the Web guide in the appendix) and tons of teaching videotapes (see page 93 for a list of the best ones) available.

Watching any video or reading a book, however, is no substitute for actually doing the Lindy with a partner. So think of the information here as a briefing, a way to familiarize yourself with what you'll hear and do in class, so that your body starts spinning and not your head.

THE BASICS

Perfecting your basics, rather than knowing 150 tricky moves, is the most crucial part of being a great Lindy Hopper. "The basic is like your golf swing. You work on it your whole life," says Paul Overton. And once you learn the basics, adds Frankie Manning, "all the other steps will come easily for you."

What exactly is a basic? There are two types, the six-count and the eight-count. Each is simply a rhythm pattern you make with your feet. You can do them in place, while moving forward or backward, and while turning in a circle. They are the foundation upon which you base everything else, from styling to specific movements. Once you can do the basics consistently, you are freed to do countless other things with the rest of your body and simply enjoy yourself. "When your feet can do the steps without even having to think about it," say Sylvia Skylar, "then you can spend all the time in the world thinking about and concentrating on your partner."

To do the basics, you'll need to get a grip on the following:

Counts: When you first start dancing you may need to count the beats of the rhythm. In swing music, the beats are syncopated. This means that there are stresses on beats that are generally unstressed. Think a-one-and-a-two. To do the Lindy you want to put emphasis on what is called the downbeat. For example, downbeats are the first beat and the third beat of a phrase, not the second and fourth. Of course, "once you get the numbers, lose the numbers," says Erin Stevens of the Pasadena Ballroom Dance Association. "And feel it."

Lead and Follow: The Lindy Hop is referred to as a lead-and-follow dance, meaning that one person, generally but not always the man, leads the movements, while the partner, generally the woman, follows them. In this chapter the leader is referred to as he; the follower as she. But this is purely for the sake of convenience. Many men dance with other men, and women dance with women. Some same-sex couples are gay; some are not. In the Seattle swing scene, for example, lead and follow is a strictly gender-neutral affair. You can also get a better appreciation for the dance by learning the "other half" of it. "A lot of girls because they're such fast learners will eventually learn how to lead too," says Debra Sternberg. "It's fun to know both."

Arm Positions: When you hold your partner's hand, you want to feel a light tension between both of you. If the follower's arms are too rigid, she isn't responding to being led. If the follower's arms are too limp, often referred to as "spaghetti arms," she won't be able to feel and respond to her partner. The right connection will enable you to be sensitive to the slightest pull and the lightest push from your partner. Also, neither partner should ever hyperextend his or her arms; you want to keep a slight bend in the arm, a gentle spring at the elbow.

Step to It: Don't plod or stomp around the dance floor. You want to keep a light, swinging feeling in your feet. No heavy shuffling, this isn't work. Also, your steps don't have to be as big as you imagine. You want to learn how to take small steps too, especially for when you're on a crowded dance floor (see etiquette rule no. 3, page 93).

Body Positions: There are two basic positions for the couple to be in: either open or closed. Open position is when you are facing and at arms' length from each other, holding either one of your partner's hands or both. For closed position, the leader puts his right arm behind his partner, his hand in the middle of her back. She rests her left hand on his right shoulder. He lightly holds her right hand in his left hand at waist height, keeping an easy tension in the arms with the elbows bent. Also, the pair should position their bodies in a slight **V**. You can also be very close together, with your torsos and

Open Position

legs touching. Think of closed and open positions as your home bases. If you're stuck for what to do next, you can hang out there for a measure or so until you figure out a new move.

Tempos: It's great when a dance band plays a mix of songs of different speeds throughout the night. If every number is at warp 10, you'll be bushed halfway into the evening, while too many slow songs is boring. That's why many Lindy Hoppers

Closed Position

prefer bands—such as Bill Elliott or Indigo Swing—that play a lot of songs at midtempo. "The Lindy Hop is really about expressing yourself, and when the tempo isn't as fast, you have more time to play with the music and put more movement into it," says Steve Conrad, of the Arizona Lindy Hop Society. Some experienced dancers will even get quite technical, wanting to know how many beats per minute a song has, and a few Web sites go so far as to list the BPM of popular swing songs. So what are the best tempos? For a nice easy swing, anywhere from 140 to 180 beats per minute. For faster numbers, they can go up to 220 beats per minute, though you may have to dance single or double time, instead of triple, to keep up.

The Six-Count Basic in Triple Time

The six-count basic is one of the most important building blocks of swing dancing. It's one of the two rhythm patterns that make up the Lindy, the other being the more challenging eight-count basic. It's also the move that most people associate with jitterbugging or East Coast swing. The basic can be done in many variations; this is an example done in closed position:

Starting in closed, do what are called triple steps on counts 1 and 2. These are syncopated movements that require three steps in two beats. If it's helpful, think to yourself as you move TRI-ple-STEP, STEP-three-TIMES, or ONE-and-TWO to get the counting right. (For speedier numbers, you may want to dance in either double-time or single-time rhythm to go faster.) For triple time however, the leader steps on his left foot, then right foot, then left again, changing his weight three times. He's not crossing his feet over each other. In fact, it should feel like you are doing the steps almost entirely in place, even though you'll move slightly forward with your partner. The follower is doing the same steps, mirroring her partner but on the opposite feet, beginning with her right foot.

On counts 3 and 4, do another set of triple steps. The leader

Triple Step

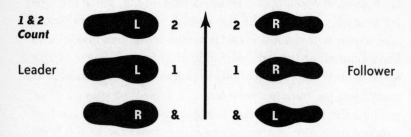

1 & 2
Count

Leader

Follower

Triple Step

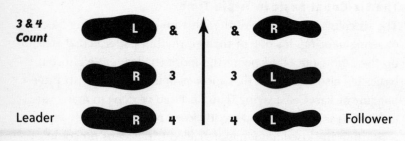

3 & 4
Count

Leader

Follower

Rock Step

5/6
Count

Leader

Follower

Six-count basic

starts with his right foot; the follower with her left. And this time, the couple moves back to their starting point.

On the next two counts, both partners do what's referred to as a rock step. The leader should give his partner's arm a gentle push with his left hand, opening up the space between the couple. As he does that, he puts his left foot behind his right on count 5, stepping only on the ball of the foot and "rocking" back on it. His partner does the same move with her right foot. At this point, both of them will have their hips more in line with each other than facing each other. On count 6 both leader and follower simply step on the other foot in place and come in close together again. Between the two steps, you should feel as if you've rocked back and forth.

The Eight-Count Basic

"Until you have learned an eight-count step, you really aren't dancing swing," says Dance Manhattan's Teddy Kern. "Because the music we're dancing to is written in four-four time, it's the eight-count in which you use up a whole phrase of music. It's fundamentally important. When you dance an eight-count, you go, 'Oh, wow, that's where the music is.'" To do the eight-count, on counts 1 and 2 take a rock step. On 3 and 4, a triple step. You single-step on 5 and again on 6 in what's called a walking step. And then on the last two counts, do a second triple step. (You can also choose to do the eight-count with the rock step coming at the end of the phrase). The eight-count can be done in numerous variations, with one of the most common involving doing a circle, beginning and ending in closed position. (Much of the Lindy, in fact, is done in circles. The dance is done, as dancers say, to all four walls.) Other eight-count variations include moving from open to closed position or beginning and ending in open position. The swing-outs come in the middle of these phrases on count 5. That's when the leader releases or sends out his partner, allowing one or both of them to do an improvisational step.

Advice for Leaders

Sure, you're the one in charge, but leading isn't about going off on some kind of power trip. In fact, it's your job to make the dance the most wonderful experience possible for your partner. And that puts a lot of responsibility on your shoulders.

1. **Reach Out and Touch Your Partner.** You'd be surprised how many guys in their first class are as shy as ten-year-olds about putting their hands on a woman. "I say, 'Okay, now you're going to have to put your arms around the ladies,'" says Manning. "And they're reluctant you know. I say, 'Fellas, touch the girl. She won't mind.'" Some men, at first, don't realize how clean, fun, and above all, safe touching in a social dance situation can be. "It's not like it's a come-on between you and your partner, though sometimes that happens," says Dance Manhattan cofounder Elena Iannucci. "It's dance intimacy." Adds Lee Moore of the Flyin' Lindy Hoppers, who often dances with his sister-in-law Tammy Finocchiaro, "It's a contact sport. There's not a part of her I don't know."

2. **Think Ahead.** Because you decide what you and your partner are doing, you always have to be planning the next move. How do you choose which comes next? Let the music inspire you. Listen to the beat, the phrasing, and especially the feeling of the song. Also, you need to dance at the level of your partner. Don't throw a slew of variations at a girl you've just met. Start simply and then begin to challenge her and see how far you can go together.

3. **Communicate Clearly with a Strong Lead.** Once you make that split-second decision on what move you're going to do, you then have to inform your partner. The way you tell her, however, is with actions, not words. Most steps have specific signals associated with them, known as leads. These precise signals are generally simple pushes, pulls, and touches. For instance, in one simple move starting in closed, you simply put your hand at your partner's waist and gently push her out into open position, just before the beat on which you want her to move. (For an idea of

how all this works, you might want to watch a leader on the dance floor, but the key is to pay attention to what he does with his hands, not his feet.) Good leading isn't wishy-washy, nor is it aggressive. The more firm and clear you are, the faster she'll pick up on your intention. The more light and sensitive you are, the more she'll enjoy your dance together.

4. Be Alert to Your Surroundings. You control where the two of you move on the dance floor, so you have to be especially aware of where you are in relation to other couples. Look for spaces between other dancers where you can swing her out. Change direction, freeze, or do a turn if another couple is heading right at you. Remember, your partner is putting herself in your hands. "I know certain partners I could dance with with my eyes closed because they would protect me," says Fredda Seidenbaum. What you want to avoid at all costs is your partner's getting kicked or jostled. You'd rather be dancing a second dance with her than running to find an ice pack, right?

5. Finally, Make It a Thrill. This is the cardinal rule. If it's a thrill for her, you're guaranteed to enjoy yourself too. "Treat her like she is the queen," says Manning, "and you are just a jester in her court."

Advice for Followers

Here's an easy one: follow. Just let go and listen to what your partner is communicating to you. Of course, you need to know your steps, but if something new comes at you, the best advice is simply to go with the flow. "If you are a good follower, you can get through any dance with some degree of success," says Debra Sternberg.

1. Listen to the Lead. It may feel odd at first to let a man tell you what to do. But give in, it's just a three-minute dance after all. Being a good follower means not worrying about what comes next. You simply pick up and respond to your partner's signals. If you feel uncomfortable being led, be aware of it and be patient with yourself. Champion Lindy Hopper Jenny Thomas recalls that she fought being a follower for almost a year when she was first learning the dance. Before she became partners with Ryan Francois, she had been a professional tap dancer but never a social dancer. "I had been trained to think, 'Oh yeah, I know what comes next.' Ryan would trip me up. For about a year, any time I recognized a step, he would change it halfway through and say, 'Don't anticipate the next move.' I used to hate it. He'd actually trip me up in front of people on a social dance floor. And it's actually made me a much better follower. I just think if you can let the lead take you on a ride, it's so much more enjoyable."

2. Don't Backseat Drive. On the dance floor this is known as back-leading. Don't do it.

3. Don't Be Stiff. But don't be a rag doll either. "We always give the equal and opposite movement of what the leader gives," say Paul Overton's partner, teacher Sharon Ashe.

It's a Two-Way Street

Whether you're the leader or the follower, you both want to be constantly sensitive to each other. Dancing is about what's best for both of you. So don't forge ahead and forget what's going on with the other person. "In a jazz band when a soloist goes on a riff, they don't just go off on their own. It relates back to what the band is doing," says Ashe. "So even though I might improvise with my feet, I want to relate it back to the song and to my partner." Just take a second and watch a few couples on the dance floor. It's easy to spot the pairs that aren't on the same page. They're the couple letting fly with the most amazing moves, but they never even look in each other's eyes. "They're dancing at each other, not with each other," says Sternberg. Nothing's less fun than having partners, "who are doing their own moves," adds Ashe. "They are doing the same thing they always do. They are being cool. Or they are grandstanding."

By contrast, a couple can be doing the simplest of moves and if the communication is intense, they will be far more pleasurable to watch than a couple that's just going through the motions, however elaborate those may be.

The Way That You Do It: Individual Styling

Whether you do Savoy Lindy Hop or one of the more smooth styles, you'll still want to put your own distinct stamp on the dance. "Everybody should do the Lindy in their own style," says New York instructor Margaret Batiuchok. "Each person who does it dances differently and has their own way of moving."

The shape of your body will help determine how you dance. Shorty George Snowden created moves that played up his small stature. By contrast, says Ryan Francois, "I'm a long-limbed, tall athletic guy. I like to use my legs and stretch out." The Flyin' Lindy Hoppers gravitated toward more athletic moves, according to Tammy Finocchiaro, "because we're short, stocky people. We adjusted the image to fit our bodies."

Beyond that, the most important consideration is bringing your own personality to the dance. "Some people are more comical, some have a little more hip-hop style," says Overton. "There are people who do a little more upright style. Different personalities start to emerge. More bouncy or less bouncy. You change your style all the time." You may bring humor to it. Or grace and beauty. Or simply whatever feelings you happen to be having that night. The Lindy is your own way of expressing yourself.

Getting Out on the Dance Floor

When you first start learning the Lindy, you want to take what you know from the classroom into a real social dance situation as soon as you can. Getting yourself out on a club's dance floor, however, can be an intimidating experience. Everyone is hopping and flying around with abandon and looking as good, to you at least, as world-class champions. But don't let it get to you. To work up the nerve to head out there, you can start out by attending the practice dances that most studios sponsor at least once a week. When you go to a real nightclub, it helps to show up with another beginner. It can also be more inspiring to go see a real band, instead of attending a DJ'd swing night. "When you dance to live music, you tend to dance better," says Manning. Finally, don't feel the need to show off on the dance floor. Swing dancing isn't about performing. Nor does it require attitude. Go in with the spirit that it's OK to mess up, have two left feet, and make a fool of yourself. Give yourself the space to be a beginner and don't be hard on yourself. "What we teach people is that every mistake is just a new move," says the Arizona Lindy Hop Society's Steve Conrad. "That's the freedom of the dance."

ADVANCED MOVES

Once you know the basics, you can then start adding variation after variation after variation. The improvisational nature of the dance means that there are endless new moves you can introduce all the time. "Social dancing is about having all these little pieces of a puzzle and you create new pictures every time you're out on the dance floor. It looks different, it feels different, it is different. You put it together your own way," says Elena Iannucci. In class, of course, you'll learn lots of moves in particular sequences. Certainly, many moves work naturally in sequence, like an underarm turn followed by a turn in which both partners go under the raised arms. But don't get too hung up on set patterns. Listen to the music and do what feels right at the time. "You shouldn't learn a move and throw it in on any swingout," says Sylvia Skylar. "People should do the styling based on what they are hearing."

Be aware, the information on different moves provided here is meant merely as a look at the options you'll have, not as a set of directives of what you should do. It is by no means exhaustive. Also, some teachers may have other names for these moves.

"There's no set-in-stone definition for a lot of this stuff," says Sternberg. Gladly, you can depend on your follower to understand your body signals, not what you happen to call a move. Relying on the international language of dance is always the best policy.

Turns

Followers, here's where you work that skirt! While the idea behind them is simple—one or both partners turn beneath the pair's raised arms—there are more varieties of turns than you'd imagine. There are underarm turns to right or left; tuck turns (in which the follower is pulled in close before then being swung out); "she goes, he goes" turns, which are just what they sound like; ones like the Texas Tommy where the partners change hands; and turns where one partner releases hands and does a double free spin. But for most turns, you'll want to remember these guidelines: Be careful moving past each other so you don't end up with an arm in the face. Keeping eye contact with your partner will help you spot as you turn. On many turns, you'll want to end up in the same place where your partner just was; both partners simply switch spots. Leaders should bring the followers in toward them on the first beat of a count and turn them on the second; these should be two distinct yet smooth movements. Lastly, the secret to making a skirt move is not to just turn with your legs but to involve your whole body in the motion, from hips to ribcage.

Spin Out

Steps

Sick of doing the rock step? As an alternative, the woman can jazz up her Lindy by doing what are called swivels, in which she pivots on one or both feet and swings her hips from one side to the other. Instead of stepping backward, either partner can also step forward. (One move, called the slingshot, involves the leader's going into a forward lunge before he sends his partner into a swingout.) Other great elements to throw into the mix include slides, where you touch your foot to the floor and slide it smoothly back, and stomp offs, where you stomp the ground like a bull and drag your foot back under you.

Kicks

In the Lindy, kicking can be any which way and loose. You can kick sideways, forward, backward, up, or out, from the knees or from the hip. You can do these with your partner in what's called a hopscotch while you turn in a circle. You can do them as part of a Charleston move (see Charleston information below). The only time it's best not to do them is during a slow song or on a very crowded floor. "The kicks are meant for when you are dancing at speed," says Francois. "When you are moving fast across the floor, it makes sense to take your feet to the air." The most important rule about kicking, though, is to be considerate of other dancers. "Do not let your feet fly without checking around you first," says Teddy Kern. "Getting kicked by a speeding Lindy Hopper can be dangerous and painful."

Hesitations and Freezes

Add a little more syncopation and surprise to your Lindy by stopping, waiting, and teasing for a beat or two. These can be done with a lot of dramatic flair. They can also be used to get you back on the beginning of a song's phrase.

Dips and Drops

While they are the most romantic and chivalrous way to end a dance, dips can be done at any time during a song. Along with so-called drops, "they are used quite a bit to emphasize the music," says Steve Conrad. "Dips are great during trumpet blasts or when saxes draw out a whole note. On the riff, you'll drop down to the ground." The key to both dips and drops is smoothness and connection. "The leader should stay with her all the way down," says Conrad. "And she should usually support her own weight with at least one of her legs." Once you learn simple dips, you can move onto advanced ones like a dip borrowed from salsa dance: "You use a lot of momentum and the girls dip down as they spin in a circle," says Conrad.

Swingout Moves

When you're doing a swingout, whether you've let go of each other's hands or not, you're free to do anything you like. You can do the twist or break-dance or mosh. Do the robot with as much sincerity or irony as you like. Whatever. Oftentimes, however, both partners will stay in mirror with each other and do some of the following moves traditionally associated with swingouts.

- ▶ SUZY Q: A challenging move that involves crossing one foot over the other while moving sideways along a line. You will look, says Francois with a laugh, "like a crab that's crushing a bug underneath its shoe and then cleaning it off while holding a stance in your upper body like Babe Ruth about to bat."
- ▶ TRUCKIN': Stepping forward and swiveling your foot in and out while holding up your index finger and shaking it.
- ▶ PECKIN': "You walk kind of like a chicken and you peck your head forward at each other, normally to the beat," says Conrad.
- ▶ SHORTY GEORGE: Invented by Shorty George Snowden, who was reputed to do it while walking between his partner Big Bea's legs. It's a very low to the ground move in which you do bent-knee kicks with pivots while walking forward with your arms up. "It looks like a drunk man walking and struggling to carry two pails down the street," says Francois.

▶ BOOGIE BACK OR FORWARD: A series of kicks and steps punctuated by clapping the hands in front of you. The emphasis on the kicks is in really using your hips for the movement.

Couple Moves

There are a number of fun, well-known moves that don't fall into any category, except that they aren't done in breakaway but in close pairings. There's the cuddle, in which the leader brings the follower back from a swingout, snuggling her up against his body, putting his right hand around her back on her right hip and his left hand holding her right hand in front of her body. You've probably seen people do the popular pretzel, in which both partner's loop and unloop their arms over their shoulders as they turn. Best of all is the mess around, which sounds as erotic as it feels. For this move, both partners hold their hips close together and move in unison around in a circle, marking beats as if pausing along the numbers of a clock.

Cuddle

Charleston Steps

Since the Charleston was one of the progenitors of the Lindy, it's perfectly natural to add its moves to your swing dancing. The most recognizable step is called the tandem or back Charleston. "The girl is in front of the guy and they are holding hands and facing in the same direction," says Louise Thwaite, a Lindy Hopper with expertise in the Charleston. "They kick and touch the toe forward with the same leg, come back to the center and then kick back and touch the toe behind, or they can do a kick with a hop for a more energetic move." Other moves are known as the Flying Charleston ("you'll pass by each other quickly as you are doing basic Charleston kicks," says Steve Conrad), side Charleston, crossover Charleston, and hand-to-hand Charleston (in which the partners are facing). The dance, which originated in Charleston, South Carolina, was popularized in an all-black Broadway show, *Running Wild,* in 1923, which included the song "Charleston" by Harlem stride pianist James P. Johnson. "In the 1920s it was the biggest dance craze the world had ever seen, and the only one that was bigger was the Lindy," says Thwaite. While it was considered a scandal in its day (the risqué Josephine Baker was one of the most famous Charleston dancers), it's now a way of adding a distinctly twenties look to your Lindy.

Charleston Kick

Aerials

Aerials, or air steps, as they are known because they are danced in time to the music, are the extreme sport of swing. They were invented by Frankie Manning back at the Savoy around 1936. Today they are perhaps the most well-known moves associated with swing, thanks to that Gap commercial. Wild, crazy, thrilling, and high-flying, they put the zing in swing. "When people first see swing the thing that grabs their attention is the aerials," says Tammy Finocchiaro of Ventura, California's aerials troupe the Flyin' Lindy Hoppers.

But air steps aren't for everyone. If you're a beginner, it will be some time before you're proficient enough to start learning them. "A lot of young kids say, 'Oh, how do you do the air step?'" says Manning. "I say, 'How long have you been dancing? Three weeks?

You know I started dancing in 1927, the first air step was done eight years later, so I had a long time to learn how to dance before the air step was even created.'"

You may in fact never be able to do them. "If you are not athletically inclined, if you do not have a sense of timing and balance, you know, forget aerials, you'll kill yourself," says Iannucci. Adds Sylvia Skylar, "There are some people who just never feel comfortable in the air. They hate being upside down."

Aerials can be dangerous. Finocchiaro and her partner, Lee Moore, have each broken their noses doing them. To be safe, aerials should be learned from trained teachers using spotters or mats or both.

Aerial

Finally, air steps should never be done in a social dance situation but only during jam sessions, contests, and performances. It's too easy for people to get hurt on a packed dance floor if someone attempts an aerial. Even at the Savoy, they were only performed in a cordoned area of the ballroom.

Don't be scared off, however. Aerials, when performed properly, are as thrilling as the best roller-coaster ride. "You get to fly," says Finocchiaro, whose group has created an amazing step in which one guy throws her over another guy's head. When you're learning, though, you'll start with somewhat less spectacular moves. Some of the most accessible steps include the side car, in which the woman has her legs together and swings from left to right facing her partner, and the lamppost, also known as over the back or the helicopter. "You bring the girl and hook her over your arm and send her over your back," says Sylvia Skylar. "It's the most common aerial." While it's fun to know which moves, such as the lamppost, were originally done at the Savoy, astounding new aerials are being created all the time too. "I do an aerial where I go fifteen feet up in the air and then I come back down head first in between my partner's legs. They call it the big dive," says champion dancer and aerial specialist Nathalie Gomes. (Again, please don't try these at home.)

So how do you do a good aerial? Work on the timing between yourself and your partner. Work on it again and again. Accidents happen when you're doing something the other person thought was going to happen five seconds before. Discuss beforehand which step you plan to accomplish. Leaders should work on getting the right grip on their partner. "Grab the hip bone. If you grab her body and it goes squish, you are in the wrong location," says the Flyin' Lindy Hoppers' Moore. Once the follower is coming back down from her flight, the leader should be sure to grab her hips again and bend in his knees to cushion her fall. "You are not only there to lift her, you are there to babysit her and help her land," says Gomes.

Most important, don't hold back. Aerials work because of a perfectly synchronous interplay of leverage and momentum. When you hesitate, everything can be thrown off. Says Finocchiaro, "You have to go without any fear." Let 'em rip.

Group Dances

So you know how to do the electric slide. But can you get out on the floor and do these group dances that are associated with the Lindy?

▶ THE SHIM SHAM SHIMMY: It's become a tradition for Frankie Manning to lead the Shim Sham Shimmy line dance wherever he's teaching. Developed originally as a tap number, it was adopted by Lindy Hoppers in the early thirties. Everyone stays facing the same wall throughout the routine, as they move through steps that include stomps, boogie backs, and the Shorty George. The best part is when the leader says "Swing." At that point you grab the nearest partner and dance the Lindy until the leader calls out "Stop." Then freeze for eight beats until the leader declares it's time to dance again. A great song for dancing the Shim Sham is Erskine Hawkins's "Tuxedo Junction."

▶ THE JITTERBUG STROLL: A more recent line dance, the Jitterbug Stroll was created by Ryan Francois to be danced to Woody Herman's "Woodchopper's Ball." It puts together such exciting moves as boogie backs, the Suzy Q, and the Shorty George, with quarter turns between the different sections. By the end of the stroll, you will have faced all four walls.

▶ THE BIG APPLE: Created in Columbia, South Carolina, around 1930, the Big Apple was once such a popular dance that there were hundreds of Big Apple clubs across the country. It requires a caller who stands in the center of a circle and shouts out a variety of moves, from Charleston to stomp off to truckin'. "It's really fun actually, even if you don't know what to do," says Sharon Ashe. "Because everybody repeats each move for a few eight-counts, you can just look around and copy people."

THE MANY STYLES OF SWING

Swing dancing has been around for more than seventy years, and like any art form, it grows and changes all the time. With its resurgence in the 1990s, people now dance many different styles of the Lindy, often depending on the city or region in which they live. Indeed, even the original Savoy-style Lindy Hop had countless variations to it. "There is no true Savoy," says Debra Sternberg. "There were thousands and thousands of people showing up at the Savoy Ballroom every night. Everybody didn't dance the same way. The people who say there is one true authentic style are the ones who are teaching now who have to sell themselves." Today the Lindy Hop includes Savoy, Dean Collins, and Hollywood styles. Plus, swing also begat a variety of other dances, including the shag, the Dallas Push in Texas, the Imperial Swing in Saint Louis, Florida's Beach Bop, and a New Orleans Lindy variant called the Jamaica. Here's a handy reference to the most well-known swing styles and related dances that are being practiced across the United States — and around the globe — all of them descendants of the Lindy Hop, which Norma Miller calls "the granddaddy" of them all.

Dean Collins Style

In the mid-1930s, one-time Savoy dancer Dean Collins moved to Hollywood to dance in such movies as *Buck Privates* and *Ride 'Em Cowboy*. Whereas Frankie Manning exemplified the Savoy style of swing, with the man keeping himself low to the ground, like a runner at the start of a race, Collins held himself more upright when he danced. In the early 1980s, dance instructors Jonathan Bixby and Sylvia Sykes sought out Collins, who had since retired from dancing, and asked him to teach them his moves. They helped popularize Dean Collins's smoother, more contained style among West Coast swingers.

Hollywood Style

Collins may have been the most well-known smooth-style dancer in the movies, but he wasn't the only one. Recently, interest has been increasing in the styles of some of his jitterbugging colleagues, most notably Jean Veloz (who appears in the cult dance instruction film *Groovy Movie*) and Lenny Smith. A few years ago LA dance teachers Sylvia Skylar and Erik Robison, inspired by the many variations done by these film dancers, including Collins, trademarked a smooth Lindy as "Hollywood style." They even tracked down Veloz at a local bar called Bobby McGee's, where many old-timers hang out. Since then the dance has been a major hit in Los Angeles and Washington, D.C., with Lindy Hoppers in other cities catching on all the time. One of its distinctive marks is the whip, in which the leader sends the follower out with a very explosive action. "Ask a West Coaster to watch us and they'll say we dance Lindy," says Skylar. "Ask a Lindy Hopper and they'll say we look West Coast."

West Coast Swing

WCS was originally called Western swing, but the name was changed to avoid confusion with country-western swing. Some dance experts claim that WCS grew out of the smoother Dean Collins style; however, Collins claimed he had nothing to do with this variant, according to Sykes. WCS is actually more rigid than Collins's style, with the couple dancing in a line or slot, which some dance historians believe developed as a response to California's extremely crowded ballrooms. It is done in an upright position and the primary moves include a push, a pass, and a whip. Since the eighties West Coast has also incorporated many elements of the hustle. WCS can be done to smoother modern music, such as R&B and pop, and can be very sultry if danced properly.

Jitterbug or East Coast Swing

The jitterbug originated in the late 1930s or early 1940s as a simplified variant of the Lindy Hop, danced primarily by whites trying to emulate the black dancers from the Savoy Ballroom. As the music of the era became faster, the triple step of the Lindy was abbreviated to a single step, and the more complex eight-count steps were eliminated. The jitterbug is essentially the same as East Coast swing, although some would argue that the latter can be done with a triple-step rhythm and also incorporates eight-count turns. Both are basically easier versions of the Lindy Hop, without all the fancy improvisations or air steps.

Modern Jive

A European swing variant, modern jive focuses on six-count steps and can be danced to contemporary music and faster tempos. Jive follows the same counts as East Coast swing but has more of a hopping movement to it, with the hop executed in anticipation of the first beat. Jive is not as leadable as a social dance, because there is a lot of movement in the shoulders and because there is a set syllabus of steps, which does not allow for improvisation. Although popular in many European clubs, jive is primarily a competitive swing dance.

Boogie-Woogie and Rock 'n' Roll

Boogie-woogie grew up in America and Europe in the 1950s as rock 'n' roll replaced swing and big band on the radio and in dance clubs. Similar to jive, boogie-woogie is a swing variant that incorporates a lot of hopping movements as well as kicks forward, almost like chorus-line kicks. A similar variant is rock 'n' roll, which is a much more acrobatic dance that incorporates many jumps and lifts. It is really intended for competitions and not for the social dance floor, notes Nathalie Gomes, winner of the French championship in acrobatic rock 'n' roll in 1987.

Shag

There are several different kinds of shag, but perhaps the two most popular are Carolina shag and Saint Louis shag. Both are linear, slotted dances that feature lots of fancy footwork and mirror patterns. The shag is danced almost exclusively in the closed position, with the couples leaning in on one another, and there is almost no vertical movement from the waist up. Carolina shag is a smoother dance style traditionally done to slow and medium-tempo music from the 1950s and 1960s. The man is often the center of attention and executes most of the spins and other flourishes. Saint Louis shag is danced to very fast music, 165 beats per minute and up, and more closely resembles the Charleston than the Lindy, with patterns of kicks and jumps.

Balboa

The Balboa is an eight-count dance done in a tightly closed position. Similar to the shag and descended from the Charleston, the Balboa incorporates very rapid footwork and hardly any movement at all above the waist. "It would look like you are ice-skating across the floor but your feet would be a blur," says Sylvia Sykes, who has helped bring the Balboa back to today's ballrooms. Because the dance does not travel much, the Balboa allows people to dress up and still dance to very fast music, she notes.

ETIQUETTE

Because the Lindy is a social dance, nothing is more important than good etiquette. Keep in mind that the dance floor is not your personal stage. Everyone shares the same space and everyone wants to have a good time. These tips will help make it happen.

1. If you would like to dance with someone, simply ask the person. There's no need to use lines more complicated than "May I have this dance with you?" In fact, it's a relief to finally be able to go out and ask someone to dance and not have it be a signal that you want to pick the person up. "I asked a guy to dance and the best I ever heard was, 'I can't. I'm here with my girlfriend. Look,' I said, 'I don't want to marry you. I just want to dance with you. This is not for eternity,'" says dancer and vintage dealer Darrow Cannizzaro.

2. If someone asks you to dance, never say no and then take the next dance with someone else. "That's absolutely unacceptable," says Teddy Kern. However, it is OK to say no to a dance if you want to take a break. You may be tired, your feet may hurt, you may want to get another drink. "You might say, 'Please find me

Dance Videos

There are hundreds of instructional videotapes on the market. So here's a sampling of the best.

► *The Frankie Manning Collection* includes tapes for beginner, intermediate, and advanced dancers, plus a video on the Shim Sham Shimmy.

► American Lindy Hop champions Paul Overton and Sharon Ashe offer almost a dozen great tapes, including ones on the Charleston.

► The series *Everybody Dances* is a super introduction to Lindy, West Coast, and shag, and includes such instructors as Manning, Louise Thwaite, Jonathan Bixby, and Sylvia Sykes. (These and many other tapes are available from Bixby and Sykes's catalog, A.R.B.S.P. Videos and Music, 1220 Mission Canyon Road, Santa Barbara, CA 93105.)

later,' 'Come back and ask me again,' or 'Please give me a rain check,'" adds Kern. "The important thing is to be gracious so the person doesn't feel that you are rejecting them." Also, try to be welcoming to newcomers. They may not be as advanced as you are, but they won't progress unless veteran dancers give them a chance. As one etiquette writer states: "Today's beginners will be the good dancers of tomorrow."

3. Be aware of space. If it's crowded, be courteous. Make adjustments by keeping your steps smaller and your kicks low. "This can be a very big dance but it also can be a very small dance if you know how to control it," says Elena Iannucci.

4. If you do collide with someone anyway, or get your foot stepped on, don't assign blame. "You don't always know who is the victim and who the aggressor. You never know. You could have gotten in their way and even if you got stepped on, it may

Dance Camps

Yes, kids, if you're really into the Lindy Hop you can even go away to swing dance camp. These are among the most popular.

- Herräng Dance Camp, held in Herräng, Sweden, every summer by the Rhythm Hot Shots. There are four weekly sessions with scores of the best international teachers, from Buenos Aires and Singapore to London and Los Angeles. (46 8 643 4058 or *www.swing.ch/herrang/camp*)
- Swing Dance Catalina, sponsored by the Pasadena Ballroom Dance Association, runs for two weeks in early summer on the beautiful island of Catalina off the coast of California. (626-799-5689 or *www.pasadenaballroomdance.com*)
- Monsters of Swing, a raucous weekend in Ventura, California, put on by the Flyin' Lindy Hoppers in March. (805-643-3166 or *www.flyinlindyhoppers.com*)
- Beantown, a two-week summer event sponsored by Boston's Hop to the Beat Dance Studio. (508-435-2363 or *www.hoptothebeat.com*)
- Camp Hollywood, a new fall camp devoted to teaching Hollywood-style Lindy. (323-874-9649 or *www.camphollywood.net*)

be your own fault," says Paul Overton. "If everybody apologizes, everybody goes home happy."

5. Don't bring drinks or cigarettes on the dance floor. You may even want to think twice about wearing a hat to hop. "A pet peeve of mine is guys who go out on the dance floor wearing a hat and it falls off and they are there grabbing for it," says Leann Wright of San Francisco's Guys and Dolls vintage store.

6. If your partner bungles a step, let it go. There's no place for lectures in the middle of a song. In fact, it's not appropriate to give another person pointers during a social dance, unless the per-

son asks for help. Conversely, if you suddenly sprout two left feet, don't sweat it, and don't feel you need to apologize profusely. Just get back in the swing.

7. At the end of a dance, always say thank you. Also, "a guy should always walk the woman back to where he asked her to dance. Don't leave her in the middle of the dance floor," says Overton.

8. Support the bands and the clubs. Take the time to applaud the musicians and singers. And if you don't drink, buy water or at least a soda at the bar. Don't bring your own water bottles to a nightclub.

9. Don't wander across the dance floor looking for someone. You become a hazard.

10. The most important etiquette advice: smile. Always be friendly, gracious, and polite to everyone.

CHAPTER 4

The Legends of Swing

*H*ere they are: the kings and queens of the original swing era. In the short biographies that follow, you'll meet the best bandleaders, the most virtuoso sidemen, the loudest jump blues shouters, and the sweetest singers. You'll find out what each musician's classic songs are. There's a bit of trivia included too, such as how Billie Holiday got her nickname Lady Day and which swing musician claims to have invented the electric guitar.

Plus, the main entries feature a recommendation of the greatest CDs to purchase for an introduction. Given the thousands of CDs on the market, from original albums and reissues to compilations and imports, starting a swing music collection can be a daunting challenge. Louis Armstrong, for example, recorded at least fifty different versions of the song "Basin Street Blues," while more than two hundred albums featuring Duke Ellington are available. Sometimes two almost identical CDs will feature the same songs by an artist, but only one will include the best performances of those numbers. These CD picks will, I hope, help you avoid getting stuck with a so-so purchase, although for many performers they only hint at the sheer volume of amazing music out there.

So think of this as just the beginning of a lifelong journey of musical discovery. But be careful: Once you start buying albums by Louis Jordan, Nat King Cole, Jimmie Lunceford, and Ella Fitzgerald, just to name a few, you won't be able to stop. These performers will enrich you, inspire you, and thrill you—and most important, make you want to get up and move. (Readers looking for more in-depth CD guides would do well to check out *The New Grove Dictionary of Jazz;* the excellent guides to swing, jazz, and lounge from the editors of *MusicHound; The Penguin Guide to Jazz on Compact Disc;* or *The Rolling Stone Blues and Jazz Album Guide.*)

FACING PAGE: *Ella Fitzgerald and Louis Jordan exchange a knowing look in the studio.* (ARCHIVE PHOTOS/METRONOME)

THE GIANTS
Count Basie

The man who made Kansas City one of the great capitals of jazz was actually raised on the East Coast. Born in the town of Red Bank, New Jersey, in 1904, Basie moved to New York in the 1920s, where Fats Waller taught him to play the organ. By the age of twenty-three, he was touring the country as part of a vaudeville show. But when the company got stranded in Kansas City, Basie stayed there. The city's nightlife, flourishing under the corrupt Pendergast political machine, and its Southwest blues music permanently changed him. "I hadn't ever played the blues," wrote Basie in his autobiography, *Good Morning Blues*. In Kansas City, Basie first joined the Blue Devils band, then the influential Bennie Moten Orchestra, which in 1932 recorded "Moten Swing," one of the most ahead-of-its-time early swing numbers. When Moten died in 1935, Basie took most of the band's best members and put his own orchestra together. Before long, word traveled to New York about the hot new sound of the Basie outfit.

What made this band distinct? Basie's piano playing was remarkably spare and lean, a challenge to the more elaborate styles of Harlem. Fronted by singers Jimmy Rushing and Helen Humes, the band completely embraced the blues. Its tremendous sidemen all became legends: tenor sax players Lester Young and Herschel Evans; trumpeters Oran "Hot Lips" Page, Harry "Sweets" Edison, and Buck Clayton; drummer Jo Jones; and the famous bassist Walter Page. But it was Page — and his four-to-the-bar bass playing — who was the force behind the band's unparalleled rhythm section, heavy on the backbeat and driving forward with unstoppable momentum. "Basie's rhythm section was nothing less than a Cadillac with the force of a Mack truck," said trombonist Dicky Wells. While Basie's pared-down, propulsive songs pointed the way toward the next wave in music, jump blues, he was forced to disband his orchestra in 1950 as the big band era came to a close. During the fifties, however, Basie bounced back, putting together a new band and creating music that ranks among his best on such albums as *April in Paris, Count Basie Swings, Joe Williams Sings,* and *Sinatra-Basie.* While he died in 1984, the memory of this charismatic entertainer—known in later years for his signature captain's hat—is as bright as ever.

Classic Songs: "Swingin' the Blues," "Taxi War Dance," "Jumpin' at the Woodside," "Dickie's Dream," and the Frankie Manning favorite "Shiny Stockings."

Swing Trivia: Basie's band could improvise much more than solos. It recorded its signature song completely on the spur of the moment. One night, when the band didn't have a number with which to end a radio program, Basie looked at the clock, shouted out "One O'Clock Jump," and the band, renowned for its cohesion, put together this now-classic number on the spot.

CD Pick: Don't skimp on Basie. Buy the three-CD set *Count Basie: The Complete Decca Recordings, 1937–1939* (Decca/GRP). "It represents the zenith of Kansas City jazz, the recordings that really brought Basie to the national forefront," says Chuck Haddix, director of the Marr Sound Archives at the University of Missouri, Kansas City.

Duke Ellington

With 1999's celebration of what would have been Ellington's one hundredth birthday, this multitalented musician was justly acclaimed as one of a handful of America's most talented composers, along with Gershwin and Copland. His songs are so ingrained in our culture that even if you think you don't know an Ellington song, you do. During a career that spanned the twenties to the seventies, Ellington composed more than two thousand pieces of music. He even popularized the word *swing* in his early classic "It Don't Mean a Thing (If It Ain't Got That Swing)." Born in Washington, D.C., in 1899, Edward Kennedy Ellington transformed himself into the elegant Duke after moving to New York in 1923, where he formed his own orchestra.

In 1927 he secured a star-making gig at the Cotton Club, where he directed the nightspot's exotic floor shows in addition to creating such memorable songs as "Mood Indigo" and "Black and Tan Fantasy." A brilliant pianist, Ellington composed songs in which he took jazz to new levels of artistry, adding an emotional depth, a lyric poetry, and an easy confidence that hadn't been there before. "He's one of the major impressionist painters of the twentieth century. His colors are as rich and subtle and sophisticated as Cezanne's or Monet's," says bandleader Casey MacGill.

Ellington's renowned sidemen over the years included trombonists Juan Tizol and Lawrence Brown; trumpeters Bubber Miley, Cootie Williams, Ray Nance, and Rex Stewart; the incomparable alto saxophonist Johnny Hodges; and clarinetist Barney Bigard, plus singers Ivie Anderson and Betty Roche. Ellington's secret talent lay in writing for the specific, and often quirky, talents of each one. The band hit its high-water mark in the late thirties with the additions of Jimmy Blanton, who imparted a new expressive voice to the bass, and tenor saxophonist Ben Webster, plus arranger/composer Billy Strayhorn, with whom Ellington formed an intense and rich musical partnership. After the end of the swing era, Ellington enjoyed a huge resurgence after appearing at the Newport Jazz Festival in 1956. Consistent with his ambitious artistic aims, he explored other types of music throughout his life, from long-form pieces to spiritual compositions. He died in 1974 at age seventy-five, a genius who defined swing but was never defined by it.

Classic Songs: "Cottontail," "Ko-Ko," "Harlem Air Shaft," "Don't Get Around Much Anymore," "Sophisticated Lady," "Solitude," and Strayhorn's "Take the 'A' Train."

Swing Trivia: According to Bill Crow's *Jazz Anecdotes*, Ellington was notoriously superstitious. He feared drafts, hated to fly, and wouldn't wear yellow. He also never gave shoes as gifts; to him they were a symbol that someone might walk away from him.

CD Pick: The three-CD set *The Blanton-Webster Band* (RCA) includes sixty-six songs, gems one and all, from the band's peak years.

Benny Goodman

Admit it, when you were a kid, his albums were collecting dust on your parents' (or grandparents') shelves and you probably thought he was lame. But now you realize the error of your ways. It's about time that the King of Swing is cool again. Without Goodman, the man most responsible for bringing the hot sounds of Harlem to the masses, there might have been no swing era. After a period of disillusionment with jazz, Goodman broke through in 1935 at the now-famous Palomar engagement in Los Angeles with his truly hard-swinging music. And he challenged the color barrier by hiring such extraordinary black musicians as pianist Teddy Wilson, vibraphonist Lionel Hampton, and guitarist Charlie Christian to play in his small combos and later in his full orchestra. His string of female singers — Helen Ward, Martha Tilton, Helen Forrest, and Peggy Lee — ranks as the best lineup any band could boast. And when it came to playing the clarinet, Goodman was so crystal clear and so passionate that he carved out a new, richer place for the instrument in the jazz world. Dressing like an egghead, famous for his prickly personality, Goodman proved that you don't have to be a flashy entertainer to become one of the most beloved and inspired musicians of all time. He died in 1986 at age seventy-seven.

Classic Songs: The swing anthem "Sing, Sing, Sing," "Christopher Columbus," "Sometimes I'm Happy," "Blue Skies," and the Fletcher Henderson arrangement "King Porter Stomp."

Swing Trivia: When Goodman became angry at one of his sidemen, he'd glare so harshly at the guy that band members talked about avoiding "the Ray."

CD Pick: The two-CD set *Benny Goodman On the Air, 1937–1938* (Columbia). "These are live broadcast performances that really capture the famous band with Harry James and Gene Krupa that played Carnegie Hall. There's much more life than in some of the studio recordings," says Loren Schoenberg, leader of the Loren Schoenberg Big Band and former director of the Benny Goodman Archive.

LOUIS, LOUIS, AND LOUIS

Louis Jordan

Squawk! The seminal R&B vocalist and alto sax player Louis Jordan recorded no fewer than three songs about chickens. And once you've heard "There Ain't Nobody Here but Us Chickens," "A Chicken Ain't Nothing but a Bird," and "Chicken Back," you'll be plucked if you don't agree that Jordan is one of the most raucously fun singers who ever lived. But Jordan wasn't just about laughs. This soulful singer's voice has astonishingly expressive range. And his flyin' combo, the Tympany Five, never failed to get a crowd's feet moving. All three qualities have combined to make Jordan the king of the neoswing movement. The reason? His influential jump blues sound—Jordan had more than fifty Top 10 R&B hits between 1942 and 1951—stands at the crossroads of jazz and rock 'n' roll, which is exactly where most of today's swing fans find themselves. (Jordan, who had played for Chick Webb, led the post–big band transition toward smaller groups.) In fact, the only thing negative that can be said about this entertainer is that, since his death in 1975, he's been in danger of overexposure. Every other new swing group seems like a Jordan cover band.

Classic Songs: "Choo Choo Ch'Boogie," which sold a million copies in 1946, "Caldonia," "Knock Me a Kiss," "What's the Use of Gettin' Sober."

Swing Trivia: According to John Chilton's biography *Let the Good Times Roll,* one old-time shtick of Jordan's was to dedicate his hit song "Is You Is or Is You Ain't My Baby?" to Errol Flynn while the actor was in the midst of a paternity suit.

CD Pick: "To me, Louis Jordan is really the most important guy out there," says Steve Lucky, leader of Steve Lucky and the Rhumba Bums, who recommends *The Best of Louis Jordan* (MCA). "These are the hits that really define the sounds of the small jump swing band, from 'Knock Me a Kiss' to 'Open the Door, Richard.' It's twenty great cuts."

Louis Prima

Get it right. It was Prima's classic "Jump, Jive, an' Wail" that was featured in the Gap's "Khakis Swing" ad, not Brian Setzer's recent cover of the song. Prima's original is the real deal, and just a taste of the rollicking musical banquet this superb entertainer has to offer. Influenced by the trumpet playing of Louis Armstrong and the jump blues of Louis Jordan, Prima created an unforgettable mix of the Dixieland sounds of his native New Orleans, the *abbondanza* attitude of his Neapolitan heritage, and a steady stream of knockout humor. Grabbing fame in the fifties in Las Vegas, Prima created a bridge from the swing era (he composed Goodman's most famous number, "Sing, Sing, Sing") into the world of lounge, especially after he hooked up with his fourth wife, Keely Smith, and wild saxman Sam Butera. The latter two still perform on the Strip, but Prima died in 1978. His memory lives on, most recently in the hit indie film *Big Night. Buona séra,* indeed.

Classic Songs: "That Old Black Magic," Prima's hit duet with Keely Smith, and "Just a Gigolo," later covered by David Lee Roth.

Swing Trivia: Prima was the voice of every kid's favorite orangutan, King Louie, in Disney's 1967 animated film *The Jungle Book.*

CD Pick: "Something you have to have in your collection is the Louis Prima *Collector's Series*" (Capitol), says Marc Berman, host of Philadelphia's *Swingtime* radio show. "It's not only an introduction, it's the essential Louis Prima, and you can find it in every store. It's got all the hits, but what it also has is Louis's version of 'Sing, Sing, Sing.'"

Louis Armstrong

Every swing musician spoke Louis Armstrong's language. With his remarkable trumpet solos and raspy but rich voice, Armstrong had an effect on jazz so profound he might as well have redirected the course of the Mississippi. Born in New Orleans in 1901 and put in a waif's home by the age of twelve, Armstrong got his start as a protégé of cornetist King Oliver and gained experience playing in bands on the Mississippi's riverboats. Early on, his soaring range was literally incredible. Armstrong hit so many high Cs and Fs, that he was occasionally accused of using a trick instrument. But it was Armstrong's gift for creating new rhythms, phrases, and harmonies, on his landmark *Hot Fives* and *Hot Sevens* recordings of the mid- to late twenties, that really shook up the jazz world. Exuberant, warm, and full of life, he appeared in scores of movies; recorded unforgettable duets with fellow legend Ella Fitzgerald; put out a seemingly limitless catalog of albums; and in 1964, seven years before his death in 1971, dislodged the Beatles' "Can't Buy Me Love" from the Billboard No. 1 spot with his rendition of "Hello Dolly." Armstrong was jazz's first international star and is arguably still its most famous.

Classic Songs: The *Hot Fives* cuts "Potato Head Blues" and "West End Blues"; "Weather Bird," with pianist Earl Hines; "Basin Street Blues"; and "What a Wonderful World," which became a hit after its appearance in the film *Good Morning, Vietnam.*

Swing Trivia: Armstrong's nickname Satchmo was taken from the song "Satchel Mouth Swing."

CD Pick: To witness the birth of the swing solo and Armstrong at his most stunning, buy *The Hot Fives, Volume 1* (which features the pioneering scat song "Heebie Jeebies"), plus *The Hot Fives and Hot Sevens, Volumes 2 and 3* (Columbia). For later Armstrong check out a great live performance, the two-CD *Complete Town Hall Concert 17 May 1947* (BMG/RCA), which includes solos by trombonist Jack Teagarden.

Tommy Dorsey (left) and saxophonist Bud Freeman watch as Louis Armstrong launches into a solo. (CHARLES PETERSON/ARCHIVE PHOTOS)

THE ENTERTAINERS
Cab Calloway

The biggest showman of them all, Calloway seemed practically possessed onstage, stomping around in his extreme zoot suit, throwing his hair back, and baring his teeth with gleeful abandon. "His spirit was life or death," says his daughter, singer Chris Calloway. "He always felt as if you owed everything to your audience." On countless songs, such as "Are You All Reet?" and "Are You Hep to the Jive?" he established himself as the avatar of rap. Calloway—who published his own slang guide called *The Hepster's Dictionary* in 1936—could rhyme, jive talk, and scat to Mars and back in the course of a three-minute number. And while the high points of his career extend from his appearances at the Cotton Club beginning in 1930 to his performance in *The Blues Brothers* in 1980, Calloway was once remembered more as a cartoonish novelty act than a serious musician. Lately, however, he's gained hugely increased respect. His stylistic influence is, of course, undebatable. From clothes to slang to songs about reefer, he practically invented the concept of hipness. But it shouldn't be forgotten that back in the day, Calloway's orchestra was one of the highest-class outfits out there, boasting such stellar sidemen as bassist Milt Hinton and sax player Chu Berry. The Professor of Jive knew how to keep 'em dancing too.

Classic Songs: The one and only "Minnie the Moocher," which made Calloway known as the Hi-De-Ho man.

Swing Trivia: One swing-era account credits Calloway's orchestra with the origin of the term *jitterbug*. A trombone player in the band was a lush who purportedly concocted a drink called "jitter sauce" to quell his shakes.

CD Pick: There's no dispute here. Fly out and buy *Are You Hep to the Jive?* (Columbia), which includes twenty-two of his all-time most righteous tunes, from signatures like "Minnie" to his teasing of violinist Yehudi Menuhin in "Who's Yehoodi?" It's even got great cover art featuring Cab in one of his widest, wildest hats.

Lionel Hampton

Pounding his mallets and sweating up a storm, Hampton is a thrilling improviser and wildly inventive rhythmist, the longest-running swing band leader in history, and an important harbinger of rock and R&B. Born in 1908 in Louisville, he grew up on Chicago's South Side, meeting everyone from Jelly Roll Morton to Bessie Smith through his uncle, who made and sold moonshine for Al Capone. After moving to Los Angeles, he discovered his fortune-making instrument, the then-unknown vibraphone (it's similar to a xylophone but has rotating fans that create a vibrato sound), during a recording session with Louis Armstrong in 1930. "Louis asked me if I could play that instrument and I was a brazen young guy and I said, 'Yeah,'" recalls Hampton, who had in fact never touched it before. Six years later he joined the Benny Goodman Orchestra, playing in the band's color-barrier-smashing quartet with Teddy Wilson and Gene Krupa. His most influential musical contributions came, however, once he started his own band in 1940. Two years later he recorded "Flying Home." The hit song featured a honking tenor sax solo by Illinois Jacquet that presaged the balls-out sax approach of late forties rhythm and blues. Hamp, as he's known, has continued performing into his nineties, celebrating his ninety-first birthday in early 1999.

Classic Songs: The rocking call-and-response tune "Hey! Ba-Ba-Re-Bop," plus the signature "Hamp's Boogie Woogie."

Swing Trivia: Perhaps the first stage dive in music history occurred during a Hampton concert. According to *Jazz Anecdotes*, the band members were always known for their leaping and dancing, but during one gig an alto player began to walk the edge of the stage during his solo. At one point, he fell and was caught by the crowd, playing all the way through.

CD Pick: The two-CD set *Hamp: The Legendary Decca Recordings* (Decca) includes all the hits. Listen for the contributions of trumpeter Dizzy Gillespie and singer Dinah Washington, both of whom were with Hampton early in their careers. Especially amusing is the song "Blow Top Blues," a trippy song about a girl losing her marbles.

THE CLASSIC BIG BANDS

How many orchestras were there at the height of the swing craze? The Big Bands Database Web site lists more than 550 of 'em, from the most candy-assed sweet outfits to the hottest barn burners and everything in between. Hell, even Chico Marx had a short-lived band. So take this short list of the most important bands as just what it is: a critical sampling and the barest of introductions.

The Dorsey Brothers

Think disputes about dance tempos are a problem today? Well, back in 1934, just such an argument helped break up Jimmy and Tommy Dorsey. The pair, sons of a Pennsylvania coal miner, had formed their own band together earlier that year. But simmering disagreements came to a head onstage one night when they couldn't agree how fast to take a song. Tommy walked off the stage and started his own band, and a long-standing rivalry ensued. While reedman Jimmy's Orchestra was known as a more jazzy outfit, Tommy's more commercial big band—he was known as the "sentimental king of swing"—earned its place as the best all-around dance band of its era. Both orchestras boasted highly popular singers. Helen O'Connell and Bob Eberly warbled for Jimmy, while Tommy's knockout pair was Jo Stafford and Frank Sinatra (who consciously modeled his singing on Tommy's melodic and perfectly phrased trombone playing). By the fifties, however, the Dorseys reunited, only to meet early death. Tommy choked to death in 1956; Jimmy died of cancer a year later.

Classic Songs: Tommy's biggest songs include the harmonizing "Marie" (with a thrilling solo by trumpeter Bunny Berigan) and Sinatra's crooner's delight "I'll Never Smile Again." Jimmy's biggest charter was "Tangerine."

Swing Trivia: How intense was their rivalry? After Jimmy hired trombonist Frank Rehak, according to *Jazz Anecdotes,* he told the musician to let loose on his solos with abandon. "Anything you can do to make Tommy mad, go ahead and do it," Rehak recalls Jimmy saying.

CD Pick: *The Dorsey Brothers: The Best of the Big Bands* (Sony) documents the pair's music before the split, while *The Best of Tommy Dorsey* (RCA) features Tommy's many hits, including three cuts with Sinatra.

Glenn Miller

The swing era's equivalent of warm milk before bedtime, Miller's orchestra is still the most nostalgically remembered band of the 1940s. With a knack for turning jazz inspiration into catchy pop, Miller, who grew up in Iowa, Nebraska, and Colorado, was a so-so trombonist but an exceptional businessman. He chased radio play relentlessly, emphasized synthesized sound over individual solos, imposed strict rules on his musicians (down to telling them what color socks to wear), and chose sweet-style songs with such an eye toward their commercial value that he's been accused of hastening the end of the big bands. But Miller unapologetically revelled in popular approval. "The majority of the people like to hear pretty tunes," he once said. Indeed, even today Miller has more well-known hits — "In the Mood," "Chattanooga Choo-Choo," "Pennsylvania 6-5000" (named after the telephone number of the famous Hotel Pennsylvania in New York), "Moonlight Serenade" — than any other bandleader. During the war, Miller formed a cherished military orchestra called the Army Air Forces Training Command Band, rallying servicemen and civilians alike. His band, wrote *Metronome*'s George Simon, was "a living symbol of what America meant to them, of what they were fighting for." After a small plane carrying him from England to France disappeared in late 1944, the forty-year-old Miller was declared missing.

Classic Songs: "Little Brown Jug," Miller's first swing success, and "Tuxedo Junction," a song first recorded (with less chart success) by black bandleader Erskine Hawkins.

Swing Trivia: According to *MusicHound Jazz,* Miller found his first instrument, an old trombone lying in the basement, while working as an errand boy for a butcher's shop.

CD Picks: The music of Miller's army band is collected on *Glenn Miller: The Best of the Lost Recordings and the Secret Broadcasts* (RCA/Victor). And while it lacks the singing of fave Miller vocalist Tex Beneke, it includes all the great chestnuts. "That was a fantastic band and much better for my money than [his earlier one]," says bandleader Bill Elliott.

Jimmie Lunceford

As popular as the bands of either Basie or Ellington in its time, the Jimmie Lunceford Orchestra was one of the most powerful, dependable, and stylishly dressed senders in the business for more than a decade. Lunceford formed his orchestra from a group of players he met while in college at Nashville's Fisk University. Launched by a six-month engagement at the Cotton Club in 1934, the band rolled out its fair share of sweet ballads, but its fast dance tunes—many set down by master arranger Sy Oliver—flew with the best of them. Lunceford's swing, wrote one reviewer, "carries a tremendous 'sock,' . . . the music parallel of Joe Louis' gloved fist." Part of the band's punch also came from the tremendous show it put on: the musicians created synchronized routines, waving, pointing, and sometimes throwing their instruments in the air, all in perfect unison.

Classic Songs: The wailin' and chargin' "White Heat," the sweet-as-pie "For Dancers Only," and a song that should be required listening for Lindy Hoppers everywhere, "Tain't What You Do (But the Way That Cha Do It)."

Swing Trivia: Guitarist, trombonist, and arranger Eddie Durham maintained that he devised music's first electric guitar in 1935 while he was a member of Lunceford's orchestra.

CD Pick: A hard choice between *Classic Tracks* (Kaz Records), which includes every major hit, and *For Dancers Only* (Decca), a critical fave of the editors of *MusicHound* that unfortunately does not feature "White Heat" or "Tain't What You Do."

Artie Shaw

One of the last surviving leaders of the big bands, Shaw is as opinionated and curmudgeonly today as he was years ago. He frequently went into highly public "retirements," saw eight marriages go bust, including betrothals to Ava Gardner and Lana Turner, and often lashed out at his audience, once calling jitterbuggers "morons." (He's also fond of taking a swipe at dancers' obsession with tempos. "You can dance to a windshield wiper," he's often said.) But all the headline-grabbing actions didn't get in the way of making some of the most exciting music of the swing era. Shaw played clarinet with such an alluring smoothness that a long-running fan argument broke out over who was the better player, he or Goodman. The debate goes on to this day. Shaw "was the greatest jazz clarinet player that ever lived," says bandleader and Shaw partisan Eddie Reed, who's styled his big band on Shaw's. "He did things on the clarinet that have never been duplicated. Period." Shaw is also known for challenging the color barrier when he hired Billie Holiday to sing for his orchestra.

Classic Songs: "Begin the Beguine," his hugely successful redo of Cole Porter's original, the Mexican-inspired "Frenesi," the novelty number "Indian Love Call," and "Nightmare," his dark, moody theme song.

Swing Trivia: During his many retirements, Shaw has worked as a farmer, translator, theater producer, and writer. He published a novel in 1965 titled *I Love You, I Hate You, Drop Dead!*

CD Pick: *Begin the Beguine* (Classic Jazz) offers all of the above-mentioned hits, plus Helen Forrest giving in to the inevitable on "Comes Love."

Chick Webb

As the house bandleader for the famed Savoy Ballroom, this human beatbox drove the music through the wall and around the block every night of the week throughout the 1930s. Sophisticated and tightly arranged, his music had a propulsive power that continually inspired the club's Lindy Hoppers, sending them to ever wilder extremes. Born in 1909 to a poor Baltimore family, Webb suffered from a spinal problem that left him short and hunchbacked. Despite these obstacles, he formed his own band in 1926 at age seventeen, eventually signing on at the Savoy. There Webb presciently hired Ella Fitzgerald when she was just a kid, established his reputation as one of the greatest drummers in swing, and took on all comers in a series of famous battles of the bands. His career ended suddenly in 1939 when he died of tuberculosis at age thirty.

Classic Songs: "A Tisket A Tasket" with Ella Fitzgerald, "Undecided," and "Stompin' at the Savoy."

Swing Trivia: At one of the most famous Savoy battles, Goodman's orchestra came to Harlem to challenge Webb. Four thousand dancers packed the house, five thousand were turned away, and by the end of the night, Webb's band had sent Goodman's packing. "I was never carved by a better player," said Gene Krupa afterward.

CD Pick: The greatest-hits package *Chick Webb and his Orchestra* (Best of Jazz) offers up early Ella and some of his hardest-driving numbers. The album includes his first recorded cut, "Dog Bottom," a thrilling nail-biter of a ride.

Gene Krupa

With his sticks a-twirling and his hair a-flying, Krupa created a lasting archetype: the slightly mad, flashy percussionist who won't ever slow down. As a member of the Goodman orchestra, he's credited with taking drums beyond their lowly status as mere timekeepers and making them a true solo instrument for the first time. In 1938 he formed his own band, having hits with famous trumpet soloist Roy Eldridge and singer Anita O'Day. A high-profile arrest and imprisonment in 1943 on a suspect marijuana-possession charge (he was later cleared) seriously damaged his career, at the same time that Buddy Rich was giving Krupa a serious run-for-the-money as a skinbeater. But his legacy is secure. Every modern rock drummer should never forget that it all started with Krupa.

Classic Songs: "Wire Brush Stomp," "After You've Gone," "Rockin' Chair," "Bolero at the Savoy," and "Drum Boogie."

Swing Trivia: Krupa didn't spend time in jail just once. According to David Stowe's *Swing Changes,* he was once jailed for throwing a punch at a restaurant owner who refused admission to Eldridge.

CD Pick: Listen to him do his stuff on Goodman's classic song "Sing, Sing, Sing." Or check out one of his two aptly titled hits collections, *Drummer Man* and *Drum Boogie.*

THE GREAT SINGERS

Frank Sinatra

The definitive male swing singer, Sinatra is ironically also credited with hastening the end of the big band era. In 1939 a slender, fresh-faced Frank got his start with the Harry James Orchestra and later joined Tommy Dorsey's group, singing such tender ballads as "Imagination" and "All or Nothing at All." Influenced greatly by Billie Holiday, Sinatra crooned his way to a stardom that no band singer had ever possessed before. Performing at a now-famous engagement at New York's Paramount Theater in the early forties, he turned bobby-soxers into love-struck fans and left the orchestra jealous for attention. That was the beginning of a revolution that ushered in such solo vocalists as Patti Page, Frankie Laine, and Perry Como. It was Sinatra who set the standard for them all, not just with his perfect phrasing but also for the way in which he could take a composer's lyrics and turn every word into his own intimate revelation. But for as much pop success as Sinatra ultimately achieved, he never left behind his jazz roots. At the height of his Rat Pack days—when he transformed himself into an icon of swaggering, womanizing, and ever stylish manhood—Sinatra recorded highly praised albums with both Basie and Ellington. And when he died in 1998 at age eighty-two, the indomitable Chairman of the Board had survived to see his music catch on once again with a hip, young audience.

Classic Songs: "Fly Me to the Moon," "My Way," "The Lady is a Tramp," and the Dorsey-era hit "I'll Never Smile Again."

Swing Trivia: During the 1950s, according to David W. Stowe's *Swing Changes,* Sinatra railed against rock music as "the most brutal, ugly, desperate, vicious form of expression it has been my misfortune to hear." Little more than a decade before, his own music had been cited by the New York Philharmonic's leader as a prime cause of juvenile delinquency.

CD Picks: You could buy a dozen and not go wrong, but here are three to get you started. *I'll Be Seeing You* (RCA) collects the best of his work with Tommy Dorsey. *The Best of the Capitol Years* (Capitol) pinpoints Sinatra's pinnacle, with masterful arrangements by Nelson Riddle and featuring such songs as "I've Got You under My Skin" and "You Make Me Feel So Young." And to hear Ol' Blue Eyes swingin' with the great Count, check out *Sinatra/Basie* (Reprise).

Ella Fitzgerald

"The First Lady of Song." "Lady Time." That's the Ella we all know and cherish. But did you know that she was also the only woman to lead a major swing band? After winning amateur contests at the Apollo Theater, Fitzgerald got her start at age seventeen singing in the Chick Webb Orchestra and soon found fame with such hits as 1936's "You'll Have to Swing It (Mr. Paganini)" and the even bigger 1938 song "A Tisket A Tasket" (based on an 1879 nursery rhyme). But when Webb died in 1939, Fitzgerald took over the leadership of his band for two years before going solo in 1942. Establishing herself as the best scat singer of all time, Fitzgerald effortlessly swung, bopped, and went pop, famously dueting with Louis Armstrong and recording album after classic album. But the most important were her so-called songbook LPs, a massive project begun in 1955 that married her brilliant jazz artistry with the work of the best American composers — Harold Arlen, Cole Porter, Rodgers and Hart, Ellington, Irving Berlin, Jerome Kern, Johnny Mercer, and George and Ira Gershwin. Called by some the greatest singer in history, Fitzgerald, who died in 1996, may sit atop the mountain of twentieth-century music, but her clear voice, her glad, warm way, and her impeccable sense of swing make her accessible to every listener.

Classic Songs: "Undecided," "Flying Home," and "Mack the Knife."

Swing Trivia: Louis Jordan, who recorded a 1945 calypso hit with Fitzgerald, "Stone Cold Dead in the Market," also romanced the singer back when both were in Webb's band. According to John Chilton's Jordan biography, *Let the Good Times Roll,* Louis had an ulterior motive. He was planning on starting his own band and hoped, without success it turned out, that Fitzgerald would come with him.

CD Pick: *The Best of the Songbooks* (Verve), drawn from the 16-CD *Complete Ella Fitzgerald Songbooks,* is a wonderful if relatively skimpy starting point with such standards as "'S Wonderful," "Midnight Sun," and "I Got It Bad and That Ain't Good." But to hear her in her early swing incarnation, buy *The Early Years, Part 2* (Decca), which covers her stint as leader of Webb's orchestra. It's a bit of a shock. Fitzgerald, not yet the full-fledged singer she later became, sounds positively girlish on such songs as "My Heart Belongs to Daddy" and the novelty number "Chew Chew Chew (Your Bubble Gum)."

Billie Holiday

Her life was anything but a holiday. Today Holiday's difficult forty-four years of triumph, decline, and more decline have been strangely romanticized. She's become the poster child for tortured, self-destructive artists the world over. And indeed, the list of her travails is exceedingly long. Born Eleanora Fagan in 1915, she was raped as a child and was put away in a home for wayward girls. She worked in a brothel as a teenager (which she forthrightly discussed in her 1956 autobiography, *Lady Sings the Blues*). After being discovered by legendary promoter John Hammond in a Harlem club, she made her first recording in 1933 with Benny Goodman. The successes and troubles followed in equal measure. She was arrested three times on drug-possession charges, spent a year in jail after the first bust, and was thereafter prevented from working in New York nightclubs because of a law forbidding felons from holding "cabaret cards." A lifetime of substance abuse—heroin, marijuana, opium, alcohol, and cigarettes—ravaged her voice and ultimately brought on her death. When she passed away in 1959 at age forty-four, she had 70¢ in her bank account and $750 taped to her leg. While it's tempting to try to approach her music apart from her life, that would be impossible. Holiday's heartache infused everything she sang. Even in her most distinctly stylized vocals, she never worked on the surface; she laid down her soul's blue pain on vinyl with an intensity and strength that are far from tragic.

Classic Songs: "Strange Fruit," her politically charged 1939 antilynching song; "God Bless the Child," her own composition; "I Must Have That Man" and "Summertime," great pairings with pianist Teddy Wilson; and, of course, the unlucky-in-love singer's signature lament, "Lover Man."

Swing Trivia: How did Holiday become known as "Lady Day"?

Lady Day sings the blues. (FRANK DRIGGS/CORBIS-BETTMANN)

As a teenager she worked in a sleazy Harlem club where wait-resses often had to use their labia to pick up tip money. Holiday, to her credit, wouldn't do it, so her coworkers began to mockingly call her "Lady." Later, Lester Young, picking up on her last name, added "Day."

CD Pick: If you can't afford the nine-CD collection, *The Quin-tessential Billie Holiday* (Columbia), buy the two-CD set, *The Complete Decca Recordings* (GRP), an easy introduction. With material recorded from the mid- to late forties, it catches Holiday at the peak of her powers. By contrast, her later recordings, done with great sidemen but wrecked pipes, have been described by *Rolling Stone* as "acid splashed against velvet."

Nat King Cole

He seemed just like the "stardust" of one of his signature hits, pure and brilliant and like a gift from another galaxy. In fact, Cole's genius was that his voice could inhabit so much space and yet at the same time never lose a bit of its warmth. But before he became known worldwide as a singer of jazz-inflected pop, Cole was one of the greatest piano players in swing. In 1937 he formed the Nat King Cole Trio, with original members Oscar Moore on guitar and Wesley Prince on bass, as purely "an instrumental group," he once said. Putting his all into his exciting keyboard work, he considered singing completely secondary. He was, in fact, rather insecure about his vocal ability. But by the fifties the trio had broken up and the astounding rise of Cole as one of music's most beloved vocalists continued until his untimely death, from lung cancer, at age forty-seven in 1965. Twenty-six years later his starry magic shone through once again on his daughter Nathalie's uncanny duet with him, "Unforgettable."

Classic Songs: His first big hit, 1946's "(Get Your Kicks on) Route 66," "Unforgettable," "The Christmas Song," "Mona Lisa," and the novelty "Mr. Cole Won't Rock 'n' Roll."

Swing Trivia: The trio was originally intended as a quartet. At one of their early gigs, they sat around waiting for their drummer to show up. According to *The Penguin Encyclopedia of Popular Music,* he never did, and they decided to just do without.

CD Pick: Now that Cole is once again appreciated for his instrumental prowess, *Hit That Jive, Jack* (MCA/Decca) is a must-have. By turns lightsome, then bluesy, it's a great presentation of the trio's work in the early forties.

SIDEMEN FRONT AND CENTER

To a degree that's hard to imagine today, it was the sidemen, not the singers, who were the real focus of the true jazz fan's admiration. Debates raged over who played the alto better. Were you a partisan of Johnny Hodges? Or of Benny Carter? What were your opinions of the relative merits of trumpeters Roy Eldridge, Bunny Berigan, Erskine Hawkins, and Harry "Sweets" Edison? And could you pick out a Jack Teagarden solo on trombone or a Barney Bigard riff on clarinet in an instant? Indeed, the swing era owes its greatness to the contributions of hundreds, even thousands, of instrumentalists, from the most obscure sideman in a territory band to the likes of pianists Teddy Wilson and Mary Lou Williams, drummer Louis Bellson, violinist Stuff Smith, bassist Milt Hinton, and vibraharpist Red Norvo, to name just a few. But there are three men who seem to stand above them all—this trio made the world think of the saxophone when it thinks of jazz. Just call them the three tenors.

Coleman Hawkins

The tenor sax was a plodding, clumsy bird of an instrument before the Hawk gave it new wings. Influenced by Louis Armstrong's trumpet playing, Hawkins is credited with turning the tenor into a star with his passionate, aggressive style. A master of harmony, he joined Fletcher Henderson's band way back in 1923 and stayed with the orchestra until 1934, but his greatest

triumph came five years later. In a stunning 1939 performance, he recorded "Body and Soul," taking listeners on a richly emotive three-minute journey. Hawkins, while embracing bop in the forties, set the swinging standard for every tenor sax player to come after him.

Ben Webster

While Webster's warm, almost airy tone meshed seamlessly with the Duke's tone-poem compositions, it took Ellington's star soloist a long time to find his perfect match. Beginning in the late twenties, Webster jumped from band to band, playing for Andy Kirk, Benny Carter, Teddy Wilson, Fletcher Henderson, Bennie Moten, and both Cab and his sister Blanche Calloway. It wasn't until 1940 that he joined Ellington's orchestra full-time, but he quickly became the first star tenor player the band had ever had. In fact, his influence, along with that of bassist Jimmy Blanton, was so profound that Ellington's group from this time is sometimes referred as the Blanton-Webster band. Excelling on ballads, Webster can best be heard on "Cotton Tail," where his spirited tones flow like the sweetest honey.

Lester Young

Standing in cool contrast to the bolder and ballsier style of Hawkins, Young was a shining light in the Basie band from 1937 to 1940. With his high, nimble playing—some said he made the tenor sax sound almost like an alto—he left his mark on such classics as "Taxi War Dance" and "Lester Leaps In." Without being a showman, Young was one of the heppest cats out there. Inventing his own slang, wearing his signature porkpie hat, and affecting an all-around mellow air, he became an early inspiration to the bebop players. He also displayed a particular affinity with singers, especially Billie Holiday, with whom he recorded such great songs as "All of Me" and "He's Funny That Way." After Young nicknamed her "Lady Day" (see Holiday's bio above), she dubbed him "Prez," short for President. His death inspired Charles Mingus to write the gut-wrenching elegy "Goodbye Pork Pie Hat."

EARLY R&B AND ROCK

Neoswing's post–big band era influences aren't limited to Louis Jordan and Louis Prima. Swingers love to listen to original rockabilly and rock stars like Elvis, Chuck Berry, Little Richard, Carl Perkins (who did "Blue Suede Shoes" before Elvis's cover took off), "Be-Bop-A-Lula" heartthrob Gene Vincent, and even Bill Haley, the man behind "Rock Around the Clock." "There's been this really broad redefinition of swing," says Lavay Smith pianist and arranger Chris Seibert, "so that it includes rockabilly and early rock 'n' roll like Bill Haley and the Comets." By the way, Haley, earlier in his career, played Western swing, another huge influence on the swing revival. Check out a greatest hits collection of Western swing giant Bob Wills's work for an introduction to this smoothly swinging music. But the dominant force behind the swing revival remains the jump blues and early R&B sound, everything from Atlantic Records' powerhouse Ruth Brown and "Good Rocking Tonight"'s Roy Brown to Ray Charles and Ike Turner (at least his stuff from before he met Tina). In addition to Jordan, here are three of the greatest in the genre.

Wynonie Harris

Working as a bartender and almost forgotten at the time of his death in 1969, Harris was one of the best-selling blues shouters of the postswing era. First a singer in Lucky Millinder's band (an important swing-to-R&B transitional orchestra), Harris went solo in 1945, recording a string of R&B hits for such "race music" labels as Aladdin and King. Harris—who by all accounts lived as wildly as he sang—wasn't afraid of taking double entrendre to the limit, singing about liquor, sex, and more sex. For an example, check out "Keep on Churnin'," in which he exhorts his baby to do it til "the butter comes!"

Classic Songs: The comic "Good Morning Judge" and "Who Threw the Whiskey in the Well?" his big hit for Millinder.

Swing Trivia: A prodigal spendthrift, Harris was known for entering bars and declaring, "Mr. Blues is back in town, and I have enough money to air-condition hell."

CD Pick: Rhino's *Bloodshot Eyes: The Best of Wynonie Harris* includes eighteen of his best down-and-dirty numbers, plus a shout-out duet with Big Joe Turner. Guaranteed to make you blush.

The Treniers

Founded by twin brothers Claude and Cliff Trenier, the Treniers are a hard-rocking, shout-out group from Alabama who've become the band to know within the hard-core swing set. Their new popularity owes a lot to the group's longevity. The Treniers, who formed back in the forties, still perform (with original members brother Claude and sax man Don Hill) in casino lounges around the world. They got their start with swing big bands—Claude sang with Jimmie Lunceford for a while—but eventually became one of the most rousing early rock bands of their time. When the Treniers shout "Go! Go! Go!" you'd better be on your feet.

Classic Songs: "Rockin' Is Our Business," which they sang in the Jayne Mansfield movie *The Girl Can't Help It,* and "Say Hey (The Willie Mays Song)," their highest-charting number.

Swing Trivia: Claude and Cliff made an inauspicious but satisfying debut while studying at Alabama State in Montgomery. "We'd go into Pope's Luncheonette and sing with the jukebox and the people would give us hamburgers," says Claude, who recently passed the eighty-year mark. "At one time we had ten hamburgers stacked up on the jukebox. We had five or six guys we hung out with and they'd say, 'We're hungry. Go in and sing a song and get some hamburgers.'"

CD Pick: *They Rock! They Roll! They Swing!* (Epic/Legacy) is a terrific collection of greatest hits. True to their billing, half of the songs have the word *rock* in the title. The CD also includes the band's off-color novelty number "Poon-Tang!" recorded in 1952. "We said 'a poon is a hug, a tang is a kiss,'" remembers Claude. "We tried to clean it up. But they wouldn't play it on the air at the time." Go figure.

Big Joe Turner

Called the Boss of the Blues, Turner backed up that claim with his unstoppable freight-train voice during his influential sixty-year career. He came out of the wild and swinging jazz scene of 1920s Kansas City, where he met up with pianist extraordinaire Pete Johnson, with whom he helped popularize the all-over-the-keyboard sound of boogie-woogie. Both R&B and rock 'n' roll owe a tremendous debt to his powerful mixing of jazz and blues. For example, Ike Turner hit it big with "Rocket 88," a song about the classic Olds, six years after Joe Turner recorded the original version "Rocket Boogie 88" in 1948. Sun Records' Sam Phillips later hailed Ike's hit as the first rock 'n' roll record.

Classic Songs: The boogie-woogie "Roll 'Em Pete," one of his first breakthroughs, and "Shake, Rattle and Roll" (Bill Haley's megahit was a cleaned-up version of this Turner tune).

Swing Trivia: Turner got his start as a singing bartender at Kansas City's Sunset Club. Before that he worked as a guide for a blind guitarist.

CD Pick: It's a tough choice between *Boss of the Blues* (Atlantic), with Johnson, which features great selections of the pair's early hits, and *Big Joe Turner: Greatest Hits* (Atlantic Jazz), a solid sampling of Turner's more rockin' work.

MORE BIG BANDS

Fletcher Henderson: Henderson laid the foundation of swing with his influential band in the 1920s, is credited with sparking Benny Goodman's breakthrough, and had the most awesome lineup of sidemen of any bandleader ever (with Louis Armstrong at the top of the list, followed closely by all three great tenor sax players, Hawkins, Webster, and Young). His famous arrangements, many put together by reedman Don Redman, include "Tozo," "Henderson Stomp," "Whiteman Stomp," and, for Goodman, "Blues Skies" and "Christopher Columbus." But huge commercial popularity always eluded Henderson, which some historians attribute to his failure to be a tough taskmaster, something Henderson himself copped to. "When I'm lucky enough to get them all on the bandstand, I've got the baddest-ass band in the world," he once said.

Fats Waller: A renowned showman, Waller established himself as a jazz giant in the preswing era of the 1920s. Born in 1904 in New York and dead of pneumonia in 1943, Waller got his start as a protégé of Harlem stride piano innovator James P. Johnson. He soon began to rival his mentor in ragtime virtuosity and wrote such enduring hits as "Honeysuckle Rose" and "Ain't Misbehavin'," which he performed with trademark flamboyance, his nimble eyebrows always highlighting his mischief-making tone. Bandleader Bill Elliott recommends buying anything and everything Waller ever recorded, an approach that Fats would have approved. Anecdotes abound of Waller's more-is-more lifestyle. Whether it's to be believed that he could eat three chickens and three steaks in one sitting is another story.

Charlie Barnet: Barnet proved that even Park Avenue could swing. A rich Yale dropout, the sax-playing Barnet formed his own big band in 1933 and struggled for a few years for acclaim. By the mid-thirties, however, Barnet—a devoted admirer of Ellington— began to really swing it. Soon *Metronome* magazine had dubbed his group "the blackest white band around." Barnet's biggest hit is "Cherokee," a hard-swinging number that had a successful second life as a bop standard after Charlie Parker reworked it and renamed it "Ko-Ko." But the band's most entertaining choice of material came after the orchestra lost its arrangements, uniforms, and instruments in the fire that destroyed LA's Palomar Ballroom in 1939. The first song the band played after regrouping was a tune called "We're All Burnt Up."

Benny Carter: One of the true geniuses of jazz, Carter led his own bands throughout the late twenties and beyond; composed and arranged tunes for Henderson, Ellington and Goodman; and along with fellow musician Johnny Hodges, carved out the distinctive place of the alto sax in swing. His song "When the Lights Are Low" became a standard, but others have failed to reach a wider audience. According to Ted Gioia's *History of Jazz,* Carter's moody, more "reflective style" was in opposition to the hot uptempo tenor of the times. Carter turned ninety-two in 1999, having had one of the longest careers in his field.

Woody Herman: An adored bandleader and reedman, Herman was as adept at reinventing himself as any nineties pop star, but he did it with leagues more depth. Nicknamed the Wood-chopper, he first scored it big in 1939 with the jaunty "Wood-chopper's Ball." After a string of swing hits — including a version of Louis Jordan's "Caldonia" and the theme song to the Gene Tierney film *Laura* — Herman's orchestra morphed by the mid-forties into a bop-influenced big band, one of the few orchestras, along with Stan Kenton's, to successfully pursue what they called a "progressive" approach to the music. The band's theme song, "Blue Flame," is inspired by a locker room trick involving a match and . . .

Earl Hines: Without Hines the jazz piano may never have existed as we know it. Known as "Fatha" Hines, this inventive player — in seminal recordings with Louis Armstrong in the late twenties — moved the piano beyond its more limited ragtime and stride structures into the looser rhythms of the swing era. In 1928 he began recording under his own name and led a band through-out the thirties that played the famed Grand Terrace Ballroom in Chicago. Hines also helped incubate bop in the late forties, hiring such greats as Charlie Parker, Billy Eckstine, Dizzy Gillespie, and Sarah Vaughan for his orchestra. His hit song "Second Balcony Jump" was purportedly inspired by a too-high cat who tried to fly off the balcony of a nightclub.

Les Brown: Known as Les Brown and His Band of Renown, Brown's orchestra made it big once it hired Doris Day as its vocal-ist. Their hits together included "My Dreams Keep Getting Better All the Time" and the touching "Sentimental Journey." Brown, who also fronted the house band on the *Dean Martin Show,* still does a radio show with his son, Les Jr.

The Casa Loma Orchestra: Formed in 1929, the Casa Loma Orchestra was one of the only white bands on the circuit that reg-ularly played hot tunes during the bleak jazz years of the early thirties. With fast-tempo hits like "Casa Loma Stomp" and "Maniac's Ball," they helped prime college audiences for Good-man's later breakthrough. And unlike most bands, the Casa Loma was run not by a leader but as a cooperative venture. How about a quarterly dividend instead of a salary?

Bob Crosby: Always performing in the shadow of his hugely famous older brother Bing, Bob nevertheless put together a real solid sender of an orchestra back in the thirties, creating a distinct swing sound with a Dixieland vibe. His best tunes, many done with his smaller combo the Bobcats, include "Wolverine Blues" and "March of the Bobcats."

Harry James: One of the most inspiring trumpeters of his generation, James enjoyed only a short honeymoon with jazz critics. A flashy high-stepping soloist, he first gained national attention with the Benny Goodman Orchestra, appearing most notably in the epochal concert at Carnegie Hall in 1938. ("I feel like a whore in church," a nervous James reportedly said before the curtain rose.) But after he left to form his own band in late 1938, he poured on the syrup, with great success. By late 1942 he had a band that topped all others in popularity, scoring hits with Helen Forrest's "You Made Me Love You," and "Two O'Clock Jump," a reworking of Count Basie's "One O'Clock" standard. The quintessential celebrity bandleader, James gained further fame the next year by tying the knot with pinup queen Betty Grable.

The International Sweethearts of Rhythm: One of the few all-female bands to break through during the male-dominated swing era, the International Sweethearts of Rhythm got its start in the thirties in Mississippi and struggled for years to be taken as more than a curiosity. It also numbered a few white musicians among its members, who attempted to pass as black during tours in the South.

Sammy Kaye and Kay Kyser: Reviled by serious jazz fans and adored by millions, both the Kyser and Kaye orchestras played sugar-cube music and laid on cute gimmicks. Kaye's band, dubbed a "Mickey Mouse" outfit by *Metronome,* let audience members come onstage and wave a baton during a musical number. Kyser had a quiz-show-themed radio show, *Kay*

Kyser's Kollege of Musical Knowledge. But history buffs will
want to hear the patriotic World War II songs each turned into
hits, Kaye's "Remember Pearl Harbor" and Kyser's "Praise the
Lord and Pass the Ammunition."

Andy Kirk and His Clouds of Joy: For a while, Kirk's outfit
gave the Basie band a run for its money in the hot Kansas City
jazz scene. Kirk's best songs include "What's Your Story, Morning
Glory?" singer Pha Terrell's "Until the Real Thing Comes Along,"
and the evocatively titled "Mess-a-Stomp." But his greatest contribution may have been to provide a roost for pianist Mary Lou
Williams, one of the only female instrumentalists allowed to
really shine during the swing era. She began as a chauffeur for
the band and worked her way up, eventually earning top billing
as "the Lady Who Swings the Band."

MORE GREAT SINGERS

The Andrews Sisters: The best-selling girl group of all time, La-
Verne, Maxene, and Patti Andrews were so magnitudinally square
—they poured so much innocent glee into their impeccable harmonies—that the group's music seems almost bizarrely tweaked
today. Nostalgic symbols of wartime America, they created a mul-
ticultural musical stew, with influences ranging from polka to
calypso to boogie-woogie bugle boys. They even sampled Yiddish
on their first big hit, 1937's "Bei Mer Bist Du Schoen." (*Greatest
Hits: The Sixtieth Anniversary Collection,* MCA, which includes
many of their famous duets with Bing Crosby, is a super collection.) But just how naive were they? The trio recorded at least two
risqué songs back in the day: "Rum and Coca-Cola"—its lyrics
were about both mothers *and* daughters in Trinidad "working for
the Yankee dollar"—and the fairly obvious "(Hold Tight) Want
Some Seafood Mama." About the former, Maxene told Fred Hall
in *Dialogues in Swing,* "We didn't have any idea what it meant."

Peggy Lee: That instant when smoke comes off a flame? Lee seemed to sing from that place all the time on such sultry hits as "Fever" and "Black Coffee." Her talent, however, lay in much more than imparting a sexy purr to a song. She joined Benny Goodman's band in 1941, finding her first big hit two years later with the sweetly goading "Why Don't You Do Right?" She had hits from there on out, culminating in 1969's Top 40 smash, "Is That All There Is?" which she recorded despite resistance from her label. A talented songwriter, she penned "Mañana," wrote part of the score for Disney's *Lady and the Tramp*, and turned "Fever" into a hit after adding some of her own lyrics. Oh, and then there's that Oscar nomination for the 1956 jazz film *Pete Kelly's Blues.* Seemingly unstoppable, she has in fact retired twice. Since falling onstage in Las Vegas in the eighties, she's been confined to a wheelchair and largely out of public view. Back in the late forties, after marrying former Goodman guitarist Dave Barbour and becoming a mother, she left the business . . . for a spell. According to *Dialogues in Swing,* after she was coaxed by producer Dave Dexter to return to recording, Lee thought about it for a moment and replied, "Well, I think I can get a babysitter."

Tony Bennett: Two words: *MTV Unplugged.* With his justly hyped special on the network and subsequent CD, Bennett's coolness quotient hit the stratosphere in 1994. Suddenly the music video generation found out what Sinatra, who always referred to Bennett as his favorite singer, had been saying for years. Discovered in 1950 by Pearl Bailey and Bob Hope, Bennett put his signature smooth touch on such hits as the country-inspired "Cold, Cold Heart," "Because of You," "I Left My Heart in San Francisco"; paired up with Basie on *Basie Swings, Bennett Sings;* and recorded critically acclaimed tributes to Billie Holiday, Rodgers and Hart, Irving Berlin, and fittingly, Sinatra. Not bad for a guy who started his career as a singing waiter.

Bobby Darin: Splish, splash? More like flip, flop. Like an earnest chameleon, Darin jumped from persona to persona. He was a Sinatra-esque lounge singer ("Mack the Knife"); a rockin' teen idol ("Dream Love," "Queen of the Hop"); and, as Bob Darrin, an antiwar folkie ("If I Were a Carpenter"). But his style hopping has become an inspiration to today's genre-straddling swing musicians. And his inspired ballad "Beyond the Sea" (recently covered by Royal Crown Revue) is an undisputed classic.

Sammy Davis Jr. and Dean Martin: Once you've got your Frankie albums, you'll have a ring-ding of a time checking out the music of his Rat Pack buddies Sammy and Dino. The pair, remembered more today for their Vegas Strip hijinks, cut their fair share of suave tunes. *Dean Martin: The Capitol Collector's Series* (Capitol) includes "Volare," "That's Amore," and "Ain't That a Kick in the Head," while *Sammy's Greatest Hits, Vol. 1* (Garland/DNA) offers up "That Old Black Magic," "Something's Gotta Give," and two numbers with drummer Buddy Rich.

Dick Haymes: A former Hollywood stunt man, Haymes once equaled Bing Crosby and Frank Sinatra in popularity. His more than forty hits—many with Helen Forrest, his former colleague in the Harry James Orchestra—include "It Might As Well Be Spring," "It Can't Be Wrong," and "I'll Get By." And Haymes certainly did that. He was married seven times, once to Rita Hayworth.

Lena Horne: Crushingly beautiful and amazingly multitalented, Horne turned up everywhere during the swing era with Zelig-like regularity. She danced in the chorus line at the Cotton Club early in her career, starred in many movies, including *Stormy Weather* and *Cabin in the Sky,* enjoyed romances with both Joe Louis and Duke Ellington, toured with Charlie Barnet, and recorded with Artie Shaw. During the war she also became the single most popular black pinup girl. More of a pop than jazz singer, Horne, who turned eighty in 1999, remains a symbol of the class and sophistication of the age.

Anita O'Day: Anything but just another canary, O'Day sings with a husky voice that imparts a knowing toughness to every number she grabs hold of. Still performing today, O'Day began her career with drummer Gene Krupa in 1941 — *Uptown* (Columbia) collects her amazing work with Krupa and trumpeter Roy Eldridge from this time — then went to Stan Kenton's band, where she had a hit with "Her Tears Flowed Like Wine." After that O'Day went solo and established herself as one of jazz's best scat singers. But as O'Day revealed in her 1981 autobiography *High Times, Hard Times*, she'd battled addictions to heroin and alcohol for years. The wine had flowed like tears too.

The Helens: Do you know how to tell your Helens apart? Four major singers of the swing era shared this first name.

- ► HELEN FORREST: The epitome of the big band girl singer, Forrest performed for the orchestras of Artie Shaw, Benny Goodman (whom she quite disliked), and Harry James. Her claret voice endowed such romantic numbers as "I Had the Craziest Dream" and "I'm Always Chasing Rainbows" with the most plaintive longing.

- ► HELEN HUMES: Succeeding Billie Holiday in the Count Basie Orchestra, Humes — known for her beautiful high voice — recorded such numbers as the sensual "One Hour with You" and later had an R&B hit, "Be-Baba-Leba" in the fifties with pianist/organist Bill Doggett.

- ► HELEN O'CONNELL: Known as the sweetest of canaries, O'Connell sang for the Jimmy Dorsey Orchestra and recorded such 1940s hits as "Green Eyes" and "Tangerine."

- ► HELEN WARD: Girl-next-door Ward, Benny Goodman's first singer, most famously sang "Goody-Goody," about the pleasure of hearing that an ex-lover (and cad) has himself gotten dumped.

Jimmy Rushing: Known as Mr. Five by Five (for his height and girth), Rushing brought blues to the big band, performing from 1935 to 1950 as the male vocalist for Count Basie. With his amazingly clear and strongly supported tenor voice, he was adept at taking lovable ballads and casting them in dappled bluesy light.

You'll hear his warm, cheerful tone on Basie's *Complete Decca Recordings* (Decca/GRP), singing such songs as "Georgianna," "Blues in the Dark," and the classic "Sent for You Yesterday."

Jo Stafford: Dreamy but sensible, sweet but substantial, Stafford was dubbed GI Jo during the war by her legion of enlisted fans. As part of the Tommy Dorsey Orchestra, she was one of the Pied Pipers, backed up Frank Sinatra on "Stardust," and had her own hits with "Manhattan Serenade" and "You Took My Love." After the big band era, Stafford's career soared, including major duets with Frankie Laine ("Hey, Good Looking") and Gordon MacRae ("My Darling, My Darling"). But she'll always be remembered for her oddball campy side too. Using the pseudonym Cinderella Stump, she sang the hillbilly curiosity "I'm My Own Grandma." And she and her husband, Paul Weston, under the aliases Jonathan and Darlene Edwards, recorded a number of albums in which they purposefully sang and played off-key, sending up everything from "Honeysuckle Rose" to "I Am Woman."

Mel Tormé: Tormé's career went in the opposite direction of most singers' of his era. Dubbed the Velvet Fog, a nickname he hated, Tormé was a gifted songwriter who had his first song, "Lament to Love," published at age fifteen after Harry James recorded it. After he began his solo career in the mid-forties, he dueted with Peggy Lee on "The Old Master Painter," penned the solid gold chestnut "The Christmas Song" (more than seventeen hundred versions of it have been recorded), and charted with such pop songs as "Careless Hands" and "Bewitched." But he soon set out to prove his chops as a jazz singer, recording acclaimed tributes to Benny Goodman, Fred Astaire, and Bing Crosby. As he once said of himself, "This syrupy, creamy bobby-sox sensation was taking the musical bull by the horns and singing the kind of music he wanted to sing." When Tormé died at age seventy-three in 1999, he was lauded for doing just that.

Dinah Washington: If she was mad at you, Washington would as likely pull a pistol on you as curse you out. Notoriously hot tempered and married at least seven times, Washington began her career in 1942 singing for Lionel Hampton when she was just eighteen. In the fifties she became known as the Queen of the Blues, admired for both her fearless gospel-influenced style, on such songs as "What a Diff'rence a Day Makes" and "This Bitter Earth," and for the way she could take a chestnut and make it new again, as she did with Nat King Cole's signature "Unforgettable." Washington's hard living caught up with her in 1959 when she died of an overdose at age thirty-nine.

Joe Williams: After knocking around with such orchestras as Lionel Hampton's and Coleman Hawkins's, Williams replaced Jimmy Rushing in the Count Basie Orchestra and was instrumental in reviving the band's fortunes during the fifties. His voice had an elegant authority and deep soulful feeling, nowhere better heard than on "Every Day I Have the Blues," the song that's considered his greatest triumph. He recorded the classic album *Count Basie Swings, Joe Williams Sings,* scatted like mad with Ella on the 1956 song "Party Blues," and in the eighties reached a whole new audience through his role as Grandpa Al on *The Cosby Show*. As Duke Ellington once wrote of Williams, who died in 1999, "He sang real soul blues on which his perfect enunciation of the words gave the blues a new dimension."

THE TEN BEST COMPILATIONS
Big Band

1. *An Anthology of Big Band Swing 1930–1955* (GRP) is a Lindy Hopper's dream. The two-CD collection not only features Henderson, the Dorsey Brothers, Lunceford, Armstrong, and Kansas City blues pianist Jay McShann, to name just a few of the giants, but also includes competing versions of "One O'Clock Jump" recorded by Basie and Goodman.

2. *Oscillatin' Rhythm* (Capitol) is the hands-down favorite of swing DJs around the country, putting such standards as "Sing,

Sing, Sing," "Smoke Rings," "For Dancers Only," "Tain't What You Do," and "Leap Frog" all on one disc.

3. *Swingin' at Capitol* (Capitol) is another great one-CD introduction, featuring a diverse lineup of swing greats, from Harry James and Les Brown to Cootie Williams and Illinois Jacquet to Ray Anthony and Benny Carter.

4. *Swing Time, the Fabulous Big Band Era* (Columbia/Legacy) is truly the swing mother lode. This indispensable three-CD set brings together the best bands and their biggest hits. From Artie Shaw's "Nightmare" to Jimmy Dorsey's "Green Eyes" to Ellington's "Don't Get Around Much Anymore," the list never stops.

Lounge

5. *Wild, Cool and Swinging* (Ultra Lounge/Capitol) is the essence of Las Vegas cool, featuring Dino singing "Volare," Wayne Newton's "Danke Schoen," Peggy Lee's "Fever," plus Lou Rawls, Bobby Darin, Louis Prima, Sammy Davis Jr., and Vic Damone. Just lie back and pretend you're sippin' a martini at the Sands.

Jump Blues and R&B

6. *Blues Masters, Vol. 5, Jump Blues* (Rhino) features eighteen wild tracks, including LaVern Baker's "Voodoo Voodoo," Wynonie Harris's "Destination Love," and Professor Longhair's friskily titled "Ball the Wall."

7. *Jump Blue: Rockin' the Jukes* (Blue Note) shows off such jump greats as Jimmy and Joe Liggins, Big Jay McNeely, Roy Brown, and Louis Jordan at their honking and shouting best.

8. *Jumpin' Like Mad: Cool Cats and Hip Chicks* (Capitol), a two-CD set, will knock the roof off the joint with such rockin' R&B classics as Helen Humes's "Be-Baba-Leba" and Louis Prima's "Five Months, Two Weeks, Two Days," plus Louis Jordan, Ella Mae Morse, T-Bone Walker, and the Nat King Cole Trio. As Peggy Lee sings it here, "Yeah, yeah, yeah."

9. *Original Swingers: Hipsters, Zoots and Wingtips, Vol. 2*

(Hip-O Records) collects Dinah Washington, Jimmy Liggins, Erskine Hawkins, Count Basie, Lucky Millinder, and Louis Jordan all on one irrepressible CD.

10. *Risqué Rhythm: Nasty '50s R&B* (Rhino) pulls together the most raunchy double entendre songs ever made, from Moose Jackson's "Big Ten-Inch Record" to Dinah Washington singing about a trombone player's "big long slidin' thing" in a song of that title, to the Toppers' "I Love to Play Your Piano (Let Me Bang Your Box)." Let yourself be shocked.

CHAPTER 5

The Most Swinging New Bands

*I*f it was difficult defining what swing was back in the thirties, it's become almost impossible to do so now. Today's swing isn't just one thing—it's pure mutt, drawing from the original era but folding in a host of other influences. There is swing with bop, hip-hop, Beatles-style pop, Dixieland, blues, R&B, rockabilly, punk, ska, hard rock, and lounge. "It's taken all we have learned about rock 'n' roll, all we've experimented with and developed in the past forty years and incorporated it into the music," says Jack Vaughn, president of the neoswing label Slimstyle Records.

The following list of bands certainly runs that gamut. From the punk-influenced Royal Crown Revue and Big Bad Voodoo Daddy to the rockabilly sounds of Brian Setzer to the big band traditionalism of Bill Elliott and Eddie Reed to scores of others, you'll be surprised by both the depth and breadth of the new swing music. Indeed, one Web site (*www.406hepcats.bukowski.com*) has links to more than 225 swing band homepages. Below you'll get an introduction to the biggest, the most buzzed about, and the ones that the dancers can't live without. They're all in here.

Plus, you'll see the results of a survey that tells you which ten albums swingers think are the most righteous. Based on the opinions of the most hep-to-the-jive insiders—the top swingzine experts and radio and club DJs—it'll let you know where to get started in building a new swing music collection. Most of the CDs are available at on-line music stores such as Amazon.com. But for harder-to-find albums, contact Hepcat Records (*www.hepcat-records.com*), the indispensable retro music distributor, which puts out a great catalog of everything from swing to surf to rockabilly. You should also check out the Web guide in the appendix for a list of which swing sites have the best links to individual bands' homepages.

FACING PAGE: *Brian Setzer strutting his stuff at the Hollywood Palladium.* (MARK JORDAN)

But let's talk priorities for a sec. Listening to the music on a CD can't replace the experience of getting out and dancing to a real band. More than anything else, live music is the foundation of the swing scene. In fact, as you'll soon find out, most swing dancers decide where to go based not so much on which club they like best as on which band is playing there that night. So head out to a dance spot. Support the bands. (But keep in mind that not all the groups listed below are as danceable as others.) And have a blast spinning your partner.

THE BIG GUNS

Big Bad Voodoo Daddy

How do you know a swing band has really made it? When other bands start playing their songs. In the past couple of years, such BBVD tunes as "You and Me and the Bottle Makes Three Tonight (Baby)" and "Go Daddy-O" have become perhaps the best-known and most-covered songs in swing. "And we've never had a radio hit," says lead singer Scotty Morris. Of course, the band hasn't lacked for exposure. After a career-making performance in *Swingers* in 1996, they've since played for President Clinton, performed with Stevie Wonder at the Super Bowl, appeared on *Melrose Place* and *Ally McBeal,* and performed in promotional spots for the NBA. Morris, a former punker who put the band together on the outskirts of LA (in Ventura) in the early nineties, can now look back and laugh at how hard it was getting BBVD started. "I was trying to convince these good players that they should come to me and play pre-bop music and they were like, 'Fuck, no way,'" he says. So what direction does this rocking high-energy band head in now that they've hit so many peaks? Getting even more rock/swing schizophrenic on their latest album. "The crazier stuff is by far crazier than anything we've ever done and the traditional stuff is more traditional," says Morris. "I even wrote a seventeen-piece big band ballad."

Cherry Poppin' Daddies

They don't try to be offensive, they just are offensive and that's the way they like it. A ska-inspired band with a big horn sound, the Daddies started doing swing soon after getting together in Eugene, Oregon, way back in 1989. Fronted by former punk rocker Steve Perry, the band would seem to have been in the wrong place at the wrong time. The Pacific Northwest was then ground zero for grunge, and the group's antics were anything but angst propelled. They'd wheel a giant phallus-shaped golf cart, dubbed the Dildorado, onstage during their shows. They put out an early album called *Ferociously Stoned,* with women on the cover so skimpily clothed they would have been at home in a David Lee Roth video. And then there was their risqué moniker, inspired by the double entendre "race" records of early R&B. "It was dirty and filthy and bad and it was funny and it swung, too," Perry has told *Lo-Fi* magazine. Needless to say, it was a little too dirty for some people. The Daddies' in-your-face attitude upset a fair share of PC types; at one point Perry even had hot coffee thrown in his face while just walking down the street. But the band made a shrewd decision in 1997. Before then they'd always mixed up ska, punk, and swing on their albums, but that year they improbably decided to put together a greatest hits CD that gathered all their most swinging songs in one place. Named for their soon-to-be-huge radio hit "Zoot Suit Riot," the CD blew out of stores in 1998, selling over a million copies. It also made the Daddies emblems of the swing scene, an odd place for the band given that they're not a favorite of the dance crowd and are more likely to be found touring with such ska bands as the Mighty Mighty Bosstones and Reel Big Fish. But the band's pop success isn't hard to fathom. In their best and most irreverent songs, they smartly marry a blasting swing sound with lyrics that gamely tackle the dysfunction of the nineties. For a signature Daddies' tune, just check out "Drunk Daddy," which opens with the following line: "Momma married a big asshole / Whiskey bottles on the floor."

Royal Crown Revue

Give 'em their props! The Royal Crowns are the true pioneers of
the swing revival, bringing their pumped-up jazz to a whole new
generation for more than a decade. (For the full story of how they
did it, check out chapter 2.) They've got the cred and the cool and
a range of influences as diverse as a Las Vegas buffet table. From
Dashiell Hammett and film noir to juvenile delinquent novels and
Jim Thompson to punk and bebop, they throw it all into the mix.
The result is that they've created a hybrid brand of music they call
gangster bop that's hard to pigeonhole. Fronted by lead singer
Eddie Nichols, they've toured with the B-52's and the Pretenders,
recorded with Bette Midler, played on the Warped Tour, head-
lined the Desert Inn in Las Vegas, performed at jazz festivals, and
even opened for Kiss. "This isn't anything like Glenn Miller would
do," says the band's trumpeter, Scott Steen. But is the band starting to show its sweet side as well? For their newest album, *Walk
on Fire,* according to guitarist James Achor, "Eddie's writing love
songs." Get ready to swoon.

Brian Setzer Orchestra

Believe it or not, you can draw a line of inspiration from Tommy
Dorsey to Brian Setzer. In the late eighties the former Stray Cat
first got the idea to take his brand of rockabilly and put a swing
band behind it after he was scheduled to appear on *The Tonight
Show.* A routine TV appearance perhaps. But the producers sug-
gested Setzer do something totally different on air. They offered
to let him strum his guitar in front of the *Tonight Show* band,
led by none other than the mighty trumpeter Doc Severinsen,
who, believe it or not, got his start back in the forties in the
bands of Tommy Dorsey, Charlie Barnet, and Benny Goodman.
And while the *Tonight Show* appearance never actually happened, the offer planted a seed in Setzer's head. Cut to the early
nineties. Setzer — with some great advance money from Warner
Records — decided to put his brainstorm into action. Putting

together what are hands-down the best musicians in the business, Setzer reinvented himself with the Brian Setzer Orchestra, which began playing its first gigs in Los Angeles in 1993. "Man, I hit a brick wall," he once told *Pulse* magazine. "It was like, what the hell are you doing? First of all, no one's gonna book a big band, there's too many guys to pay. Then they'd ask, 'What is a big band? Is that two drummers and four backup vocalists?' They didn't know what it was!" Indeed, Setzer's first two albums failed to spark. But the third, *The Dirty Boogie*—released in 1998 just as swing was about to hit critical mass—became a monster hit, no doubt helped immensely by the fortuitous redo of Louis Prima's "Jump, Jive, an' Wail," released at the same time as the Gap commercial, featuring the original. But has Setzer—who won two Grammys in 1999 for *The Dirty Boogie*—really reinvented himself? Get beyond the Prima cover and this is still greaser rock, music that isn't really that far afield from "Rock This Town" and "Stray Cat Strut." Not that that's a problem. What could be better than getting to carry on the tradition of Bill Haley and Eddie Cochran in two successful incarnations? This cat's got at least a few more lives.

Squirrel Nut Zippers

While they've been credited with convincing radio execs that retro music can be a hit—with their landmark 1996 calypso-tinged song "Hell"—the Squirrel Nut Zippers, contrary to popular belief, aren't really a swing band. In fact, they've strenuously resisted being tagged with the swing label. Instead, this North Carolina band is a bunch of alt rock eccentrics who like to play twenties hot jazz. Since forming in 1993, they've put out three albums, *Hot, Inevitable,* and *Perennial Favorites,* but the latest CD to look out for is *Jazz Squad,* the solo album from singer and resident banjo player Katharine Whalen. With her high but wry tone, she covers such pre–World War II gems as "Deed I Do," "Sugar," and "Just You, Just Me."

DANCERS' FAVORITES
Bill Elliott Orchestra

Perhaps the most dancer-friendly bandleader out there, Elliott started falling in love with Benny Goodman's music when he was ten and Fats Waller's piano playing when he was sixteen, and he hasn't stopped swinging since. Modeling his Los Angeles–based fifteen-piece group on the orchestras of Tommy Dorsey and Artie Shaw circa 1939, Elliott plays a traditional big band style of swing. He's got great sidemen, a thrilling way with the keyboard, and a vocal group called the Lucky Stars who call to mind the Pied Pipers. And he's also an acute observer of the rapidly evolving swing scene, which shouldn't be too surprising. Elliott—who's also a successful composer of movie and TV scores—started a jump blues band back in Boston two decades ago. So what keeps his music fresh? Often it's because he takes inspiration directly from Lindy Hoppers. In fact, he recently wrote a song called "Shim Sham Shimmy" inspired by the dance of the same name. "Not every band can play at a medium tempo and have it really cook," he says. "I take pride in the fact that we can do music that isn't fast but is still exciting."

Indigo Swing

One of the most in-demand dance outfits in the country, San Francisco's Indigo Swing plays more than three hundred live shows a year. And it's not hard to see why. Lead singer Johnny Boyd's crooning voice is smooth as buttermilk. The band members—who look for inspiration from folks like guitarist Charlie Christian and pianist Earl Hines—walk a fine line between tradition and invention. And Indigo Swing's modern-day lyrics are all about good old love and heartache. "What my band does is real, honest postwar boogie-woogie swing," Boyd has said. Look for the band's fourth and most recent album, *Red Light,* or better yet, dance to 'em live.

One of the top neoswing albums, Come Out Swingin' *by Steve Lucky and the Rhumba Bums.* (PHOTO: TRACY HATCH)

Steve Lucky and the Rhumba Bums

When swing music really swings, according to the Rhumba Bums' alluring guitarist Carmen Getit, "it makes you moist." Oh, behave. Or don't. Carmen's sirenlike ways and pianist/vocalist Steve Lucky's handsome looks certainly make this band a must-stare. But it's their original boogie-woogie pieces and unexpected jump covers that keep you coming back for more. In the last couple of years, this San Francisco band has held the coveted

Wednesday night slot at LA's Derby nightclub and has even done parties for Whoopi Goldberg and the casts of *Party of Five* and *ER*. Of course, this music's nothing new for Lucky, who fronted a jump blues–style band back in the early eighties, when Ann Arbor, Michigan, had its own microscene going. "We don't do a lot of the songs that we used to, like 'Caldonia' and 'Choo Choo Ch'Boogie,' because they are the chestnuts of swing," says Carmen, who can always be counted on to be fresh.

The Eddie Reed Big Band

How did a rockabilly fanatic come to revere Artie Shaw? Reed was one of the first to make the musical journey from the starting point of fifties roots rock back to the big band era. After fronting a rockabilly band in the eighties called Eddie Reed and the Bluehearts, this multi-instrumentalist began exploring further back in time. He was soon listening to Benny Goodman and Tommy Dorsey but really got hooked when his young son had him listen to "Traffic Jam" by Shaw. "It blew my mind," he says. By 1993 Reed, who plays clarinet, guitar, and piano, had his own orchestra up and running. A true traditionalist, he has hooked up with such greats as Anita O'Day, Helen Forrest, and his idol, Shaw himself (who has even given some of his original charts to Reed). And he has consciously catered to the dance community (even listing the beats per minute of his songs in the liner notes of his CDs). "In my opinion," says Reed, "if you write a song and it doesn't appeal to someone's physical body, if it doesn't make them want to tap their toes, then you are leaving part of the equation out."

Lavay Smith and Her Red Hot Skillet Lickers

Two bars into one of Lavay Smith's songs, you realize one thing you'll never forget. This gal can sing, with a voice that's both forceful and dazzlingly warm. One of the most authentic jazz singers in the scene, Smith has been entertaining San Francisco crowds since 1989 and has crossed over into the mainstream jazz festival circuit. "I don't even look at it as swing. I look at it as jazz," says Smith, who's known for her signature look, a va-va-voom style that's all about fishtail dresses and gardenias behind the ear. But what's most impressive is the depth of musical knowledge of Smith and her partner, arranger and pianist Chris Siebert. "We have thousands and thousands of records," says Smith, whose commitment to her music involves listening to as little rock as possible. "The rhythm of rock is a lot different. It's a bad influence for me. I have to be surrounded by good music and listen to it all the time. The more you listen to Billie Holiday and Dinah Washington, the better the swing will sound."

THE TOP BANDS — BY REGION

From Seattle to Orlando, each city or region has its own distinct dancing scene. Because swing is a movement that thrives on live music, there are many great bands in almost every major town across the United States, Canada, and England. Some have national followings; some are local secrets. Here are the best ones to look out for near where you live.

Arizona

Kings of Pleasure: Arizona was one of the first states after California to get caught up in the Lindy craze, and the Kings of Pleasure were there from the beginning. Started in 1996, this five-piece group is a dancer's delight, playing a mix of swing and rocked-out jump blues and having fun on such signatures as "Are You Buyin' Wine" and "Havana Hop."

   Plus: Swingtips — the favorites from Phoenix — boasting a big horn section and even a Christmas album, *Santa Swings;* **Swing 42,** a traditional big band; **Heavenly 7,** swing with a George Clinton funk twist; and **Hipster Daddy-O and the Handgrenades,** a hard-core ska/swing band.

Atlanta and the South

Lost Continentals: With the sultry vocals of lead singer Amy Pike, the four-member Atlanta band Lost Continentals is revving up the Georgia scene. And while they've got only a bass, drums, and a guitar, they swing with a big sound on their popular CD *Moonshine and Martinis.* Among the best cuts are quirky romantic numbers like "Please, Please" — as in "please give me another chance" — and "Love Roller Coaster." Get ready for a great ride.

Plus: Nashville's **Badabing Badaboom,** featuring an Andrews Sisters–style vocal group; Memphis's classic swing band the **New Memphis Hepcats;** New Orleans's **Amy and the Hank Sinatras,** who mix swing with country and R&B; Athens, Georgia's ska-meets-swing powerhouse **Seven Foot Politic;** and Atlanta's **League of Decency,** with a sound that ranges from jump blues to James Brown.

Boston and New England

Bellevue Cadillac: On their lyrically ambitious album *Prozac Nation,* Bellevue Cadillac riffs on the overcaffeinated and mood-enhanced 1990s. Fronted by terrifically smooth lead singer Doug Bell, this seven-piece band has a relaxed, swinging sound that's been described as a confluence of "sixties Memphis R&B and forties swing." After hearing such simmering songs as "Pull the Plug" (it's about euthanasia), "Cuppa Joe," and "Call of the Wild," you definitely won't be needing coffee.

Plus: Connecticut's **Eight to the Bar,** a six-piece band that swings from Kansas City to Motown, and Boston's New Orleans–influenced **Love Dogs.**

Canada

Johnny Favourite Swing Orchestra: Who'd have ever imagined that one of the hottest new swing bands would come out of Halifax, Nova Scotia? A ten-piece group of mostly twentysomething Canadian lads, this band is fronted by singer Johnny Favourite, nicknamed Young Blue Eyes, a sweet bad-boy who grew up loving David Bowie's swingesque *Let's Dance* music and wearing suits in high school. Just three years since he started the band in 1996, the orchestra has put out two CDs, including the latest, *Holiday Romance;* signed a deal with Universal; and won a Juneau Award, the Canadian equivalent of a Grammy, for best new group. "It's nice to find out you're not a freak," says Favourite, whose image now is anything but. "We're not some retro guys. We're not like 'Hey, Daddy-O' or any of that stuff. For the most part, the band is comprised of shit-kicking Canadian guys that drink beer, like to surf and ride fast cars, and love this music. Sometimes we'll rock out and sometimes we'll do like a real nice Benny Goodman number. It just really varies."

Plus: The popular **Big Rude Jake,** a thoughtfully provocative songwriter whose brash humor shows up most forcefully on his song "Let's Kill All the Rock Stars"; Vancouver's peerless Western swing and rockabilly outfit **Ray Condo and the Ricochets;** Montreal's crooning **Swingtown Sinners;** Calgary's top swing band the **Dino Martinis** (their humorously titled CDs include *The Bottle Collector's Lounge* and *Steak and Comedian Night*); Vancouver's the **Molestics,** who throw everything from Jelly Roll Morton jazz to Hawaiian, calypso, and polka into their musical blender; and last but far from least, north-of-the-border star **Colin James,** a blues-based rock guitarist who's recorded two great swing albums with his Little Big Band.

Chicago

Rhythm Rockets: The title track of the Rockets' CD *Come Ride the Rocket* says it all. Plying the suggestive lyrical terrain of late-forties jump blues, the seven-piece Rockets play everything from original material to the best of Cab Calloway and Louis Jordan. Fronted by singer Lesley Byers, they're a hit not just with hoppers, they've also entertained the Chicago Bulls. What makes them distinct? A big-time sound provided by the group's three saxophonists.

Plus: The wonderfully danceable **Blues Swingers;** the New Orleans–influenced **Speak Easy Swing; Three Cent Stomp,** who swing from Ellington to Sinatra on their CD *Jimmy Primo Livin' At Large;* the rockin' **Chicago Jump Company; Alan Gresik's Swing Shift Orchestra,** a traditional late-thirties big band; and the band that swingers love but that for some reason hates being known as a swing band, the **Mighty Blue Kings.**

Denver

Money Plays Eight: Colorado native sons Money Plays Eight, taking the name of their band from a gambling term, bring a little Las Vegas glamour to the Mile High City. They play fast, dress sharply, and perform constantly at Denver's top swing clubs.

Plus: The **Hot Tomatoes Dance Orchestra,** a big band; and the jump blues groups **Papa Grande and His Double-Wide Jumptet, David Booker and His Swingtet,** and **Chris Daniels and the Kings.**

Detroit

Atomic Fireballs: Charging through lyrics with his deep raspy voice, Atomic Fireballs' lead singer John Bunkley sounds like Tom Waits . . . if Waits had a swing band. This high-octane eight-piece group recently signed a major-label deal with Lava/Atlantic and appeared in the Matthew Perry/Neve Campbell movie *Three to Tango.* It's not hard to see what the buzz is about. On their album *Torch This Place,* they fire up their fast call-and-response style on such songs as "Man with the Hex," "Lover Lies," and "Drink, Drank, Drunk." Says *Swing Time* magazine's Michael Moss: "They have anything anybody could want in a live show. They rock like rock stars and swing like maniacs."

England

The Ray Gelato Giants: Sounding almost like Louis Prima reincarnated, Ray Gelato is one of the major pioneers of the swing

music revival. Back in the early eighties—even before Joe Jackson
went swing—Gelato was in the influential English jump blues
band the Chevalier Brothers. After London's eighties swing scene
came and went, Gelato kept perfecting his brand of Las
Vegas–inspired music, and he's now gaining a strong following
stateside. A singer and tenor sax player, he's recorded six albums,
including one in Italian and his latest, *The Men from Uncle*.
"Swing is difficult to define," says Gelato. "I think it just means
really great music and lots of people Lindy Hopping to it."

The Big Six: The ultimate British retro rockers, the Big Six mix
up swing, ska, rock, and R&B into one potent ball of fire. Influenced by everyone from Bill Haley and James Brown to the
Skatalites, they're the one band that's guaranteed to bring swing
and rockabilly fans into the same club. And they do it all in the
loudest, maddest plaid suits known to man. They aren't bluffing
when they shout out on their signature song, "We the Boys Will
Rock Ya!"

Plus: The entertaining **Jive Aces,** the Scientologists of the swing
scene; the blasting jump band **King Pleasure and the Biscuit
Boys;** the doo-wop group the **Senti-Mentals; Sophie Garner and
Her Swing Kings,** swinging à la Carmen Miranda; **Blue Harlem,**
influenced by everyone from Jimmie Lunceford to Ruth Brown;
and the recently reconstituted jumpin' blues group **Sugar Ray's
Flying Fortress.**

Florida

Swingerhead: With a name like Swingerhead and an infectious
lounge/swing sound, Florida's powerhouse retro band is starting
to gain national attention. Singer and bandleader Michael
Andrew first came up with his band's irreverent moniker in 1996
when he wrote and performed in an Orlando musical called
"Mickey Swingerhead and the Earthgirls," about a lonely guy living on another planet, where, horror of horrors, swing music is
forbidden. Thankfully, the situation's a little better back on earth.

In fact, *Rolling Stone* has called Swingerhead's "Pick Up the Phone"—from the hot CD *She Could Be a Spy*—one of the two best songs on the *Swing This, Baby* compilation album. Andrew lists Frank Sinatra, Burt Bacharach, Herb Alpert, and Tom Waits among his inspirations. "But for me," he says, "Bobby Darin is absolutely number one." Unlike many swingers, Andrew—the former bandleader of New York's famous Rainbow Room—isn't a rock refugee. Says Andrew: "All I've ever listened to is swing."

Plus: Felix and the Buzzcats, a Prima-influenced group that's secured the right to use the animated Felix's trademarked mug on their bandstand; Sarasota's jump-blues band **Dan Electro and the Silvertones;** the rock-edged **Swingin' Mooks** of Tampa; and Orlando's **Johnny Cool and the Mobster Swing Band.**

Los Angeles and San Diego

Alien Fashion Show: "We didn't set out to be a quote swing band," says Eldon Daetweiler, the lead singer of this lounge-from-another-planet quintet. "We came up with this concept of, 'What if Frank Sinatra grew up in the town of Twin Peaks or hung out with David Bowie?'" Formed in 1996, Alien Fashion Show adds a postmodern banquet of influences—from surf and rockabilly to trip-hop and Angelo Badalamenti—to their cocktail-culture style of swing. But these sharkskin-loving guys—who even cover the Kiss tune "Detroit Rock City" as "Detroit Swing City"—always keep in mind where it all started. Eldon and his drumming brother Jeff have a green-and-purple psychedelic portrait of Gene Krupa hanging over their living room sofa.

Big Time Operator: The swing kings of San Diego, Big Time Operator is a jump blues band fronted by Sinatra-esque crooner Frank Lovell, who sails like a pro on such covers as "Fly Me to the Moon," "Leap Frog," and "Calloway Boogie." But where did their name come from? During World War II, Big Time Operator was a nickname for the B-17 bomber.

Jumpin' Jimes: What else can you call it but swingabilly? The

Jumpin' Jimes, a Derby favorite, made up of vocalist Mark Tortorici and six terrific musicians, always seem like they're having fun, whether they're rocking it out or swinging it up. And they do a lot of both on their high-spirited CD *They Rock! They Roll! They Swing!*

Mora's Modern Rhythmists: Givin' you good old-fashioned swing, Dean Mora's ten-piece orchestra is as purist a band as they come. Covering songs from 1929 to 1936, they send dancers with the works of Fletcher Henderson, Jimmie Lunceford, and *early* Benny Goodman. They even wear tuxedos just like the old bandleaders did.

Red and the Red Hots: Red's got cred. A Texas-born boogie-woogie pianist, Red Young was part of a swingy jazz vocal group called the Stepsisters that came together in Los Angeles in 1983. The group soon found themselves opening on tour for Linda Ronstadt and legendary Sinatra arranger Nelson Riddle. That experience was so great it inspired Young—who's also played piano for everyone from Sonny and Cher to Tanya Tucker and Joan Armatrading—to start his own band, the Red Hots. With their distinctive sound—this big band's got three lead vocalists—and their effortless melodies, Red and the Red Hots know how to rev up Lindy Hoppers.

Plus: Like a championship NBA team, dance-obsessed Los Angeles has the best and deepest bench of bands of any city in the country. Among the city's other hot players are the swinging jump blues groups the **Swing Sinners, Blue Plate Special,** the **Chrome Addicts,** the **Jumpin' Joz Band,** the **Eric Ekstrand Ensemble,** and **Flattop Tom and His Jump Cats;** the nostalgic **Pete Jacobs and His Wartime Radio Revue,** who even dress in armed-forces-style khaki uniforms; two traditional groups, **Johnny Crawford and His 1928 Society Orchestra** and the **Don Miller Orchestra;** boogie-woogie pianist **Rob Rio;** and last but certainly not least **Candye Kane,** a big-lady singer who bills herself as "two hundred pounds of fun."

Minneapolis

The Senders: The jump blues band the Senders, a critics' pick of the editors of *MusicHound Lounge,* has been having a blast mixing up swing and jump blues for more than a decade. But lately they're starting to get attention outside the Twin Cities as well. And it's not just because they lured legendary blues pianist Charles Brown to guest on their album *Jumpin' Uptown.* Their lead singer, Charmin Michelle, has an endearing Betty Boop–like voice, put to fun effect on standards by the likes of B. B. King and Wynonie Harris.

Plus: **Hot Heads,** whose influences range from the twenties to the fifties; and local lounge/swing bands the **Jaztronauts** and **Vic Volare.**

New York

The Camaros: "Our female fans are the ones who really get it. They're rabid," says lead singer Jen Jones, who founded this "swingabilly" group in 1997. But who really needs categories anyway? The Camaros' lyrically entertaining songs take a stance on love with which anybody can identify: if you get burned by romance, hang tough. And while Jones won't reveal which certain someones in the New York scene inspired the sardonic tunes on the Camaros' debut CD *Evil,* she will say, "It's what female blues singers have done all the time, which is not take any shit and not let yourself be beaten down. You come back with some wit and some humor and create a space to say it."

Flying Neutrinos: Breaking out of the jump blues mold, the Flying Neutrinos came to the Big Apple from the Big Easy in 1992 and have carved out a real niche for themselves playing New Orleans–influenced swing. "If I could clarify one thing, it's that New Orleans music can swing just as much as jump blues. Swing isn't any particular style of music, it's a certain type of feel," says the band's Billie Holiday–influenced lead singer Ingrid Lucia. No argument here. On their album *I'd Rather Be in New Orleans,* the Neutrinos get just the right mix of the sultry and the swingin'.

George Gee and His Make-Believe Ballroom Orchestra:
Billing himself as the only Asian-American bandleader in the
business, Gee fronts a seventeen-piece orchestra that pridefully re-
creates the jump swing of Count Basie. And boy do they have the
chops. Boasting a slew of veteran musicians (who've played in the
bands of Basie, Goodman, Xavier Cugat, and Hampton), this
orchestra hit new peaks in 1999. They faced off against Bill Elliott
in two high-profile battles of the bands, swung the crowd at
Frankie Manning's eighty-fifth birthday party, and even toured
Japan. "For someone who's been in the business twenty years,"
says Gee, who started a band while in college at Pittsburgh's
Carnegie-Mellon University, "I'm living in a fantasy world now."

Jet Set Six: Many bands claim to mix lounge and swing, but
the Jet Set Six may be the one band that most truly *melds* the two.
Yes, they've got a suave sophistication that does justice to their
foremost inspiration, Tony Bennett. But this isn't sit-back-with-a-
martini music. It makes you want to get up on your feet and
dance. And while the band began back in 1989 under the name
Beat Positive, they thankfully aren't changing their style just to
ride the zoot suit bandwagon. As lead singer John Ceparano told
Swing Time magazine: "We've always been a sharkskin band."

Ron Sunshine and Full Swing: With zero irony and on-the-
money musicianship, the experienced band Full Swing — formed
in 1991 — plays swing from the other side of the tracks. Not
sophisticated nightclub stylings, the songs on its album *Straight
Up* sound like they were laid down at a modern-day roadhouse.
The honky-tonk feel gets a great boost from Ron Sunshine's
inspired harmonica playing.

Yalloppin' Hounds: With a barking big sound, the Hounds
have torn up New York City in the last couple years like a pack
on the hunt. They've not only got three musicians who've played
with sax legend Illinois Jacquet, they're pioneering a compelling
new hybrid: swing with rap elements (not as much of a stretch
as you might think, considering how much both Cab Calloway

and Louis Jordan are deemed forerunners of rap). "They are the only band I know of right now that not only deeply care about pleasing dancers," promoter "Lo-Fi" Lee Sobel has enthused, "but [are] also willing to risk everything to infuse hip-hop into some of their material."

Plus: The original pioneers of swing in New York City, **Nick Palumbo and the Flipped Fedoras;** the jump blues faves **Set 'Em Up Joe,** the **Blues Jumpers,** and New Jersey's **Crescent City Maulers; Bim Bam Baby,** featuring blond chanteuse Shawn Sobel; the gangster bop boys **Dem Brooklyn Bums;** the traditional swing of the **Blue Saracens;** and the jazzy R&B group the **Delegates.**

Ohio and Indiana

Wolfgang Parker: Columbus's most devilish swing bandleader, Wolfgang Parker turns swing into a full-out head-bangers ball. He's even coined his own term for his heavily punk-influenced music: "acid swing."

Plus: Columbus's **Honk, Wail and Moan,** from big band to Sun Ra and Miles Davis, and the classic swing outfit **Tenors Head On;** Cleveland's jump blues groups **Dukes of Wail** and **Blue Lunch;** Cincinnati's best dance band, **Rich Uncle Skelton;** Toledo's the **Mighty Meaty Swing Kings** and **Hepcat Revival;** and Indianapolis's **Kelly Jay Orchestra.**

Saint Louis

Vargas Swing: A favorite of *Swing Time* magazine, the eight-piece band Vargas Swing, fronted by soulful singer Pete Bold, has its roots in funk. Now they are swinging themselves and the city up with such hot, jumping numbers as "Fire" and "Satan."

San Francisco

Jellyroll: Jellyroll, a stylish six-piece combo, goes beyond just Louis

Jordan jump blues. On their well-liked album *Hep Cats Holiday*, and in their great live shows, soulful singer Belinda Blair brings back lesser-known gems by such early R&B singers as Helen Humes, Tiny Bradshaw, Ella Mae Morse, and Big Mama Thornton.

New Morty Show: Morty Okin and his extroverted band put on one of the best live shows in the business. With po-mo abandon, they excel at swinging up hard-rock classics, making you sway instead of grind to such songs as Metallica's "Enter Sandman" or Poison's "Unskinny Bop." Says Okin, the bandleader and trumpeter of New Morty Show, "We'll do a straight-ahead tune and in the middle of it we'll put in a ripping metal part or a punk part and then go back into swing." But don't worry, this Louis Prima–inspired band's got real musical chops too. Their trombonist Van Hughes has recorded with Ellington and toured with Woody Herman. And both Okin and vocalist Vise Grip were in a band called St. Vitus Dance during the early days of the swing revival in San Francisco. Says Okin: "We live in the nineties and it's nice to incorporate lots of different music with a backbone of swing."

ACME Swing Company: Unlike some swing bands, the guys in ACME Swing Company don't sound like they're trying too hard. On the CD *California Premium Hops!* bassist and singer Tom Beyer and his six sidemen kick back, have fun, and create a real party album with twelve all-original tunes.

Plus: The Goth-inspired showstopper **Lee Press-on and the Nails; Ambassadors of Swing,** a Cab Calloway tribute band; **Mitch Woods and his Rockets 88's,** led by boogie-woogie pianist Woods, who's played with both Joe Liggins and John Lee Hooker; **Blue Room Boys,** hitting all the right Ellington and Basie notes; local jump swing crowd pleasers **Swing Session, Chazz Cats,** and the **Johnny Nocturne Band,** with fabulous singer Kim Nalley; and retro pioneer **Connie Champagne**'s new band the **Magnum Brutes.**

Seattle

Casey MacGill and the Spirits of Rhythm: You certainly can't accuse Casey MacGill of jumping on the bandwagon. This accomplished songwriter and keyboard/ukelele player had a swing band way back in 1971 in Southern California. "We used to open for Lily Tomlin at the Ice House in Pasadena," he recalls. In the early eighties he fronted a second swing group, a trio called Mood Indigo, that showed up in the thirties period piece *Frances,* starring Jessica Lange. Now, after what he calls a few years of "oblivion" in the Pacific Northwest, MacGill has emerged in his most successful incarnation yet. His band's new swing and boogie-woogie CD *Jump,* featuring jitterbugged-out songs like "Git It (In the Groove)" and "Jump Up," has been one of the most buzzed-about releases of 1999. He's also written an original number, "Kitchen Mechanics' Night Out," for *Swing,* the Broadway musical. The tune is inspired by the Thursday evenings at the Savoy, the night that black chauffeurs, maids, and cooks tended to have off from work. "'Kitchen mechanic' was the nickname they used for the cooks," says MacGill, adding, "I love the energy of fifties rock 'n' roll done with the style of thirties music. That's where I'm at."

Plus: The dancer-friendly **Lance Buller and the Monarchs;** the Sinatra-esque **H. B. Radke and the Jet City Swingers; Jump Up!** from classic swing to bebop and rhumba; and the jumpin' blues of **New York Jimmy and the Jive Five.**

Texas

8¹/₂ Souvenirs: Austin's vibrant "roots" music scene counts the 8¹/₂ Souvenirs quintet as one of its brightest stars. Founded by Olivier Giraud, a French guitar player and singer, the band plays swing music with an international flair. Not surprising, given that their greatest influence is Django Reinhardt, the Gypsy guitarist who was one of Europe's jazz pioneers. The band describes their music as "cosmopolitan swing pop," and you can tune in to their sophisticated stylings with their CD *Happy Feet,* which includes four classic Reinhardt tunes.

Plus: Austin's popular dance band **Lucky Strikes,** which boasts a lead singer who croons like Tony Bennett; **Johnny Reno and the Lounge Kings,** who make Dallas swing and sway, starring frontman Reno, Chris Isaak's former saxophonist; Austin swing bands **Rocket 69,** the **Jive Bombers,** the **Day Jobs,** and the **Nash Hernandez Orchestra;** the bawdy ten-piece Austin swing-meets-country group **Asylum Street Spankers;** and Dallas bands, the jump outfit **Lakewood Rats,** the Sinatra-and-Dino-style **Mr. Pink,** and red-headed rockabilly queen **Kim Lenz and the Jaguars.**

Washington, D.C., and Pennsylvania

J Street Jumpers: A veteran swing and jump blues band, the J Street Jumpers came together in the early nineties and have quickly been embraced by Washington's strong dance community. Led by bluesy singer Marianne Previti, they travel comfortably between traditional Count Basie swing and more devilish R&B classics.

Plus: Washington's traditional big band, the **Tom Cunningham Orchestra;** Mechanicsburg, Pennsylvania's jump blues band **Big Tubba Mista;** Philadelphia's classic band the **City Rhythm Orchestra;** and Pittsburgh's **Dr. Zoot,** which adds a dose of Latin to their swing.

THE TEN HOTTEST NEOSWING CDS

Here they are: the ten albums that swing's top DJs and swingzine reviewers have picked as the best you can buy.

1. The Bill Elliott Swing Orchestra, *Calling All Jitterbugs!* (Wayland Records): This album is a dancer's dream, featuring fourteen midtempo tracks with a classic big band sound. The vocals are on the sweet side, but the music is full-bodied, with hot-blowing horns and sliding piano. Except for a cover of "On the Atchison, Topeka, and the Santa Fe," all the numbers are original compositions by Elliott but sound like the real deal, with great arrangements and stunning vocal performances.

2. Indigo Swing, *All Aboard!* (TimeBomb Records): This collection of originals encompasses everything from piano-based ballads to boogie-woogie and jump blues, all topped off with Johnny Boyd's smooth, soulful vocals. The midtempo melodies make this a favorite with the dancers, and the innocent lyrics capture a certain sweet sincerity that has been lost in modern times.

3. The Ray Gelato Giants, *The Men from Uncle* (Hepcat Records): In the tradition of Louis Prima and Frank Sinatra, Ray Gelato is a smooth crooner with huge swing appeal. *The Men from Uncle* offers up crowd-pleasing chestnuts, such as "Angelina/ Zooma Zooma," along with well-crafted originals, including the jumpin' "Givin' Up Givin' Up." The instrumental title track roars in true big band style, while songs like "Let's Face the Music and Dance" hark back to the dulcet tones of Tony Bennett.

4. Royal Crown Revue, *Mugzy's Move* (Warner Records): RCR's gutsy CD starts off with a bang, as the pounding drums and blasting brass of "Hey Pachuco!" work the listener into a frenzy right from the start. It is followed by the pulsing rhythms of "Zip Gun Bop," the high-octane title track, and ten more hard-hitting numbers. This is punk rock–style swing at its punchiest.

5. Lavay Smith and Her Red Hot Skillet Lickers, *One Hour Mama* (Fat Note Records): Sounding as seductive as Lena Horne and throwing in some of the power of Billie Holiday, diva Lavay Smith delivers a varied selection of jazz standards, including "Blue Skies" and "Between the Devil and the Deep Blue Sea." Smith's vocals are what make this album truly remarkable, and thanks to Chris Siebert's innovative arrangements, these classics swing in new and unexpected ways.

6. Steve Lucky and the Rhumba Bums, *Come Out Swingin'!*

Swing and the Jazz Community

Back in the days of the original big bands, swing and jazz were one and the same. Duke Ellington, Louis Armstrong, Benny Goodman: all are considered jazz greats, and all are revered among swing lovers. But the renaissance of swing in the early 1990s witnessed a rift with the modern jazz community. In part this was because many neoswing performers, such as Brian Setzer, Scotty Morris of Big Bad Voodoo Daddy, and the Cherry Poppin' Daddies' frontman Steve Perry, came from a punk or rock 'n' roll background rather than a jazz upbringing. "The swing scene kind of came about without some of us in jazz knowing about it," says Rob Gibson, executive director of Jazz at Lincoln Center in New York City. Many jazz musicians simply had a hard time taking the new swing kids seriously.

Fortunately, in the past few years, members of both communities have made attempts to reach out to one another, learn from each other, and help the new swing movement to grow. Bands like Royal Crown Revue and Big Bad Voodoo Daddy are attempting to woo traditional jazz audiences with appearances at major jazz festivals and are seeking the advice of musicians from the old school. Royal Crown Revue traveled to Las Vegas to meet sax great Sam Butera, Big Bad Voodoo Daddy played with Tex Beneke, and Lavay Smith has performed with R&B great Ruth Brown. On the other hand, when Chris Calloway, Cab's daughter, was looking to start her own swing band she called a neoswinger who is Lavay's arranger and pianist, Chris Siebert, for advice. "I said, 'Could you fill me in on the scene, what's happening, and who are the acts,'" says Calloway, who recently formed the Hi-De-Ho Orchestra, as a tribute to both her father and her aunt Blanche Calloway, who had her own band before Cab did.

(Rumpus Records): From the opening toe tapper, "Jumptown," straight through a dozen more good-time tracks, *Come Out Swingin'!* will keep listeners on the dance floor all night long. The songs place a strong emphasis on guitar and sax and feature delightful call-and-response vocals by Steve Lucky and Carmen Getit that sound as good as Louis Prima and Keely Smith in their prime.

7. **The Eddie Reed Big Band,** *Hollywood Jump* (Royal Big Mac Records): Following the adage "If it ain't broke, don't fix it," the Eddie Reed Big Band brings new life to traditional arrangements from the likes of Krupa, Basie, and Ellington. Reed and his crew exhibit some of the highest-quality musicianship out there and treat these classics with great respect, playing the album's twelve tunes with sincerity, vivacity, and passion.

8. **Jet Set Six,** *Livin' It Up* (Mutiny Records): Straddling the line between swing and lounge, the debut CD from Jet Set Six would be a welcome addition at any party. The eleven songs, most of which were written by singer John Ceparano, reveal influences of R&B, jump blues, rockabilly, and a hefty dose of Sinatra. With catchy lyrics and clever wordplays, this New York combo has rocketed to the top ranks of the new swing movement.

9. **Big Bad Voodoo Daddy,** *Big Bad Voodoo Daddy* (Coolsville Records): BBVD's hopped-up neoswing emphasizes full-bodied horns and slick piano licks, but it's Scotty Morris's whiskey-tinged voice that gives this band their edge. Their self-titled major label debut features eleven kickin' originals, like "You and Me and the Bottle Makes Three Tonight (Baby)" and the rollicking "Jump with My Baby," as well as a richly done cover of "Minnie the Moocher" that would make Cab proud.

10. **Swingerhead,** *She Could Be a Spy* (Colossal Music and Film): Think James Bond crossed with Wayne Newton and wearing a leopard-print dinner jacket and you've got Swingerhead frontman Michael Andrew. On the band's debut release, Andrew croons his way through a selection of campy originals, including

Indeed, today's swingers are beginning to realize that if they love George Gee and Bill Elliott, they'll also enjoy the Lincoln Center Jazz Orchestra's homages to Duke Ellington or music by such traditionalist bandleaders as Loren Schoenberg and Ken Peplowski. If you've gone out to dance and fallen for Lavay Smith's singing, you might also want to check out jazz star Diana Krall's *All for You,* a tribute to the Nat King Cole Trio, or diva-on-the-rise Elena Bennett's collection of standards, *A Wrinkle in Swingtime.* And don't forget to support the best ghost bands, which carry on the names and traditions of such deceased legends as Count Basie, Duke Ellington, and Tommy Dorsey.

Countless other musicians, young and old, are now working together to make the new swing movement every bit as dynamic and exciting as it was in its heyday. Swing "has emotion. It has depth. It has pain. It has joy," says jazz singer Ann Hampton Callaway, whose albums include the fabulous *To Ella with Love.* "It's not just fun, it's fun and magnificent."

the loungy "Lady with the Big Cigar," the Latin-tinged "He Just Wants to Cha Cha," plus a couple numbers that really swing, most notably "Pick Up the Phone."

Ten More Survey Faves: Johnny Favourite Swing Orchestra, *Holiday Romance;* George Gee and His Make-Believe Ballroom Orchestra, *Swingin' Live;* The Big Six, *We the Boys Will Rock You;* Jellyroll, *Hep Cats Holiday;* The Blue Saracens, *What's a Saracen?;* Blues Jumpers, *Wheels Start Turning;* The Lost Continentals, *Moonshine and Martinis;* The Brian Setzer Orchestra, *The Dirty Boogie;* Big Time Operator, *High Altitude Swing;* Mora's Modern Rhythmists, *Mr. Rhythmist Goes to Town;* The Jive Aces, *Planet Jive.*

THE BEST COMPILATIONS

The Hi-Ball Lounge Sessions, Vol. 1 (Hi-Ball): San Francisco's top bands, including Steve Lucky, ACME Swing Company, Lavay Smith, and Lee Press-on and the Nails, all recorded live at the city's famous Hi-Ball nightclub.

Hipsters, Zoots and Wingtips: The '90s Swingers (Hip-O/ Universal): With everything from Royal Crown Revue's "Hey Pachuco!" to Diana Krall's "Hit That Jive Jack" to Bill Elliott's "Bill's Bounce," this CD is a wonderfully varied mix.

House of Blues Swing (House of Blues): From Saint Louis's Vargas Swing to England's Jive Aces, with a little bit of Western swing thrown in, courtesy of Big Sandy and His Fly Rite Boys' "Feelin' Kinda Lucky."

New York City Swing (Lo-Fi Records): The best of the Big Apple, including Set 'Em Up Joe, Ron Sunshine and Full Swing, the Crescent City Maulers, Jet Set Six, and the Camaros.

Swing This, Baby! (Slimstyle/Beyond): *Swing Time* magazine picks the best cuts by such bands as Big Bad Voodoo Daddy, the Cherry Poppin' Daddies, Bellevue Cadillac, and Swingerhead.

SWINGIN' SOUNDTRACKS

Cotton Club (Geffen): Film composer John Barry successfully adapts Ellington and Calloway standards. Plus, star Gregory Hines sings one tune, "Copper Colored Gal."

Malcolm X (Warner Bros.): Where else can you hear Arrested Development, Aretha Franklin, Billie Holiday, Ella Fitzgerald, Louis Jordan, John Coltrane, and Lionel Hampton all in one place?

The Mask (Sony Music): An outlandish potpourri of contempo cuts (Vanessa Williams), neoswing (Royal Crown Revue's "Hey Pachuco!"), and jivin' covers (Cab Calloway's "Hi-De-Ho"), plus snippets of Jim Carrey dialogue.

Swing (RCA Victor): Lisa Stansfield was born to do a swing album. This wonderful accompaniment to the 1999 indie film *Swing* boasts Springsteen sax great Clarence Clemons, a sultry "Baby I Need Your Lovin'," and four original tunes by Stansfield.

Swing Kids (Hollywood Records): A lively mix of traditional swing, featuring James Horner's score and some choice Benny Goodman numbers.

Swingers (Hollywood Records): The soundtrack that launched Big Bad Voodoo Daddy is also a great tribute to such lounge kings as Dean Martin and Bobby Darin.

CHAPTER 6

From the Andrews Sisters to Zoot Suits:
The Guys' and Dolls' Guide to Retro Style

O K, so you know how to get down with some gritty moves on the dance floor. You're already keepin' time with the Duke, the Count, and the King of Swing. Now you're ready to fly out to the hottest nightspot in town, right? Wrong. To make the scene it's always fun to look the part too. "You really live the fantasy when you dress up," says Annamarie Firley, co-designer of Revamp, a reproduction clothing collection. "You can feel you've just walked into the past."

Putting on a vintage look—whether authentic or reproduction—may feel a bit like Halloween at first. But remember, what makes the clothes of the thirties and forties so knockout is that they were costumelike even back then. Just think about Cab Calloway at his mightiest and most righteous. His zoot suit jacket hung below his knees, his chain dropped even farther than that, his hat was like a small spaceship, and his bow tie jutted out like whiskers. And while Calloway represented the extreme, men's clothing, especially by the late forties, was designed to make a guy look bold and larger than life. Shoulders soared up and out. Lapels were at their widest. The drape of a jacket tapered down to the hips. The whole build was exaggerated. And hats increased a gent's height. These are clothes to be worn with confidence, even to swagger in. But don't get too cocky. These duds weren't rudely hypermasculine. They required polish and sophistication, forethought and savoir faire to wear correctly. You needed to know how to knot a tie just right and how to fold a handkerchief with flair. You had to be able to choose and coordinate hats, handkerchiefs, ties, tie clips, shirts, cuff links, suits, and shoes, all of which came in a startling array of styles and colors. Dressed to the nines, men could really be cool cats.

Gals were bolder too, but in a different way. Just think of the feminine extreme—Joan Crawford. A dancer herself, Crawford had a look that defined the era. It wasn't all about man-pleasing

FACING PAGE: *Cab Calloway in full regalia on the set of the film* Stormy Weather. (CULVER PICTURES)

The War's Effect on Fashion

During the war, everyone was expected to do his or her part, and that included cutting back on the use of fabric. Silk was needed for parachutes, and wool for uniforms. In March 1942, the U.S. war production board announced limitation order L-85, with the goal of reducing domestic fabric consumption by at least 15 percent. The use of natural fibers was decreased, leading to a high demand for synthetics like rayon and viscose. Women's heels were required not to be more than one and a half inches in height, while the three-piece suit became the two-piece suit, without cuffs on the trousers. To meet the fabric restrictions, skirts became straight, jackets shorter. Stockings were often hard to find at all. "When nylons were rationed, [women] would take eyeliner and draw a line up the back of the leg to draw the seam in," says swing musician Carmen Getit. "My mother still has a bottle of leg makeup. It's foundation for your legs in a matte color that women would put on. It actually did look like you had stockings on."

But in addition to specific mandates, the board made

curves. In her big-shouldered suits, Crawford was sharply defined and unequivocally imposing. With straight, more defined lines, clothing began to markedly reflect the increasing independence of women, who by the time of World War II were going to work in unprecedented numbers. These were sensibly sexy outfits that both looked great and commandeered respect. A new athleticism came to the fore also. Those freer clothes included both bobby socks and the knee-length skirt, which was neither so long as to be restrictive nor so short as to leave nothing to the imagination. Although some critics have called the forties look a bit plain, women at the time certainly didn't skimp on dressing up their pronouncements against innovation in fashion, hoping to slow the pace of change in the style world so that clothes didn't go out of vogue quickly. This partly explains why the look of the forties seems so distinct today; the fashion stayed nearly frozen. With new clothes hard to come by, people made do by constantly reworking old pieces, often adding different details and stitching. "A lot of the clothes from the war era are so obviously worked and reworked and refit. If I turn a garment inside out, I can tell how many times it's been remade," says costume designer Harper Della-Piana. Inevitably, however, once the war was over, a reaction occurred. "People went nuts. They could suddenly use as much fabric as they wanted and clothes went completely overboard," says Revamp's Firley. In 1947 Christian Dior's "New Look" revolutionized the fashion world, ushering in bigger skirts, softer romantic looks, and an hourglass figure. By the beginning of the fifties, the straight skirts had fallen by the wayside, replaced by voluminous circle skirts. "A circle skirt can take up to five yards of fabric," adds Firley. Goodbye Rosie the Riveter. Hello Jayne Mansfield.

outfits with a panoply of sexy accessories, from flowers or bows in their amazingly curled hair to gloves, seamed stockings, and scads of jewelry. But even if you admit these clothes are a touch on the plain side, perhaps for women at the time it was a bit of a relief. After all, this was one of the very few periods in fashion history when gents were expected to be peacocks too.

And preen they did. Swing's best-known bandleaders were notoriously concerned about looking their best. Tuxes and white tails were often the preferred outfits. Stories abound of careless sidemen being called on the carpet — or even being kicked out of a band — for showing up with a stain on a shirt or a pair of shoes in need of a shine. The suavely elegant Duke Ellington was noted for putting on a different pair of shoes for each set of the evening. Wearing the latest style was so important that legendary trumpeter Roy Eldridge would buy himself a new suit every two weeks during the time he played at the Savoy. "You had to be band-box perfect," says Frances Lynne, a singer who performed with both Gene Krupa and Charlie Barnet. "Every band I was with was glamorous." Or as Bing Crosby warned in his hit duet with Louis Jordan: "Tain't no use son, cause your sox don't match."

Of course, you don't need to dress up to enjoy the music and the dancing. But after slumming all day at work on casual Fridays, it can be a thrill to pull out all the stops when you hit the town on the weekend. Men and women are once again enjoying getting togged to the bricks — an expression for wearing your fanciest clothes. "I just love being able to dress up to the nines and go out. There are just no other excuses to do that anymore," says style aficionado Harper Della-Piana, key costumer for ABC's *Spin City*. And if you don't want to do it for yourself, remember that your clothes are just as important as your dancing in making your partner look good. (Besides, many clubs have dress codes that prohibit T-shirts, jeans, and sneakers; some require jackets as well.)

Don't forget one other thing: these clothes have come back for a reason. "Period stuff is so much better made. The fabrics were really wonderful and a lot of them just are not made anymore. You can't find rayon like that anymore," says Della-Piana. "That's why everybody in the swing crowd loves the older clothes." But are the fashions of the swing era really so retro after all? Today they seem more timeless than ever. "You don't put on a great-looking suit of that era and look back at pictures of yourself and go, 'Oh man, what was I thinking?'" says Big Bad Voodoo Daddy's Scotty Morris. Adds Leslie Rosenberg, editor of the swingzine *Atomic*: "It's not about what's hip, it's about what endures."

THE REAL DEAL: TIPS ON SHOPPING

1. Run out to the nearest vintage store and start your education on what's authentic retro clothing and what's not. A "Union Made" label is usually a good sign an item is old. Cuts, styles, and stitching were different back then compared with today. To find out how to pick out clothes from particular decades, quiz the store's owners, who are usually experts on the subject. Keep an eagle eye out for dead-stock — a term for clothing from the period that's been sitting in warehouses and has never been worn. Patronize the old mom-and-pop hat shop in the neighborhood. And make sure to hit vintage stores when traveling to out-of-the-way places. In the biggest cities, period clothes are nowhere near a bargain anymore. You can also check out on-line sites like eBay for clothing auctions. (A list of fashion Web sites, for buying both reproduction and vintage clothing, is included in the appendix.)

2. Do the movement test. You should make sure that clothes not only fit well (guys especially need to pay attention here — nothing looks worse than a poorly fitted suit) but also move well. You should try on the clothes and move around in them in the store. Do a turn and see if you can really work that skirt. Swing your arms in a big circle. "And then do a test kick," says Leann Wright of San Francisco's vintage boutique Guys and Dolls.

3. Be willing to stray into other decades. Many regulars in the swing scene will wear only forties clothing. A few are so strict, in fact, they've been unkindly branded "retro nazis." "Some people will look at a tag and see fifties and not buy it," says Wright. Adds Meredith Trailor of San Francisco's Martini Mercantile, "You could have the perfect vintage suit but be wearing reproduction shoes and people might be snobby about it." But don't let that bother you. Branching out into the twenties, the fifties, and even the sixties is not only more and more common, it's a great challenge trying to mix and match. Bands like Alien Fashion Show and Jet Set Six prefer sixties sharkskin suits. Great Gatsby caps are more popular than ever. And fifties skirts — which are much more full than

♫ The Best Vintage Find Ever

It's fashion kismet when you hit the right store at just the right time and make a dream discovery. A few style aficionados reminisce here about their all-time greatest hits, from oddball items to art pieces.

"I was in a store where they hadn't realized what this coat really was. It didn't have the designer label in it. It had a fancy ladies store label. But I figured out immediately that it was an Elsa Schiaparelli thirties full-length wool evening coat. It was from a collection she did that was based on Jean Cocteau. It has two beaded white doves on the front of it. I freaked out. It's a museum piece. Every once in a while I look at it and go, 'Oh my god, how did I find that?' It's luck."

— HARPER DELLA-PIANA, key costumer for *Spin City*

"Back in the early eighties I was shopping in LA and I found a pair of medium-toned denim pants, real forties baggy pants. The waistband is about eight or nine inches wide with four sets of belt loops and four matching denim belts. It comes up

those of the forties—"are almost more fun to dance in," says Wright. Adds singer Lavay Smith, "I just like bombshell clothes. I get things modeled after Jayne Mansfield's dresses."

You may also want to consider wearing quality reproductions, since fragile period clothing falls apart very easily on the dance floor. "I've ripped an armhole from just tossing back a martini," says Sarah Franko, codesigner of Manifesto, a small San Francisco clothing line that designs dresses for dancers with more room in the shoulders. Adds Autumn Carey-Adamme, codesigner of Revamp, which creates period looks in breathable modern fabrics

♫

like a straitjacket over my chest. It's got the button fly. It's heavy-duty old denim. They were stiff as a board, you could stand them up. I mean, these are the most outrageous pants you've ever seen."

— SAVOIA MICHELE, suit designer extraordinaire

"The one thing that I love the most are these fifties-style earrings that have these little mink-fur balls that are hung at the bottom of a series of pearls. I found them in Michigan and I paid like two bucks for them at Value Village. We joke that they double as fishing lures. They always get the best reaction."

— CARMEN GETIT, singer and guitarist for Steve Lucky and the Rhumba Bums

"I found this baby blue woman's suit that was just incredible. It was made by Turk, who did a lot of Western stuff for rock 'n' roll artists in the fifties and sixties. It was heavy-duty gabardine and had black detailing with arrows. The work on it was so amazing."

— GRACIELA RONCONI, owner of San Francisco's
Guys and Dolls vintage store

♫

for such singers as Lavay Smith and Carmen Getit, "A lot of vintage is wool, which looks great, but who really wants to dance in heavy wool?" And if you like to do it yourself, look out for old sewing books, Simplicity patterns at garage sales, and *Everyday Fashions of the Forties as Pictured in Sears Catalogs,* a great resource book.

4. A cheap way to get started is with accessories. One killer-diller hat, a flipped pair of cat's-eyes glasses, or a jazzy tie can really dress up an otherwise nineties-looking outfit. "You could have a Macy's or Nordstrom's double-breasted suit, but if you wear a hat,

people see it as retro," says Al Ribaya, the owner of Martini Mercantile. "Using accessories is a much easier way to go."

5. The music and the dance are about improvising, so why shouldn't the clothing be too? Buy something off the beaten track. At the Monsters of Swing dance camp in Ventura, California, the rip-roarin' styles have included guys in sailor suits, women in Marlene Dietrich–style menswear, bowling shirts worn with ties, and couples in totally retro clothes tweaked out with fluorescent dyed hair. "I love dressing up in a men's double-breasted suit, a bustier, and a fedora," says Darrow Cannizzaro, owner of New York's Darrow vintage store. What's important is to learn all the fashion rules and then have fun with them and mix it up a bit. Because it's not about just entering a time machine. It's about taking something old and creating something new: your own distinctive style.

GUYS

Starter Kit: The easiest way to avoid squaresville is to get yourself this basic outfit: Buy a white French-cuffed shirt with a pointy collar and a pair of high-waisted Hollywood-style pants. Find a screamin' tie that fits your personality. Add a pair of regulation red suspenders and a gently worn-in fedora. Then slip your dogs into a pair of comfortable spectator shoes. You're ready to boogie.

The Basics

Dress Shirts: You can't show off your new Betty Page cuff links without a proper shirt. Look for a finely woven shirt with French cuffs and a long, pointed forties collar. Some of the best, though most pricey, reproductions are made by H. Freeman and Son in Philadelphia and in New York by Savoia Michele. (Walking into Michele's East Village men's shop is like stepping into an old-time haberdashery, from the bolts of fine fabric on display to the rotary phone.)

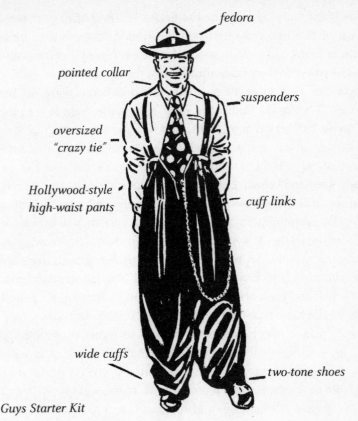

fedora

pointed collar

suspenders

oversized
"crazy tie"

Hollywood-style
high-waist pants

cuff links

wide cuffs

two-tone shoes

Guys Starter Kit

Hats: Take your time finding the perfect topper. "A hat is your personality," says Marie Lee, who's run her brimming store, Tophatters, in San Leandro, California, with her husband, Ted, for fifty-two years. And no matter what your personality is like, there's bound to be a hat to match it. There are endless styles to choose from, including fedoras, gamblers, panamas, homburgs, bowlers, and newsboy caps. But what's most important to pay attention to is the brim width, and given the shape and size of your head, how the hat fits. It shouldn't be too tight or too loose. The most popular brim width is two and three-eighths inches, but they can be very wide (think Cab Calloway, or Jim Carrey in *The Mask*) or narrow, down to one and one-quarter inches (called stingy brims, these became Frank Sinatra's signature hat in the fifties). Which brand should you get? If you can afford top-of-the-line Borsalinos (which sometimes cost more than two hundred dollars), pony up the money. "They're the Cadillac of hats," says Marie. Next best thing: Biltmore. Or Stetson and Dobbs. And whether you buy a new one or vintage, make sure it's fur felt and not wool felt. "Oh, that's the cheapest," says Ted Lee with disdain. The most popular colors are black, gray, and brown, but brighter shades such as burgundy, red, and sapphire are a blast too. Most have a pin and a small feather (Siegel's, a retro department store in San Francisco, will match the color of the feather to your suit). The ribbon around the crown generally matches the hat but is just a shade darker, though there are also contrasting ribbons, like yellow on a blue hat or black on a white hat, and even ones with stripes or polka dots. Here's a short take on the basic types of chapeaux you'll want to consider.

- ▸ FEDORA: the granddaddy of hats in terms of popularity, both in the forties and today; it's the best one to start with. There are two main styles: one with a crease down the middle of the crown and a pinch in the front, and one with just a crease. All have snap brims that can be pushed down in the front to create the perfect rakish angle.

- ▸ PORKPIE: a favorite of tenor saxophonist Lester Young, this stylin' hat is similar to a fedora but has a lower crown.

- ▸ HOMBURG: a somewhat more formal style, it has an upturned brim that, unlike the fedora, does not snap down.

- ▸ CAPS: sneaking up on the fedora as a fave, the cap — referred to as a Gatsby or newsboy — can't be beat for a casual, fresh-faced look. The best-made have eight sections stitched together. The wildest is the oversized Big Apple, a favorite of Royal Crown Revue's Eddie Nichols.

- ▸ PANAMAS: the perfect summer hat. The ones of highest quality have the most tightly woven straw.

► TANDOS: these exaggerated hats are basically fedoras that are almost as big as sombreros. "The one that Cab Calloway wore was about six inches wide in the brim. We cut it down to four," says Smiley Pachuco of El Pachuco Zoot Suits in Los Angeles. Also called zoot hats, these outrageous chapeaux can be taken all the way out to the edge in a color like royal blue and trimmed with two-, three-, and even eight-inch feathers. Says Smiley: "If you are not wearing that hat with your zoot suit, you are only eighty percent."

Pants: What's a Hollywood-style waist? Like nothing else you've worn before. The slacks of the era had a waist so high it came all the way to the bottom of your rib cage. The pleats went up to the top of the pants, so there's really no waistband. And the belt loops are very small, set a bit below the top. If you want a more casual nineties style, however, check out BC Ethic's tux slacks with stripes down the side. Or to really go retro, think about thirties campus pants, a wide trouser with thirty-six inches of fabric around each cuff. "I didn't really like them the first time I saw them," says Annamarie Firley of Revamp, which makes a fine reproduction, "until I saw them move."

Shoes: Give your dogs a good home by investing in a forgiving pair of spectators. Fred Astaire always looked impeccable in these two-toned shoes. According to fashion historian Colin McDowell in *Shoes: Fashion and Fantasy*, spectators, in their signature black-and-white color combination, "echoed the surface mood of musical racial harmony" during the swing era. Today, while vintage pairs can still be found, at way-out prices, there are two shoe companies that divide the reproduction market. Dancers seem to find Bleyers more flexible; scenesters think Stacy Adams's styles look cooler. Black-and-white is, of course, de rigueur, but don't be afraid to try the more subtle brown-and-white or wilder combinations like yellow, red, or blue with white. Get them in either captoe or wingtip. Other good brands include Brenton, John Fleuvog, and

Going All the Way: The Forties Lifestyle

For some swing fans, wearing period clothing is just the beginning. A love of retro fashion can often evolve into living a whole retro lifestyle. Believing firmly in the saying "They don't make 'em like they used to," swing scenesters like New Morty Show singer Vise Grip, tailor Savoia Michele, *Swing Time* magazine photographer Mark Jordan, and Royal Crown Revue founder Eddie Nichols collect the furniture, the cars, the books, and the radios of the thirties, forties, fifties, and sixties. "I love living that way, as long as you are having a good time with it," says Mr. Lucky, a singer and one of the original founders of the retro scene in San Francico. But he adds that some people take it so far that they have to be VC. What's that? "Vintagely correct. They are out for a historically correct experience," he says. Which goods turn a home into a time machine? Here's a sampling.

- Detective novels by Dashiell Hammett, Mickey Spillane, and Raymond Chandler
- Old issues of *Confidential, Life, Look,* and *Photoplay* magazines
- Depression-era glass and Fire King bakeware
- Home bars and martini mixers
- Late-thirties Buicks, 1950s Cadillacs, and 1960s Chryslers
- Old-fashioned refrigerators (Admiral, Frigidaire), stoves (Dixie), and fans (Zero)
- Blond streamlined Heywood-Wakefield furniture
- Art deco sofas, Eames chairs, and other midcentury furniture (à la *Wallpaper* magazine)
- Rotary dial phones, vintage turntables, and Bakelite radios
- Pinup art, especially Betty Page photos and illustrations by George Petty

the top-of-the-line Murrows and Allen-Edmonds. There's also a tougher-looking alternative: a spectator with a Doc Marten–style thick sole. And once you've got your spectators, get a dependable pair of black wingtips too. Then add a pair of white bucks for summer. And what about some brown alligators? Once you start, there's no stopping.

Suits: Whatever style you choose—whether it be double-breasted or single, three-button or four, pinstripe, fleck, or a solid color (blue serge was one of Cab Calloway's favorites)—the most important consideration is fit. Back in the swing era, it was common for men to have all their suits custom-made. "They called it a drape suit because the fabric was actually draped on the gentleman," says Savoia Michele, whose custom period-style suits can run up to two thousand dollars. Another source, in the LA area, is Jorge Avalos of Tin Tan Tailor Made Suits in Long Beach who designs suits for such bands as Royal Crown Revue, Big Bad Voodoo Daddy, and Eddie Reed. Of course, not everyone can afford custom work. But even off-the-rack vintage suits can run up to four hundred, five hundred, or eight hundred dollars. So it's worth making sure someone with a keen eye checks you out when you try on the suit. You should also plan on taking it to a local tailor for some slight alterations to get it just right. For a regulation forties look, the shoulders should be big. It should drape nicely down the body and come in at the hips, creating a V-shape. Also, look out for things like exaggeratedly peaked lapels, pleated pockets, or jackets with belted backs, the kind of detailing that makes a suit really special. As Duke Ellington and Billy Eckstine once proved, you can never have enough suits. When the pair worked together at New York's Paramount Theater, they engaged in a battle of the closets instead of a battle of the bands. "For four weeks," Ellington once recalled, "neither of us wore the same suit twice. . . . People were buying tickets just to see the sartorial changes."

Suspenders: It's a sorry sight to see a pair of pants left to hang by themselves. They need suave suspenders holding them up to really fly. Make sure to choose the classier ones that attach to the pants with buttons, not clip-ons. And if you can find authentic forties pairs—they're stretchier and narrower (three-quarters to one inch wide) than most kinds today—grab 'em. "You don't need extra-wide suspenders when you've got a wild tie on," says Michael Gardner, president of Siegel's department store. What's a snazzy color combination? A black dress shirt with total-contrast white suspenders.

Ties: In the 1940s, neckties were the undisputed kings of menswear. Sherman Billingsley, owner of the exclusive Stork Club, was renowned for his collection of more than three thousand. Men even belonged to tie-swapping clubs, and it's not hard to see why. To call them art wasn't an overstatement. Inspired by everything from deco to cubism to surrealism (Salvador Dali did his own line of ties, which today can cost more than four hundred dollars), ties were wild, oversized, crazy, beautiful, loud, you name it. Indeed, some had such inspired patterns that they were called ham-and-eggs ties "upon which sloppy eating wouldn't be noticed," according to *Fit to be Tied,* a must-have coffee table book on neckwear of the era. Among the many types worth searching out are classic art deco styles with lightning bolts and leaping gazelles; hunting and fishing motifs; tropical styles with palm trees or Hawaiian prints; and landscapes, from scenes of San Francisco to painted-desert sunsets. And if you really want to spend the money, track down such hard-to-find winners as a Countess Mara signature tie, a classic California hand-painted number (the authentic ones actually say Hand-Painted on the back); a pinup girl tie (some of the coolest have the cutie printed inside the back of the tie); and a line called Personali-ties that included ties endorsed by Bob Hope.

Be aware that the most authentic ties from the war years are made of rayon, not silk (which was requisitioned to make parachutes). Make sure that the tie is the standard forties width, about four inches, or even four and a half inches, across at the widest. And don't worry if your new find seems really short once you tie it. It was designed that way to be worn with those high-waisted pants. To stand out from the crowd, wiseguys and entertainers used to wear them even shorter.

Zoot Suit: The height of sartorial indulgence, zoot suits have almost become cliché emblems of the swing revival. But in their time they were powerful social statements of defiance, predating by decades such shock-the-bourgeoisie fashions as long hair on hippies in the sixties and multiple piercings in the nineties. Worn by disadvantaged and disaffected Hispanic and African-American youths in Los Angeles and Harlem, the zoot suit was an absurdly exaggerated look. Suit coats had peaked lapels and high shoulders and dropped all the way to the knees. Pants began at the rib cage, flowed out at the knees, and tapered in dramatically at the ankles. "It was quite a real, real zinger as a suit," Cab Calloway has said. Adding to the extravagance were long chains, wide-brimmed hats topped with feathers, pointed shoes, and oversized cuff links. The outfit even required a certain stance. "Hat angled, knees drawn together, feet wide apart, both index fingers jabbed toward the floor," wrote Malcolm X in his autobiography, recalling how a zoot suit was worn. "The long coat and swinging chain and the Punjab pants were much more dramatic if you stood that way."

Such a display, however, provoked a harsh reaction from mainstream society during the war years. Zoot suits flaunted reams and reams of material at the same time that consumer goods, especially fabrics, were being rationed. Inevitably, they were deemed an unpatriotic affront to the war effort. "To wear clothes that used up that much fabric represented a way of saying we don't care," says Annamarie Firley of Revamp. By 1943 the Los Angeles City Council had gone so far as to effectively make them illegal. Quickly the conflict turned violent, as servicemen stationed in LA began beating up zoot wearers and destroying their suits. Police often looked the other way. At the conclusion of the average rumble, zoot suiters more often than not were the ones who ended up going to jail. Incidents spread to New York,

hat feather

wide-brim topper

wide tie

swing chain

long jacket

baggy tapered pants

two-tone shoes

The Zoot-Suiter

Philadelphia, San Diego, and Detroit. (For more on the history of the zoot suit, check out the essay "The Zoot Suit and Style Warfare" in the anthology *Zoot Suits and Second-Hand Dresses* or rent the 1981 movie *Zoot Suit* starring Edward James Olmos.)

Today an authentic vintage zoot from the forties is as impossible to find as a live Elvis. Very few still exist, and most that do reside in museums. "I've been in this business ten years and I've never seen one," says Graciela Ronconi of Guys and Dolls. But many stylin' reproductions are available, from stores like El Pachuco, Siegel's (which even does zoot tuxedos in all white), and Suavecito, at prices from two hundred dollars to five hundred dollars and up. Colors run the gamut: black or white, royal blue or hot red, and, of course, pinstripe. Caution: Beware of counterfeiters trying to ride the trend: "People are taking a coat and adding six to eight inches to it and calling it a zoot suit," says Smiley Pachuco.

All the Extras

Bow Ties: They weren't just for eggheads. Cab had his wild ones, and Nat King Cole and Fats Waller were just as spiffy in more traditional bow ties. And while you can buy clip-ons, wouldn't you be more proud of yourself if you learned how to tie a real one?

Belts: The belts of the period were usually skinny, not wide. "With those thin belt loops, you wore a belt of between half an inch and an inch," says Savoia Michele. Some of the sharpest come in black alligator or white leather. "The shoes to wear in the summer were white bucks. And men always matched their belts to their shoes," he adds.

Casual Shirts: After World War II, many men stopped wearing ties after work and the leisure era was born. Among the cool offerings from the period are gabardine shirts that have a tab at the collar instead of a buttonhole, bowling shirts, short-sleeve camp shirts, Cuban-style embroidered guayaberas, and the ever-popular Hawaiian shirts. Companies making quality reproductions include the Hi-Ball Lounge, Cruisinusa, Swave and Deboner, Devlin (incredible two-tone shirts), Johnny Suede (look for their flaming martinis), Siegel's (which does a great tiki number), Trāc Edwards, and the most authentic, Da Vinci, which reproduces shirts based on their own original patterns from the period.

Chains: Up to sixty inches long, chains are the accessory of choice for a zoot suit. "The chain is part of the uniform," says

Smiley Pachuco. "The coat should not be buttoned, so that the chain shows." To jazz the look up even further, consider buying a double, triple, or even quadruple chain.

Cuff Links: To run with your own Rat Pack, you've gotta show cuff. And that means amassing your own collection of cuff links (Sinatra's hoard was legendary). There are thousands upon thousands of designs out there. So take the time to look through those glass cases in the thrift shop for a few pairs that suit your personality—or your mood. For snappy reproductions, check out Winky and Dutch's cool sets with everything from pinups to martini glasses to dice on them. And don't be afraid of oversized cuff links. The real zoot-suiters were known for strutting down the street wearing rock-sized pairs on their wrists.

Hair: For a basic forties look, just keep your hair short and slick it back (with either grease or pomade). To get fancy, try a pompadour—zoot-suiters wore ones with ducktails. In the fifties (and on the New Morty Show's Morty Okin) they were higher. But whatever you do, don't go to a salon for a cut. "If you are a guy, go to the oldest barber you can find in town," says retro hairstylist Kim Long, owner of San Francisco's W.A.K. Shack. "The older barbers will know what to do." And for real authentic flair, you may even want to try the pencil-thin mustache seen on Cab Calloway and Nat King Cole. Talk about walking a thin line.

Hollywood Jackets: Also called leisure jackets, Hollywood jackets were casual unconstructed sport coats, made of rayon or wool gabardine, that came into popularity in the late 1940s. The classiest boast a two-tone look, such as a cream jacket with contrasting brown-and-cream houndstooth sleeves and collar. Some were also belted. The most desired vintage labels are Mr. California and a line endorsed by bandleader Xavier Cugat. Jackets by C. Joseph, a label available at San Francisco's Martini Mercantile, are among the best reproductions.

Pocket Squares: Frank Sinatra was fastidious about pocket squares. He'd even go up to other guys and fix 'em if they weren't worn right. Pocket squares should puff out from the jacket's pocket a bit, while simple white handkerchiefs are worn crisply folded. Pocket squares come in all colors and fabrics (the classic is silk). Choose one that coordinates especially well with your tie, along with your shirt and jacket.

Socks: Ever thought you'd be wearing men's hosiery? Yeah, you heard it right. Guys often wore just as much nylon as gals back in the forties. The favorites were sheer nylon ribbed socks, often humorously referred to today as pimp socks. The best finds are dead-stock—from all-American brands like Gold Toe—or the well-made reproductions by Stacy Adams. "They come in every color you could think of," says Siegel's Michael Gardner, who sells them in traditional black or brown, but also in red and sapphire. "People tend to forget that in fashion in the thirties and forties, color was really big."

Spats: Spats were originally designed to protect one's shoes while walking in rainy weather. These leather ankle cover-ups, usually chosen to complement your shoes, give an instant period feel.

Sweaters: Hey, junior, want to be the B.M.O.C. (Big Man on Campus)? Throw on a collegiate-style sweater such as an argyle vest, a long-sleeved tennis sweater, or a pullover with an oversized varsity letter on the front. You can really make the grade by topping it off with a smart bow tie.

Sweat Rags: A sweat rag isn't as unimportant (or gross) as it sounds. If you're one of those guys whose mop-top sweats too much from doing the hop, you'd better carry a rag to stay neat. But no need to get fancy here. Just grab a small white towel from the gym and tuck it into your pocket. Or better yet, stuff it in the back of your suspenders.

Tattoos: Many neoswing observers have remarked on the seeming incongruity of tattooed Gen X-ers wearing forties clothes. But it's not such an anachronistic mix after all. Before tattoos ruled the mosh pit, they were the province of sailors and sharpies

slicked-back hair

argyle vest

thin belt

high-waist pants

two-tone shoes

The Collegiate Guy

during the war years and earlier. "The tattoo thing was a big part of the swing period," says Savoia Michele. "They were called flash tattoos. It was all about pinup girls and dice designs."

Tie Clips: Nothing looks better than a tie held down with a great clip—witness Vince Vaughn in the Vegas scenes in *Swingers.* They range from simple (a basic bar) to expensive (with diamonds) to trompe l'oeil swords (designed to appear that they have been stuck through the tie).

Underwear: Boxers, of course, in silk or rayon. "But it's also kind of fun to wear a pair of nylon underwear with a matching pair of nylon socks," says Siegel's Gardner.

DOLLS

Starter Kit: Step into a floral rayon forties dress with a straight skirt, a pair of open-toe chunky heels, and some seamed stockings. Tuck a gardenia behind your ear. Add a pair of Bakelite button earrings. Apply bright red lipstick. You're ready for your pinup.

The Basics

Dresses and Skirts: It don't mean a thing if your skirt ain't got that swing. Whether you go for straight knee-length skirts of the forties (like the pleated styles brought back by designer Marc Jacobs) or the fuller fifties circle skirts (the New York label Tuleh is successfully reviving the look), you'll want an item that moves as well as you do. "Some dresses look great but don't move," says Graciela Ronconi, owner of San Francisco's Guys and Dolls vintage store. "Like a Marilyn Monroe dress with long sleeves that's off the shoulder and tight with a narrow skirt. That's good for wallflowers only."

Classic styles—dresses usually have fitted waists and often belts—include floral prints, ginghams, checks, and polka dots and, in a nod to Carmen Miranda, anything with fruit, especially cherries. "Cherries go fast," says Leann Wright of Guys and Dolls. But what really defines a forties dress is the fabric. The cheapest and easiest to find are dresses in rayon, either in crepes or gabardines. "They are easy to move in and shouldn't be that expensive—maybe forty to sixty dollars," adds Wright. Considerably more expensive are such rare finds as originals by Christian Dior, Adrian (the famous movie costume designer opened his own shop in Beverly Hills in 1942), and Elsa Schiaparelli. Don't count on finding one anytime soon. Most are in museums.

Because vintage dresses can often be quite fragile, buying a reproduction or making your own dress is often a good alternative. "Our line is designed specifically for the well-dressed dancer," says Revamp's Firley, "so that you can go out and not have to worry about your clothing falling apart on the dance floor."

Hair: Getting your locks to look like Betty Grable, Veronica Lake, or the Andrews Sisters isn't easy. Back in the day, setting hair into intricate forties styles took lots of time and even more know-how. The era's hairdos were like living sculptures, usually including pin-curled bangs piled high in the front, hair pulled back on the side, and cascading waves flowing down the back of the head. Setting the hair required using wet sets and painstakingly creating each invidual curl.

But don't be scared off. The W.A.K. Shack's Kim Long advises tracking down photos in vintage magazines and watching old movies to see examples of the many varied styles. "I know plenty of girls who just find pictures and learn by doing," she says, adding that "you should find the place in town where the old ladies get their hair done." Also, many swingzines regularly run features on setting hair in an authentic period style. And don't forget that one of the nice benefits of styling hair this way is that the do should last for a couple days. (Once the hair is set, it's best to do a movement test. Hop around a bit, and if a curl falls out of place, spray it back down.)

Should you not want to submit to the full monty—an authentic forties hairstyle can take more than forty-five minutes to complete—celebrity hairstylist Kevin Mancuso, author of the book *The Mane Thing,* recommends a simpler approach. "As long as the hair is a little bit polished and turned under and has a little bit of a wave to it and it's pulled back on the sides, it automatically becomes that forties thing. You could achieve a similar silhouette with a curling iron or hot rollers and lots of product. Sculpt the hair with your hands, pin it or roll it, and create the shape you want. It should look soft and full, done but a little bit

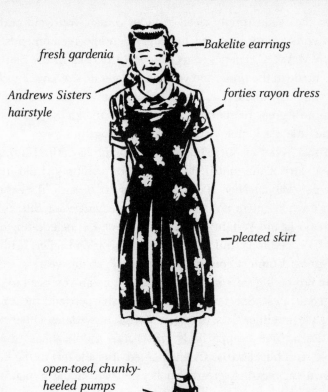

fresh gardenia

Bakelite earrings

Andrews Sisters
hairstyle

forties rayon dress

pleated skirt

open-toed, chunky-
heeled pumps

Dolls Starter Kit

undone." Either way, making the effort goes a long way. "Nothing looks worse than wearing a nice vintage dress and having a plain straight hairdo," says Kim Long. "Nothing completes an outfit better than having your hair done and nothing makes it as polished."

Makeup: "Basically the makeup is like a very subtle drag queen's," jokes Angella Mendillo, a makeup artist who's researched forties looks. "It's very extreme, even though it's not a lot of makeup. You want to do a very clean face, a sheer foundation with a good powder. You need high arched eyebrows—no bushy eighties brows. Curl the lashes and put on lots of mascara, though keep the eyelids pretty clean. And, of course, you want outlined lips with a very bold red lipstick." Mendillo recommends reds from M.A.C. Cosmetics, plus Revlon's Cherries in the Snow. "It was made in the fifties and you can still get it," she says. Finish off the face by making a black beauty mark—or buy some of Temptu's great temporary tattoo beauty marks. Says Mendillo: "One little black mole really brings it all together."

Tops: What's a sure-shot way of looking like Rita Hayworth? Tie a shirt at the midriff like the famous pinup girl did in *You Were Never Lovelier*. "I love tying a shirt because it's easier to dance when you're not worried about keeping your shirt tucked in," says Leann Wright. Other can't-lose styles include tiny cardigans, beaded tops, and simple horizontal-striped sailor T-shirts.

Shoes: Comfort comes first (so think about wearing insoles too). But taking care of your feet doesn't mean you need to sacrifce stylishness. Spectator shoes are the sharpest and most popular style, in either flats, open-toe pumps, or wedgies. Other possibilities include strappy heels, fifties-style saddle shoes, or Mary Janes with buckles (the shoe is named after the girl in the Buster Brown cartoons). A greater challenge for dancing is platforms, which, believe it or not, weren't invented in the seventies. Ferragamo made unbelievable pairs—some with rainbow stripes— way back in the thirties. What makes a forties shoe distinct? The blunt toe and a slightly chunky heel that isn't too high. Those pointy five-inch stilettos didn't become popular until the fifties. "I personally recommend dancing in either very low heels or flats. It's a whole lot easier on your legs," says Annamarie Firley of Revamp. "Also, if you end up stepping on somebody it's nicer not to have a stiletto heel plunge through the center of their foot."

All the Extras

Eyeglasses: Who cares about the forties when fifties specs are so much more fun? Grab a pair of cat's-eyes glasses—with faux jewels on the rims—and prowl for the perfect partner. (Forties

Words for a Hep Cat: Swing Lingo

If Cab Calloway were around today, he'd still want to know if you were hep to the jive. Of course, since slang changes so quickly, what's mad today is lame tomorrow. So one word of caution when boning up on the lingo of the thirties and forties: it's great to learn, but only a few people really get away with using it when speaking. Even back in the day, jazz insiders sometimes ridiculed the overuse of such words as killer-diller (a thriller) and skinbeater (a drummer). One writer called most jazz lingo "false shoptalk." On the other hand, Calloway, the heppest cat of them all, not only used jive extensively in his music and shows, he published his own *Hepster's Dictionary* in 1936. (It's appended to his now out-of-print autobiography, *Of Minnie the Moocher and Me*.) Today's compendiums of swing slang (posted all over the many swing sites on the Internet) combine words from many sources: Harlem lingo, detective novels, juvenile delinquent pulp fiction, and terms used by the Rat Pack. Much of yesterday's slang has now passed into everyday use, though some terms can still seem completely foreign. Check out this short list of some of the most colorful swing slang.

Alligator: A fan of swing

Beat up the chops: Talk a lot

Belly-warmer: Necktie

Big Sleep: Raymond Chandler's coinage for death

Blip: Good or great

Blower: Telephone

Bright: A day

Bring down: Something depressing

Calamity cubes: dice

Canary: A female singer

Cat: A guy, or specifically a musician

Chicago overcoat: A coffin

Collar: To get, acquire

Conk: Head

Dead hoofer: Poor dancer

Dogs: Feet

Drape: Clothes, outfit

Fall out: To be overcome with emotion

Flimflam: Swindle

Flippers: Hands

glasses tend to be more square.) The range of styles is limitless. "The coolest glasses I ever saw," says Leann Wright, "were these white shades with red Bakelite cherries hanging from them."

Gloves: Nobody wears gloves today, goes the common lament. So help bring these stylish accessories back. The most popular are black, though gloves were often dyed to match a dress, so they can be found in scads of colors. And try them in all sizes, from short to evening length (the most difficult to find in vintage).

Hair Accessories: Once you've got your bangs and pincurls set just right, nothing adds to the forties feel more than a scarf, a bow, or some flowers, especially gardenias. And don't buy the buds yourself—send your gent to the florist to get 'em. But if you want to try a truly remarkable look, slip your hair into a snood, the classic thick hair nets from the period (generally available in black, white, and natural). How did a hair net become a trendy accessory? Snoods became popular after famed costume designer Adrian put Hedy Lamarr in one in the 1940 film *I Take This Woman*. During the war they became a quick, easy way for busy women to wear their hair. "It very distinctly says the war years," says Al Ribaya, owner of San Francisco's Martini Mercantile vintage chain. "In factories, women had to keep their hair from being caught in machines or tools."

Handbags: The choices are legion, but among the coolest handbags to watch out for are forties pieces that have wooden clasps (metal was scarce during the war) and those unbeatable hard plastic Lucite bags from the fifties. How about a clear pink one with rhinestones?

Hats: Don't follow any rules here. Just find a hat you love. Women's hat styles are as varied as flowers in the garden. But keep an eye out for those quintessentially forties hats worn by Wacs (in the Women's Army Corps) and women in the Red Cross.

Jewelry: In the mid-thirties, more than two thirds of the costume jewelry sold in the United States was made from Bakelite, a plastic created by chemist Leo Bakeland early in the century.

Frame: Body, dance partner
Frolic pad: Nightclub
Gasoline: Liquor
Glad rags: Best clothes
Gumshoe: Detective
Hep: Cool, in the know
Hophead: Drug addict
Ice: Diamonds
Icky: Overzealous swing fan
Jelly: Free, on the house
Kicks: Shoes
Licks and riffs: Hot musical phrases
Lid: Hat
Lombardo: Schmaltz
Nails: Cigarettes
Off the cob: Out of date
One on the city: Glass of tap water
Pipes: Vocal cords
Pulleys: Suspenders
Reet: All right, fine
Righteous: The best
Ring-a-ding: Adjective for a beautiful woman
Send: To move emotionally
Solid: Great, OK

Stompers: Shoes
Tea: Marijuana
Togged to the bricks: Dressed in your best clothes
Twirl: Girl who's wild about dancing
Unhep: Out of it
Ville: As in coolsville, jailsville, nowheresville, dullsville, endsville, bombsville, scramsville
Voot: One of the many nonsensical slang inventions of singer Slim Gaillard, the man behind the swing hit "Flat Foot Floogee."

Not to mention the many slang terms for "man": **Gate, pops, daddy-o, gee, jasper, jack, egg, player, jobbie, bird**
— And for "woman": **Skirt, dame, broad, barbecue, angel cake, kitten, sister, jane, queen, pigeon, barn burner, dish, doll, bim, ankle, babe, bree, chick, fine dinner, mouse, looker, zazz girl, tomato**

Because so much was produced, vintage necklaces, pins, bracelets, and button earrings are readily available and not that expensive. The easiest colors to find are orange, green, red, black, brown, and yellow, while purple, blue, and pink are more rare. The plastic can be clear, tortoise, or opaque, smooth, or carved. Bakelite is the simplest, cheapest way of completing a retro look.

Perfume: Wear Chanel No. 5 to bed as Marilyn Monroe did. But to go to the nightclub, think about a forties scent like Fracas or Jungle Gardenia. Now that's attention to retro details.

Bakelite earrings
school sweater
white shirt
plaid skirt
bobby socks —
saddle shoes

The Bobby-Soxer

Socks: The classic still remains bobby socks. Slip on a pair with some saddle shoes and imagine swooning over a fresh-faced, bow-tied Frank Sinatra.

Suits: Suits are generally better for posing, not for dancing. But nothing beats looking like Rosalind Russell in *His Girl Friday*. Look for a suit in a fine wool with a short jacket that boasts sexy peplums (that's the slightly flared part at the bottom of the coat). And scream for joy if you happen across a reasonably priced Lilli Ann, a San Francisco label that began production in 1933. The most coveted vintage brand out there, Lilli Ann suits can go for between two hundred and four hundred dollars. A hat, gloves, and a snood complete this great look.

Undergarments: Get ready to unleash the exhibitionist within. One of the most fun parts of swing dancing can be showing off a chic or shocking item of lingerie. In fact, that's one reason to find a skirt that really twirls. For a basic outfit, consider wearing a pair of vintage seamed stockings (dead-stock is still fairly easy to find) with a garter belt, or a girdle with garter straps. "It all depends on whether you want to show your knickers or not. The more modest girl might wear a slip," says Annamarie Firley of Revamp (which, under the label Dark Garden, makes innovative garter belts with two extra straps to help hold up the stockings of even the most athletic dancers). But even if you don't want to show off, it's fun "dressing vintage inside and out," adds Firley.

Other possibilities include tap pants, flouncy crinolines, fishnets, and fifties Betty Page–style bullet bras. At the wild and popular Monsters of Swing camp in Ventura every spring, styles get even more outrageous. The brashest women have brought down the house wearing leopard garters, panties with shiny blue polka dots, and once even a pair that read "Hi, Lee," a surprise message for festival organizer Lee Moore of the Flyin' Lindy Hoppers.

CHAPTER 7

A Night on the Town:
The City-by-City Guide

*F*rom the local club to far-flung spots from Sweden to Singapore, swing is everywhere. Arranged alphabetically by state, followed by international entries, here's the most comprehensive list so far of where the coolest places are to dance and hang out with fellow Lindy fans, who the swing dance teachers are in your city (instructors will often have varying specialties; make sure to inquire before you sign up for a class), plus which Web pages to check for the most up-to-date listings of area swing events. (My apologies to those clubs and instructors who aren't on the list. In some cases, clubs have been selected based on longevity and popularity. For certain cities, just a Web site is listed.)

Before heading out to a club, it's recommended that you call ahead. Nights and locations change. (Bars also aren't always consistent about supporting swing nights since dancers don't drink very much.) Better yet, check those Web pages religiously. If you give them your e-mail address, the most organized sites will send out weekly notices detailing upcoming swing events. Keep on swinging!

FACING PAGE: *Hollywood-style dancers and instructors Sylvia Skylar and Erik Robison at Swing Dance Catalina.* (LISA C. BOREL)

United States

ARIZONA

▶ **Phoenix-Scottsdale Area**

NIGHTSPOTS

Backstage
7373 Scottsdale Mall
Scottsdale
602-949-1697
Call for details

The Bash
230 Fifth Street at Ash
Tempe
602-966-8200
Swing three nights a week, with a DJ on
Tuesdays, live music on Thursdays and
Saturdays

Bobby McGee's
7000 East Shea
Scottsdale
602-998-5591
Lessons and DJ on Tuesdays

The Rhythm Room
1019 East Indian School Road
Phoenix
602-265-4842
Long-running swing events; call for nights

Rockin' Horse
7136 East Stetson
Scottsdale
602-949-0992
Live music and lessons Wednesday
through Saturday, age 18+

DANCE CLASSES

Steve Conrad, cofounder of the
Arizona Lindy Hop Society, and
Aaryn Green
888-494-8932 (within Arizona)

Paul Maranto, cofounder of the
Arizona Lindy Hop Society, and
Kristi Bullock
602-222-9493

WEB SITES

www.azls.com
Homepage of the Arizona Lindy Hop
Society, with statewide listings

www.rhythmandmoves.com
Paul Maranto's Web site on the swing
scene in the Phoenix area

www.lauricon.com/lindycircle
Steve Conrad's Web site for Lindy events

▶ **Tucson**

NIGHTSPOTS

Club Congress
311 East Congress
520-622-8848
Books live bands; call for nights

Rialto Theater
318 East Congress
520-740-0126
Books swing bands approximately once a
month

DANCE CLASSES

Irene Stojanov and Brian Fabig
602-263-7553

WEB SITE

www.azstarnet.com/~lstrojny
West Coast swing site also provides info
on Lindy in the area

CALIFORNIA

▶ Fresno

WEB SITE
www.hepcentral.com
www.webfresno.com/swinglink/
Guides to events in the Fresno area

▶ Los Angeles Area

NIGHTSPOTS
Bobby McGee's
200 South State College Boulevard
Brea
714-529-1998
Great old-timers and youngsters mixer
with DJ music; call for nights

Carillo Recreation Center
100 East Carrillo
Santa Barbara
805-569-1952
Thrown by renowned instructors
Jonathan Bixby and Sylvia Sykes, this
dance is held every first and third Friday
of the month (with free lesson)

Coconut Club
Beverly Hilton
9876 Wilshire Boulevard
310-285-1358
Great bands and dancing on Saturdays

Conga Room
5364 Wilshire Boulevard
323-656-8363
   (Swing Set hotline)
Heidi Richman's Wednesday-night
Swing Set dance

The Derby
4500 Los Feliz Boulevard
323-663-8979
LA's premier swing nightclub offers live
music every night of the week in the
gorgeous building once occupied by the
famous Brown Derby

Memories
1074 North Tustim Avenue
Anaheim
714-630-9233
Swing dancing Mondays, Tuesdays,
Fridays, and late on Saturdays in this
forties-style supper club

Nicholby's
404 East Main Street
Ventura
805-653-2320
Home turf of the Flyin' Lindy Hoppers;
Wednesday swing nights

Pasadena Ballroom Dance
   Association
Fellowship Hall
997 East Walnut
   (in back of Lutheran Church)
Pasadena
626-799-5689
Long-running event held on Saturday;
no age limit

Rhino Room
7979 Center
Huntington Beach
714-892-3316
Wednesday swing nights with lessons
and live music

Satin Ballroom
Veterans Memorial Building
4117 Overland Avenue
Culver City
310-358-6935
Hundreds of swingers boogie once a
month on a seven-thousand-square-
foot floor

Twin Palms
101 West Green Street
Pasadena
626-577-2567
All-ages dance on Sundays

DANCE CLASSES
Jonathan Bixby and Sylvia Sykes
Santa Barbara
http://www.reson.com/dance/
tj&s.htm
805-569-1952

Kim Clever and David Frutos
805-641-3676

Flyin' Lindy Hoppers
Terri Moore
Ventura
www.flyinlindyhoppers.com
805-643-3166

Rusty Frank and Peter Flahiff
Swing Shift and On Tap!
818-753-7968

Steven Mitchell
818-468-9995

Pasadena Ballroom Dance
   Association
Erin and Tami Stevens
http://home.earthlink.net/ ~ pbda1
626-799-5689

Sylvia Skylar and Erik Robison
213-389-6691

Audrey Wilson
Irvine, Orange County
http://home.earthlink.net/
~ audreydancin/
714-551-3443

WEB SITES
http://home.earthlink.net/
~ margiekate/swingspots.html
Margie Cormier's super-comprehensive
Southern California Lindy Society
homepage

www.nocturne.com/swing/
swing.shtml
A cool guide to Los Angeles after dark

http://welcome.to/laswing
This LA guide offers club listings, links,
and a music and book store

▶ **Riverside–San Bernardino**

WEB SITE
www.pe.net/ ~ jstairs/
Riverside Station's guide to inland south
California swing

▶ **Sacramento**

WEB SITE
www.midtownswing.com
The capital's swing guide

▸ **San Diego Area**

NIGHTSPOTS
Belly Up
143 South Cedros
Solana Beach
619-481-9022
Occasional Friday and Saturday happy
hour with swing music

Cannibal Bar
Catamaran Hotel
3999 Mission Boulevard
Pacific Beach
619-539-8650
Hops on most Wednesdays with live
music (usually Big Time Operator)

Characters Bar and Grill
La Jolla Marriott
4240 La Jolla Village Drive
619-597-6394
Saturdays with a big dance floor

The Flame
3780 Park Boulevard
619-295-4163
Mondays with free lessons

Papa Jack's
502 Fourth Avenue at Island
619-696-7272
Swing on Sunday nights with live music

The Rocket Club
3094 El Cajon Boulevard
North Park
619-447-7247
Spacious all-ages club features live
music either Friday or Saturday, DJ on
casual Tuesdays

Tio Leo's
5302 Napa Street
Bay Park/University of San Diego
619-542-0562
Rockabilly swing nights Thursdays plus
occasional live shows

DANCE CLASSES
Swing Time San Diego
Meeshi Sumayao
619-271-7061

Emily Belt
619-677-0353

Jamie and Elisha Exon
760-734-4875

Jon Costa
760-720-0491

Elizabeth O'Grady
760-633-1510

WEB SITES
www.swingtimesd.com
Web site for Swing Time San Diego—
complete guide to venues, classes, and
other events

www.anyswinggoes.com
San Diego–based on-line swing magazine

www.angelfire.com/ca/SDLindyHop
San Diego Lindy Hop Society homepage

▸ **San Francisco Area**

NIGHTSPOTS
Allegro Ballroom
5855 Christie Avenue
Emeryville
510-655-2888
Call for details

Bimbo's 365 Club
1025 Columbus Avenue
415-474-0365
This club's occasional swing nights are
worth waiting for; it's got an amazing
dance floor

Café Cocomo
650 Indiana Street
415-824-6910
This small club in Potrero Hill offers
classes and bands on Wednesdays

Café du Nord
2170 Market Street
415-861-5016
The home turf of singer Lavay Smith;
call for details

Club Deluxe
1509 Haight Street
415-552-6949
Small art deco lounge where the
neoswing movement first took off

Cocoanut Grove
400 Beach Street
Santa Cruz
831-423-2053
Call for information

DNA Lounge
375 Eleventh Street
415-626-1409
Saturday night's Swinging with Spencer
in the Ultra Lounge draws the hard-core
scenesters

Hi-Ball Lounge
473 Broadway
415-397-9464
The swankest spot in North Beach and
San Francisco's only six-night-a-week
swing club; offers great classes too

330 Ritch
330 Ritch Street
415-522-9558
Wednesday night classes

Top of the Mark
Mark Hopkins Hotel
999 California Street
415-392-3434
Catch the best views of the city at this
recently renovated club ; lessons on
Tuesdays

DANCE CLASSES
Broadway Studios
435 Broadway
415-291-0333

Paul Overton and Sharon Ashe
The International Center
50 Oak Street
415-626-0255

Metronome Ballroom
1830 Seventeenth Street
415-252-9000

Michael Marangio and Persephone
Shagtime Dance Instruction
www.zootsuitswank.com
510-528-7858

Micah Jacobson and Jena Chalmers
1-800-97-MICAH

Rob van Haaren and Diane Thomas
Swing Central
650-367-9464

Belinda Ricklefs and Ken Watanabe
East Bay
belindy@sirius.com
510-893-1519

WEB SITES
www.eswing.com
The best events calendar for northern
California and beyond

www.lindylist.com
Weekly listings of dances and band
appearances

www.maybe.com/swingside
An opinionated guide to a week in
the life of Bay Area swing

COLORADO

▶ **Denver**

NIGHTSPOTS
Bluebird Theater
3317 East Colfax Avenue
303-322-2308
Call for listing of swing events

Mercury Café
2199 California
303-294-9281
Swings on Thursdays and Sundays with
local bands, DJ on Tuesdays

Ninth Avenue West
99 West Ninth Avenue
303-572-8006
Swing and supper club has featured
many of the country's best bands;
call for details

DANCE CLASSES
Matthew Donalen
303-382-6997

James Glader
www.allswingevents.com
303-861-8094

Victor Ward
303-280-1807

Russell Enloe
303-733-2237

Karen Lee Dance Studio
303-825-1116

Marcy and Keith Hellman
Contact c/o Mercury Café
303-294-9258

WEB SITES
www.swingcolorado.com
Good listing of weekly events plus
in-depth coverage of clubs in and
around Denver

www.oneimage.com/~dswing
Another source for swing info in
the Mile High City

▶ **Fort Collins**

DANCE CLASSES
Eden Ellman and Diane
    Montgomery
970-493-3718 or 970-493-3741

WEB SITES
www.jivecats.com
Site for Fort Collins swing dancers

http://lamar.colostate.edu/~swing
Homepage for Colorado State University
swing club

CONNECTICUT

NIGHTSPOTS
Cinedrome 360 Nightclub
Foxwoods Resort and Casino
Route 2 near Norwich
860-312-4231
Live music and dancing on Sundays; age
21+ only

Connecticut Swing Dance Society
AMC Hall
University of New Haven
420 Orange Avenue
West Haven
203-458-6772 or 203-985-1112

Hartford Swing Dance
West Hartford Town hall
50 South Main Street
West Hartford
860-649-0482
Live music and dancing the first Friday
of the month

Shoreline Swing Dance Society
East Lyme Community Center
Society Road
East Lyme
860-739-0697
*www.havetodance.com/
    shorelineswing*
Live music and dancing the third
Saturday of every month

Wethersfield American Legion Hall
275 Main Street
Wethersfield
860-563-8723
Thursday dances, plus Swing Jam fourth
Saturday of the month

DANCE CLASSES
Jane Dumont aka Jitterbug Jane
Hartford area and also New Haven
www.havetodance.com/danceworks
860-267-0613

WEB SITES
*http://www.havetodance.com/
    dancect.html*
Dance venues and instructors
throughout the state

*www.havetodance.com/
    hartfordswing*
Jane Dumont's weekly listings

www.ctswing.org
Homepage of the Connecticut Swing
Dance Society

FLORIDA

▶ **Melbourne**

WEB SITE
*http://ddi.digital.net/ ~ gtjj/
    swing.html*
Swing info for all of Brevard County

▶ **Miami–Fort Lauderdale**

NIGHTSPOTS
Dezerland Hotel
American Classics Lounge
8701 Collins Avenue
Miami Beach
305-865-6661
Tuesday dance sponsored by the South
Florida Swing Dance Society

Manray Lounge
4301 Federal Highway
Pompano Beach
954-788-2345
Miami's main retro club has lessons and
dancing for an 18+ crowd on both
Wednesdays and Fridays

O'Hara's Jazz Café
1903 Hollywood Boulevard
Hollywood
954-925-2555
Afternoon lessons and dancing
(small floor), on Sundays

DANCE CLASSES
Alfred "Mr. Dance"
954-733-2623

Randy Atlas
305-756-5037

Angela Nuran Gokturk
954-234-3262

WEB SITE
www.swingsouthflorida.com
South Florida Swing Dance Society,
info on Miami and Fort Lauderdale

▶ **Orlando**

NIGHTSPOTS
Atlantic Dance
Boardwalk Resort
Disney World
www.atlanticdance.com
407-939-2444
Swings seven nights a week in this
spacious period-looking nightclub;
live music Friday through Monday,
lessons Tuesday through Thursday

House of Blues
Downtown Disney, West Side
1490 Buena Vista Drive
407-934-2222
Features occasional concerts by
national acts

DANCE CLASSES
Rhythmic Harmony Productions
Alberto and Selena Hoyos
407-465-0617

Dancin' III
Altamonte Springs
407-261-1300

WEB SITES
www.neoSwing.com/orlando/
The most complete swing site for
Orlando

www.angelfire.com/fl/fourtree
In-depth list of swing nights in Orlando

▶ **Tallahassee**

WEB SITE
www.geocities.com/BourbonStreet/
    Delta/7610
All the news on swing in northwest
Florida

▶ **Tampa–Saint Petersburg**

WEB SITES
www.swingnews.com
http://members.xoom.com/Bigsby
http://www.geocities.com/
    SunsetStrip/Stadium/3409/
Guides to events and bands in the
Tampa area

GEORGIA

▶ Atlanta Area

NIGHTSPOTS
Blue Moon Supper Club
1255 Johnson Ferry Road
Marietta
770-579-3131
Wednesday and Sunday night dancing

Club Anytime
1055 Peachtree Street
404-607-8050
Friday and Saturday nights

Hot Rod's Grill
4805 Highway 29
770-638-1954
Mondays and Wednesdays

Masquerade
695 North Avenue NE
404-577-8178
Lessons and DJ dancing on Sundays

Swinger's Club
3049 Peachtree Road
Buckhead
404-816-9931
Swing on Mondays through Saturdays,
18+ Mondays and Tuesdays

DANCE CLASSES
Atlanta Dance World
770-604-9900

City Lights Dance Studio
770-451-5461

WEB SITES
www.swingtown.org
Weekly listing of bands and bars

www.dragonnet.net/swing
The homepage of Atlanta Swing

ILLINOIS

▶ Champagne-Urbana

WEB SITE
http://guava.physics.uiuc.edu/
   ~tychay/swing
Homepage of the Champagne-Urbana
Swing Society

▶ Chicago Area

NIGHTSPOTS
C-Shop Java Jive
Reynolds Club Building
University of Chicago
5706 South University Avenue
312-409-4911
Friday dance presented by the Chicago
Swing Dance Society

Frankie's Blue Room
16 West Chicago Avenue
Naperville
630-416-4898
Dancing four nights a week, mix of DJ
and live music

Green Mill
4802 North Broadway
773-878-5552
Live swing music Tuesdays and
Thursdays

Liquid
1997 North Clybourn Avenue
773-528-3400
Chicago's most reliable swing nightclub
with dancing up to six nights a week

Willowbrook Ballroom
8900 South Archer Avenue
Willow Springs
708-839-1000
Live music and lessons on Wednesdays
(with the Rhythm Rockets) and Sundays

DANCE CLASSES

Chicago Dance Ballroom
3660 West Irving Park
ballroom@chicagodance.com
773-267-3411

Chicago Swing Half-Breeds
www.slohand.com
312-409-0039

Hep Cat Swing
Joe Gerrits and Joey Honsa
www.hepcatswing.com
773-929-1067

Swing Out Chicago
www.chicagoswing.com
773-782-1927

WEB SITES

http://rainbow.uchicago.edu/~ykim/
Chicago Swing Dance Society homepage

*www2.uic.edu/stud_orgs/sports/
swingit/*
Swing events in Chicago

www.swingset.net
Monthly calendar of live swing music
appearances in the Chicago area with
great links

www.hail.icestorm.net/chicagoswing
Events listings for Chicago and national
band schedules

IOWA

▶ **Des Moines**

NIGHTSPOT

Val Air Ballroom
301 Ashworth Road
West Des Moines
515-223-6152
Monday classes and dances on
Thursdays on an eight-thousand-square-
foot floor in this 1939 art deco ballroom

DANCE CLASSES

Jennifer Malcom
Keepondancing@hotmail.com
515-223-6152 (Val Air Ballroom)
515-943-2220
800-481-8488 (within Iowa)

Randy and Sarah Reid
515-274-4676

WEB SITES

www.swingdesmoines.com
The Swing Des Moines homepage

*http://members.aol.com/jmsracing/
eiaswing*
The swing guide for eastern Iowa (Iowa
City and Cedar Rapids)

KANSAS

▶ **Kansas City Area**

NIGHTSPOTS

Grand Emporium
3832 Main Street
Kansas City, Missouri
816-531-1504
www.grandemporium.com
Tex Houston and Kurt Wegner teach
every Tuesday, with a mix of rockabilly
and swing

Raoul's Velvet Room
7222 West 199th Street
Johnson County
913-469-0466
Wednesday night swing dancing to the
sounds of the Dave Stevens Swing Band

The Swing Set at Bottleneck
737 New Hampshire
Lawrence
785-841-5483
Sunday live music nights run by the
Swing Set

DANCE CLASSES
Cats Corner
www.kcdance.com/catscorner

Jean Denney
816-640-2564

Frankie Hoang
913-683-4275

Alan Clements
913-299-3517

Tex Houston
816-561-3424

Kansas City Swing Dance Club
6101 Martway
Mission
913-831-7964

WEB SITE
www.kcdance.com
Excellent site for everything swing (and all dance) in Kansas City

MARYLAND

▶ **Baltimore**

NIGHTSPOTS
Friday Night Swing Dance Club
www.erols.com/hepcat
410-583-7337
Swing club with dances and live music most Fridays, some Saturdays; location varies

Swing Baltimore
410-377-7410
Swing dances every other Saturday; call for location

DANCE CLASSES
Friday Night Swing Dance Club
410-583-7337

WEB SITES
www.charm.net/~dadamia
Links to other swing sites in Baltimore

www.swingbaltimore.org
Web site for Swing Baltimore

*http://home.earthlink.net/~glacial/
     swing*
Swing Crossroads, a Web site for Baltimore info

MASSACHUSETTS

▶ **Boston Area**

NIGHTSPOTS
Boston Swing Dance Network
Saint James Armenian Church
465 Mount Auburn Street
Watertown
617-924-6603
Boston's swing dance society's once-a-month dance

Johnny D's Uptown Lounge
17 Holland Street, Davis Square
Somerville
617-776-2004
Live music on Mondays

Ken's Place
The First Baptist Church
5 Magazine Street
Cambridge
Bands and dancing every Tuesday

The Roxy
279 Tremont Street
617-338-7699
This grand 1920s ballroom boasts a thirty-thousand-square-foot dance floor and features national acts on its Friday swing nights

Upstairs Lounge
69 Lancaster Street
North Station
781-458-3521
Swingers' hangout, with dancing on
Thursdays

DANCE CLASSES
Best Foot Forward Dance Studio
Sara Brodsky
*http://www.havetodance.com/
    bestfootforward*
617-522-1444

Boston Swing Dance Network
Elks Lodge
268 Arlington Street
Watertown
www.bostonswingdance.com
617-924-6003

Dancing Feats Studio
190 Oak Street
Newton
http://www.dancingfeats.com/
617-52-SWING

Hop to the Beat Dance Studio
Tony and Aurelie Tye
http://www.hoptothebeat.com/
508-435-2363

Rugcutters Dance Studio
Ron Gursky
*http://www.havetodance.com/
    rugcutters/*
617-923-0220

Tempo Dance Center
Gail Rundlett
*http://www.havetodance.com/
    tempodc.html*
617-783-5467

WEB SITES
www.havetodance.com
Listings of all dance venues in the Boston
area, along with names of instructors
and places to practice; includes weekly
and daily calendar

www.totalswing.com
Guide to events in the Boston area plus
northern New England

MICHIGAN

▶ **Ann Arbor**

DANCE CLASSES
Michael Finegan
Ann Arbor Dance Classics
734-975-9055

Joyce Stoughton
734-973-2575

▶ **Detroit Area**

NIGHTSPOTS
Clutch Cargo
65 East Huron Street
Pontiac
248-333-2362
Swinging the weekend on Friday and
Saturday

Token Lounge
28949 Joy Road
Westland
734-513-5030
Call for details

Velvet Lounge
29 South Saginaw
Pontiac
248-334-7411
Mondays, Tuesdays, Fridays, and
Saturdays swingout

DANCE CLASSES
Paulette Brockington
hoofer2@ibm.net
313-869-9385

Barry Douglas
http://www.i-hustle.com
1-888-IHUSTLE

WEB SITES
www.danceaway.com
Dance site for all of Michigan

http://hometown.aol.com/dancealert/
index.html
All kinds of dancing in the Detroit–Ann Arbor area

MINNESOTA

▶ **Minneapolis–Saint Paul**

NIGHTSPOTS
Famous Dave's
3001 Hennepin Avenue
Minneapolis
612-822-9900
Let the Senders send you on Wednesdays

Fine Line Music Café
318 First Avenue North
Minneapolis
612-338-8100
Hop to the sounds of Vic Volare and the Volare Lounge Orchestra on Tuesdays

Lee's Liquor Lounge
101 Glenwood Ave
Minneapolis
612-338-9491
Free lessons plus the Jaztronauts on Mondays and Wednesdays

Mario's Keller Bar
2300 University Avenue
Minneapolis
612-781-3860
Free lessons and DJ on Sundays, live bands on Tuesdays (rockabilly)

Wabasha Street Caves
215 South Wabasha Street
Saint Paul
651-224-1191
Dancing inside actual caves, a former Capone hangout, on Thursdays, all ages

DANCE CLASSES
Cindy Geiger and Terry Gardner
612-722-9976

Land O'Loon Lindy Hoppers
612-920-7648

WEB SITES
www.tcswing.com
Listing of everything swing in the Twin Cities

www.i-swing.com
Calendar listing of local swing nights with news updates

MISSOURI

▶ **Saint Louis**

NIGHTSPOTS
Blueberry Hill
6504 Delmar
314-727-0880
Call for details

The Casa Loma Ballroom
3354 Iowa Avenue
314-664-8000
Lessons and dancing Wednesdays

Jukebox Party Club
2140 Schuetz Road
314-993-5449
Tuesdays (Saint Louis's Imperial swing)

DANCE CLASSES
Just Dancing
Jane Humphrey
Woods Mill Road and Manchester
Manchester
314-227-7202

WEB SITES
*http://digdug.dar.net/swingme/
   swingin/main.html*
Swing Me Saint Louis's guide to dancing
in the Show-Me state

*http://members.aol.com/stlballrm/
   dring.htm*
Links to all types of dance venues in the
Saint Louis area

*http://www.rescomp.wustl.edu/
   ~ballroom/*
Washington University's Dance Club
offers swing and some Latin dance
classes on most Sundays

NEVADA

▶ **Las Vegas Area**

NIGHTSPOTS
The Beach
365 Convention Center Drive
702-731-1925
The Sinn City Daddies, plus lessons, on
Tuesdays

Bellagio
Fontana Lounge
3600 Las Vegas Boulevard South
702-693-7075
888-987-7111
The coolest spot in town, with Jump, Jive,
n' Wail performing daily except Mondays

Desert Inn
Starlight Lounge
3145 Las Vegas Boulevard South
702-733-4444
Great dance floor, occasional swing
bands

New York, New York
The Big Apple Lounge
3790 Las Vegas Boulevard South
702-740-6969
Occasional swing bands; call for events

Sunset Station
1301 West Sunset Road
Henderson
702-547-7777
Live music on Tuesdays

DANCE CLASSES
Arthur Murray Dance Studio
Maryland Parkway at Harmon
Amurray@achieve4U.com
702-650-5275

WEB SITES
www.ilv.com/swing/
Full info on the Vegas swing scene

www.wizard.com/~thecage
Hip-looking guide to the city

NEW HAMPSHIRE
AND VERMONT

WEB SITES
*www.databasewebworks.com/
   swingdance*
The National and New England Swing
Dance Server homepage

www.savoystyle.org/index.html
New Hampshire and Vermont's Upper
Valley Swing Dance Network

NEW JERSEY

NIGHTSPOTS
KatManDu
50 Riverview
Route 29/Executive Park
Trenton
609-393-7300
Lessons and dancing on Sundays

The Leopard Lounge
Club Bene
Route 35
South Amboy
732-727-3000
Live music on Saturdays

Trump Marina
Huron Avenue and Brigantine
  Boulevard
Atlantic City
609-441-2000
800-365-8786
Booking some of the scene's best swing
bands; call for nights

WEB SITE
www.njswing.com
Information on dancing and music in
northern New Jersey

NEW MEXICO

WEB SITE
www.highaltitudeswing.com
Events and classes in both Albuquerque
and Santa Fe

NEW YORK

▶ **Buffalo**

WEB SITE
www.nywebshop.com/lindyhop
Homepage of the Buffalo Swing Dance
Network

▶ **Long Island**

WEB SITE
www.sdli.org/index.html
The homepage of Swing Dance Long
Island

▶ **Manhattan**

NIGHTSPOTS
Cotton Club
656 West 125th Street
212-663-7980
Monday and Thursday night swing
dancing in Harlem at this re-creation of
the famous club

Irving Plaza
17 Irving Place
212-777-6817
Long-running Sunday-night party
sponsored by the New York Swing Dance
Society

Rodeo Bar
375 Third Avenue
212-683-6500
East Coast and Western swing; call ahead
for schedule

The Supper Club
240 West Forty-Seventh Street
212-921-1940
Art deco dance palace hops after
midnight on Fridays and Saturdays

Swing 46 Jazz and Supper Club
349 West Forty-Sixth Street
212-262-9554
New York's only seven-nights-a-week
swing club; home to George Gee and His
Make-Believe Ballroom Orchestra

Wells Restaurant
2249 Seventh Avenue
212-234-0700
Uptown landmark serves up chicken,
waffles, and the Harlem Renaissance
Orchestra every Monday night;
reservations recommended

Windows on the World
1 World Trade Center
212-524-7011
More than one hundred stories above
the financial district, this club offers
spectacular views and dancing Fridays
and Saturdays

DANCE CLASSES
Margaret Batiuchok
Cofounder of the New York Swing
Dance Society
238 East Fourteenth Street
212-598-0154

Sandra Cameron Dance Studio
20 Cooper Square
212-674-0505

Dance Manhattan
39 West Nineteenth Street
212-807-0802

Nathalie Gomes
Yuval Hod
Hop, Swing, and a Jump
132 Crosby Street, Second Floor
www.hopswingjump.com
212-343-8515

Shall We Dance
200 Church Street
212-566-1081

Stepping Out
1780 Broadway
212-245-5200

WEB SITES

www.yehoodi.com
New York's most stylish on-line event guide

www.swingout-ny.com
A comprehensive listing of teachers and events

www.users.interport.net/ ~ zebra/ nysds/index.html#bottom
New York Swing Dance Society homepage

www.nyc-swing.com
Guide to events sponsored by NYC promoter "Lo-Fi" Lee Sobel (hotline: 212-462-3250)

▶ **Rochester**

WEB SITE

www.rit.edu/ ~ swingwww/
Homepage of the Rochester Institute of Technology swing club

▶ **Syracuse**

WEB SITE

http://syrswingdance.org
Homepage of the Syracuse Swing Dance Society

NORTH CAROLINA

▶ **Charlotte**

NIGHTSPOT

Swing 1000
1000 Central Avenue
704-334-4443
Swing supper club and restaurant, Tuesdays and Wednesdays

OHIO

▶ **Akron**

NIGHTSPOT

Sloopy's
1232 Weathervane Lane
330-869-2855
Call for details

DANCE CLASSES

Anita Converse
330-869-2855

▶ **Cincinnati**

NIGHTSPOTS

Havana Martini Club
580 Walnut Street
513-651-2800
Swings on Fridays

Jefferson Hall
1150 Main Street
513-723-9008
Live music and lessons on Wednesdays plus a monthly dance contest

Swing Lounge
1203 Main Street
513-665-4677
The city's original club offers live music Thursday through Saturday; lessons on Thursdays

DANCE CLASSES
Cincinnati Lindy Circle
Erich Gansmuller
KandE@ix.netcom.com

Rhonda Flora
513-533-4379

David Stewart
937-298-5770

WEB SITES
http://come.to/cincyswing
Cincinnati Swing Dancing listings and
more

http://w3.one.net/ ~ mslentz/swing/
Vertical Expressions: a guide to bands,
clubs, and more

► Cleveland Area

NIGHTSPOTS
Dick's Last Resort
1096 Old River Road
216-241-1234
Live music on Sundays

Grogshop
1265 Coventry Street
Cleveland Heights
216-321-5588
Not much room to dance but they book
swing bands

Spy Bar
1261 West Sixth Street
216-621-7907
Music and lessons on Thursdays

Wilberts
Corner of Saint Claire and Ninth
216-771-2583
Books occasional swing bands; call for
information

DANCE CLASSES
Get Hep Swing
Valerie Salstrom and Joel Plys
216-883-4519

Karl Knopp
330-626-2129

► Columbus

NIGHTSPOTS
Barrister Hall
560 South High Street
614-621-1213
Live music and free lessons on
Wednesdays

Counterfeit Heist
2619 North High
614-261-0043
Swing events approximately once a
month

Jitterbug Café
5200 Riding Club
614-866-5195
Swing meets line dancing and karaoke

94th Aero Squadron
5030 Sawyer Road
614-237-8887
Rick Brunetto's Big Band plays every
Thursday

DANCE CLASSES
Jessica Tupa and Chul
614-421-7338

Ballroom Plus Dance Studio
5815 Emporium Square
614-891-0807

WEB SITE
*http://205.133.80.114/music/
    sugarfoot/*
The resource for swing in the capital

► **Dayton**

NIGHTSPOTS
El Diablo
135 East Second Street
937-331-9096
Leopard-skin and tiki-themed club with
a suspended dance floor, swings on
Wednesdays and Fridays

Yellow Rose Night Club
852 Water Tower Lane
937-866-7765
Longest-running dance in town, on
Wednesdays

DANCE CLASSES
David Stewart
937-298-5770

WEB SITES
www.eldiablolounge.com
Guide pages for the city

*http://www.siscom.net/ ~ scot/swing/
    main.html*
Homepage of Dayton Swing

► **Toledo**

NIGHTSPOT
CitiLounge
217 North Superior Street
419-242-2484
Open seven nights a week, lessons
Mondays, live music weekends

OREGON

► **Portland**

NIGHTSPOTS
Berbati's Pan
213 Southwest Third and Ankeny
503-248-4579
Live music and lessons on Tuesdays

Crystal Ballroom
1332 West Burnside
503-225-0047
Swingers pack this huge, gorgeous dance
floor on Sundays

DANCE CLASSES
Jeff Freeman
503-221-1613

Denise Steele
www.thejointisjumpin.com
541-543-4443

Guy Wallman and Carrie Whipple
503-236-8289

WEB SITE
http://swingout.net
The central site for swing info in Portland

PENNSYLVANIA

► **Philadelphia Area**

NIGHTSPOTS
Café Chicane
15 South High Street
Westchester
610-696-6660
Thursday swing lessons at this swank
bar

Edge Restaurant
4100 Main Street
Manayunk
215-483-4100
Free lessons and dancing to live music
on Wednesdays

The Five Spot
5 Bank Street
215-574-0070
The house band at Philly's premier club
serves up swing five nights a week

Lehigh Valley Swing Dance Society
Fearless Fire Company Starlite
  Ballroom
Front and Susquehanna Streets
Allentown
610-974-8804
Sponsors a dance the third Saturday of
the month

Philadelphia Swing Dance Society
Commodore Barry Club
6815 Emlen Street at Carpenter Lane
215-843-8051
Lessons and live music twice a month,
every other Saturday

DANCE CLASSES
Bob Butryn
215-477-0997

Donna Reinhart
215-542-0463

Jane Leibman
215-576-0345

Jim Zaccaria
www.swingon.com
609-953-9248

Jacob Morris
www.swankdaddy.com

Ashley Paine
215-568-3045

Professional Dance Academy
Monique Legare and Morley Leyton
215-659-0917

WEB SITES
www.swingdance.org
Philadelphia Swing Dance Society
homepage

www.pennsylvania65000.com
Swing calendar for Philadelphia, on-line
magazine, and lots of other links

www.swankdaddy.com
Another listing of Philadelphia nightspots
and lessons

▶ **Pittsburgh**

NIGHTSPOTS
Chauncy's
Station Square on Carson Street
412-232-0601
Long-running night with live music by Dr.
Zoot on Wednesdays

Edgewood Club
1 Pennwood Avenue
412-731-3443
Lessons and dancing every second and
fourth Sunday of the month

The Pollinator Lounge
At the Beehive
Oakland
3807 Forbes Avenue
412-687-9428
Sunday night lessons and DJ dancing

Wightman School Community
  Building
Wightman and Solway
412-341-0292
Saturday lessons and dancing, all ages

DANCE CLASSES
Ron Buchanan
Swing Pittsburgh
622 College Avenue
412-441-1441

Bob Dunlap
412-341-0292

John E. Hill
412-243-4639

WEB SITES
http://www.pittsburghswing.com
Fun site, lots of pictures and good
calendar of events

http://swinginstyle.netwebz.com/
Another swing guide for the city

RHODE ISLAND

NIGHTSPOTS
The Call
15 Elbow Street
Providence
401-751-2255
Thursday and Sunday swing dances

Hepcats
Auburn American Legion Hall
7 Legion Way
Cranston
401-727-3385
Live music and lessons the fourth
Saturday of the month

Swing Newport
Elks Lodge
Corner of Bellevue Avenue and
    Pelham Street
Newport
401-846-0815
Monthly dances with live music and
lessons; call for schedule

DANCE CLASSES
Jeff Allen
dancebook@earthlink.net
401-828-2273
Based in Cranston and teaches at various
locations in Rhode Island, Connecticut,
and Massachusetts

Ed Slattery
508-336-4617

Sarah Sloane
http://rihepcats.webjump.com
401-727-3385
Teaches in Providence, Kingston, and
Cranston, Rhode Island, and Worcester,
Massachusetts

WEB SITES
www.havetodance.com/danceri
Complete information on teachers and
where to dance in the state

www.ridance.com
All things dance-related in Rhode Island

TENNESSEE

▶ **Knoxville**

WEB SITE
http://web.utk.edu/ ~ ksda
Homepage of the Knoxville Swing Dance
Association

▶ **Memphis**

NIGHTSPOTS
Café Bizmarck
704 North Highland
901-452-8511
Lessons and live music on Saturdays

Elvis Presley's Memphis
126 Beale Street
901-527-9036
Live music and dancing on Saturdays

Hi-Tone
1913 Poplar Avenue
901-278-TONE
Lessons and live music (with the New
Memphis Hepcats) on Mondays, age 18+

In the Grove
2865 Walnut Grove
901-458-9955
Supper club with dancing every night,
lessons on Thursdays, age 18+

DANCE CLASSES
D'Arcy Bryan-Wilson
Dkmurphy@juno.com

Sean Leone
901-527-4265

Neil Gallagher
901-757-1451

Chris and Jen Steinmetz
901-452-8511

Ballet Memphis
901-737-7322

Ron and Carrie Griffin
601-393-4914

WEB SITE
http://members.xoom.com/
  SwingMemphis
Updated listing of all swing nights in
Memphis

TEXAS

▶ **Austin**

NIGHTSPOTS
Carousel Lounge
1110 East Fifty-Second Street
512-452-6790
Lessons by local troupe Four on the
Floor on Wednesdays

Caucus Club
912 Red River
512-472-2873
Live music four nights a week at Austin's
central swing club

Continental Club
1315 South Congress Avenue
512-441-2444
Occasional live swing music; call for
schedule

Jake's Seafood and Steaks
3825 Lake Austin Boulevard
512-477-5253
Live music on Wednesday nights at this
nightclub/restaurant

DANCE CLASSES
Four on the Floor
Lessons in Austin and San Antonio
www.fouronthefloor.com
512-453-3889

WEB SITES
www.fouronthefloor.com
Austin's home of swing and Lindy Hop
(with info on San Antonio too)

www.austindance.org/swing
This dance guide includes information
on swing

▶ **Dallas**

Red Jacket
3606 Greenville
214-823-8333
Live music and lessons, by Smiley's
Lindy Hoppers, on Thursdays, with
house band Johnny Reno and the
Lounge Kings

The Sand Castle
2629 West NW Highway #330
214-956-8282
Swing six nights a week, Tuesdays
through Sundays

Sons of Hermann Hall
3414 Elm Street at Exposition
214-747-4422
All ages dancing, with lessons, on
Wednesdays

DANCE CLASSES

Jules Tulloch
Tulloch@airmail.net
214-320-3258

Smiley's Lindy Hoppers
Elaine Hewlett and Jeff Miller
upswing@rocketmail.com
214-922-7850

WEB SITE

www.dsds.org
Web site for Dallas Swing Dance Society
— comprehensive listing of Dallas scene
with links to clubs and teachers

▶ **Houston Area**

NIGHTSPOTS

Melody Club Ballroom
3027 Crossview
713-785-5301
Sunday and Thursday dances sponsored
by Houston Swing Dance Society

SSQQ Dance Studio
4803 Bissonnet
Bellaire
713-861-1906
Lessons and dancing on Mondays

DANCE CLASSES

Houston Swing Dance Society
hsds@usa.net
713-662-3861

SSQQ Dance Studio
dance@ssqq.com
713-861-1906

WEB SITE

www.hsds.org
Web site for Houston Swing Dance
Society — listing of clubs and lessons
in Houston

WASHINGTON, D.C., AREA

NIGHTSPOTS

America Restaurant
Tyson's I Shopping Center
Junction of Route 123 and Route 7
Tyson's Corner, Virginia
703-847-6607
Live music and dancing Fridays, DJ
Sundays

Chevy Chase Ballroom
5207 Wisconsin Avenue NW
202-363-8344
Home base of Tom Koener and Debra
Sternberg, the deans of swing dancing in
D.C.; DJ and dancing on Mondays

Lulu's Club Mardi Gras
1217 Twenty-Second Street NW
202-861-5858
Lessons and dancing on Wednesdays

Nick's
642 South Pickett Street
Alexandria, Virginia
703-751-8900
Swing dancing all weekend long on two
dance floors, Friday and Saturday;
Hollywood-style swing on Thursdays

Spanish Ballroom at Glen Echo
7300 MacArthur Boulevard
Glen Echo, Maryland
301-340-9732
Dances three Saturdays a month (first
and third sponsored by the Washington
Swing Dance Committee) in this
spacious, gracious ballroom

Vienna Tap Room
146 East Maple Avenue
Vienna, Virginia
703-255-6800
Tuesday Lindy and Wednesday jitterbug
sponsored by the Potomac Swing Dance
Club

DANCE CLASSES

Donna Barker
Ken Haltenhoff
www.erols.com/swing4me
703-978-0375

Fidgety Feet
At the DC Dance Collective
202-362-7244

Flying Feet
Ellen Engle
Marc Shepanek
www.erols.com/flyfeet
301-299-8728

Tom Koerner and Debra Sternberg
www.gottaswing.com
703-527-6734

John "Psychoboy" McCalla
www.psychoboy.com
410-875-9147

Frank Morra and Carole Berghers
202-363-2239
www.jitterbuzz.com

WEB SITES

www.jitterbuzz.com
Frank Morra and Carole Berghers's
extensive site; not only local and
national listings but swing album
reviews too

www.gottaswing.com
Listing of events sponsored by Tom
Koerner and Debra Sternberg

www.wsdc.org
Homepage of the Washington Swing
Dance Committee

WASHINGTON

▶ **Seattle Area**

NIGHTSPOTS

Century Ballroom
915 East Pine Street, Capitol Hill
206-324-7263
Beautiful classic ballroom offers swing
nights on Mondays, Wednesdays, every
other Friday, and some Saturdays

Club Rat Pack
The Aristocrats Club
220 Fourth Avenue South
206-748-9779
Swing meets lounge (with dress code)
on Wednesdays

Fenix Club
315 Second Avenue South
206-467-1111
"Club HiDeHo," Seattle's original swing
night, on Mondays

Seattle Center Saturday Night Big
    Band Dance
Center House, 305 Harrison Street
206-684-0765
Wednesdays all-ages dance; Saturdays
lessons and dancing

Showbox
1426 First Avenue
206-628-3151
Call for details

Swingin' Saturdays at the Savoy
The Eagles Hall
5600 Twenty-Fourth Avenue NW
Ballard
206-784-4390
Live music, lessons, and dancing on
Saturdays, with a huge dance floor

DANCE CLASSES
Dave Atkinson
www.daswingdance.com
206-782-3698

Ron Bolin
206-464-9500

Keith Hughes
206-547-2721

Living Traditions
206-781-1238

Savoy Swing Club
206-547-7676

Tanya Surface and Theo Davis
206-523-1221

WEB SITES
www.lindyhype.com
Guide pages for Seattle

*http://students.washington.edu/
    swingkd/*
University of Washington swing kids
page

*http://www.cs.washington.edu/
    homes/paul/sk/*
Swing Seattle links page

www.eskimo.com/~savoy
Homepage of the Savoy Swing Club

www.bluelizard.com/csl/
DJ Leslie Price's Cat Swingin' Lounge
guide to swing in Seattle, with great links

www.nwrain.net/~paralex/jk/
The guide pages for Tacoma

WISCONSIN

▶ **Madison**

WEB SITE
www.blueroomrevue.com
Mad City Swing's guide pages

Milwaukee

DANCE CLASSES
Jumpin' Jive Club
Maureen Majeski
414-54-SWING

International

AUSTRALIA

WEB SITES
http://members.xoom.com/asds
The Australian Swing Dance Society's
countrywide listings

http://home.vicnet.au/ ~ swing
Melbourne swing information

www.swingout.com.au
Sydney Lindy Hop page

CANADA

▶ **Montreal**

NIGHTSPOTS
Blue Sax
7062 St-Laurent Boulevard
514-272-9990
Swing night every other Friday; fifties
atmosphere

Jello Bar
151 Ontario East
514-285-2621
Mix of DJ and live music on Mondays,
with free lessons; famous for their
martinis

Lion d'Or
1676 Ontario East
514-526-6849
DJ and live music every third Friday of
the month

Swing Ring
4848 St-Laurent Boulevard
Biggest dance floor in Montreal;
Saturdays

Tokyo Bar
3709 St-Laurent Boulevard
514-842-6838
Mix of DJ and live music on Wednesdays

DANCE CLASSES
Kurt Hemmings and Cleo Binette
Swing Express Dance School
swingexpress@hotmail.com
514-285-4594

Hi-Ball
Sean Metcalf
smetcalf@total.net
514-851-2916

Miss Wolff's Jiving School
www.jiving.com
514-CUB-CAVE

WEB SITES
www.swinginmontreal.com
Great-looking retro site on the Montreal scene

www.montrealswing.com
Information on Montreal Swing Dance Society . . . in French

www.swingexpress.com
Site run by Cleo Binette and Kurt Hemmings

▶ **Saskatchewan**

WEB SITES
www.swingkids.com
www.angelfire.com/sk/hepcatz
Events in the Saskatoon area

▶ **Toronto**

NIGHTSPOTS
The Palais Royale Ballroom
1601 Lake Shore Boulevard West
416-532-6210
Call for details

Reservoir Lounge
52 Wellington Street East
416-955-0887
Dinner, dancing, and live music Tuesday through Saturday

DANCE CLASSES
Peter Renzland
peter@dancing.org
http://dancing.org
416-323-1300

Martin Nantel and Jane Jedlovsky
aristocatsdance@yahoo.com
http://www.jedor.com/aristocats.html
416-208-3279

Lisa Jacobs
swing@interlog.com
http://www.interlog.com/~swing
416-693-0125

WEB SITES
*http://dancing.org/
   toronto.swing.html*
The city's guide to upcoming events and local teachers

http://www.dancing.org/tsds/
Homepage of the Toronto Swing Dance Society

▶ **Vancouver**

WEB SITE
www.bluelizard.com
The guide to dancing and bands in British Columbia

FRANCE

▶ **Paris**

WEB SITES
www.danse-a-2.com/paris/
Guide, in English and French, to *le jive à Paris*

http://perso.cybercable.fr/bosset/
More swing, *en Français*

GERMANY

▶ **Munich**

WEB SITES
www.swing.org
www.swinging-world.com/sww/
Guide to events in Munich

JAPAN

▶ **Tokyo**

WEB SITE
www.impetus.ne.jp
Homepage of the Tokyo Swing Dance
Society

NETHERLANDS

WEB SITE
www.jive55.nl/
Jive dance in the Netherlands

NEW ZEALAND

WEB SITE
http://members.tripod.com/
~jitterbugs
Events and classes in and around
Auckland

SINGAPORE

WEB SITE
www.jittersbugs.com/
Champion dancer Sing Lim's "Jitterbugs
Singapore" site

SWEDEN

WEB SITE
www.swedish-swing-society.a.se/
Homepage of the Swedish Swing Society
(established in 1978)

SWITZERLAND

WEB SITES
www.swing.ch/
The Swiss Swing Dance Society's site
includes an international events listing

UNITED KINGDOM

▶ **London Area**

NIGHTSPOTS
Hellzapoppin' Club
Cecil Sharp House
2 Regent's Park Road
Camden
0171-485-2206
Once a month on Saturday, 8:00 P.M. to
midnight, DJ

Notre Dame Hall
6 Leicester Place
0171-734-4019
Jitterbug on Wednesdays, 7:30 to 11:30
P.M.; DJ and occasional live music

Saturday Night Fish Fry
Windeyer Hall
46 Cleveland Street, near Telecom
   Tower
0171-359-2800 (LeJive hotline)
Swing dances, sponsored by LeJive, the
second Saturday each month; "Zoot Suit
Riot" lessons and dancing every Tuesday

Stompin' at the 100 Club
100 Oxford Street
0171-636-0933
Live music and DJ on Mondays, run by
the London Swing Dance Society

DANCE CLASSES

Robert Austin and Claire Hilliard
www.lejive.com
0171-359-2800

Jane Eliot and Martin Ellis
www.swingland.com
0171-357-6891

Ryan Francois and Jenny Thomas
www.zoots.demon.co.uk
0181-761-0843

Julie Oram
0181-809-5507

WEB SITES

www.swingland.com
Great Lindy Hop Web site covering classes, DJs, bands, and fashions

www.jivenet.org
"Modern jive" Web site for Jitterbugs, London's Swing and Lindy Hop Club. Site includes *Swing Time* on-line magazine and complete listing of all swing events in London

www.lejive.com
Web site for LeJive's many events throughout the United Kingdom

Further Information

SWING WEB SITES

Swing rules on the Web. For the easiest entrée to the retro Internet world, just go to the Swing, Swing, Swing (In a Ring) Web site, *www.webring.org/ cgi-bin/webring?ring=daddyo&list,* which lists more than 240 swing sites. Here are some of the most popular individual pages for music, dance, fashion, news, and more.

General Sites

www.anyswinggoes.com
   Any Swing Goes: Swing lover Doug LeClair manages this site, which includes articles, an interesting news library, album reviews, and MP3 files.

www.eswing.com
   eSwing: Calendar of California swing events.

http://home.earthlink.net/~margiekate/swingspots.html
   Southern California Lindy Society: Margie Cormier's extensive information page includes band contact information, clothing resources, events in Southern California, fashion history, and more.

www.jitterbuzz.com
   Lindy Week Review: Frank Morra and Carole Berghers's Washington D.C.–based guide to the city's swing scene, also reports on the Midwest and features extensive links and information on vintage shopping nationwide.

www.neoswing.com
   neoSwing: Information on bands, style, and CDs, plus chat listings.

www.nocturne.com/swing
   The Los Angeles Swing Times: Karen Wilson's guide to the nightlife of Los Angeles, plus record reviews, links to swing radio shows, and hairdo tips.

www.pennsylvania65000.com
   Pennsylvania 6-5000: An extensive international database, with listings of bands, vintage clothing sources, nightclubs, DJ top ten lists, and *Swank Daddy,* an on-line swing magazine.

www.retroactive.com
   Retro: The Magazine of Classic Twentieth-Century Popular Culture: An
   on-line lifestyle magazine.

www.swingset.net
   Swing Set: A very comprehensive on-line guide for events in California,
   New York, Las Vegas, and Chicago. Search for events by club or band;
   look at band links and the swinguistics guide.

Dance Sites

www.cs.cornell.edu/Info/People/aswin/SwingDancing/Swing_Dancing.html
   The U.S. Swing Dance Server: This site features everything from articles
   on swing dancing to information on styles of dancing, how to do steps,
   and dance societies nationwide.

www.dancetv.com/tutorial/index.html
   Ballroom Dance Group: On-line instruction in the basics of such dances
   as East Coast swing, the waltz, and the foxtrot, as well as video and CD
   sales and links to other dancing sites.

www.databasewebworks.com/swingdance
   The National and New England Swing Dance Server: Features search
   options for finding swing events and teachers by state, as well as
   listings for champion swing dance teachers.

http://members.tripod.com/DeanCollins
   The Hollywood Jitterbugs: This club of street dancers is dedicated to
   preserving Hollywood-style Lindy.

www.5-6-7-8.com
   5678: The World of Social Dance: This site features articles, reviews,
   discussions, and event and club listings for those interested in all types
   of social dance, including swing.

www.halcyon.com/lindyhop/WLHF/wlhfa.html
   World Lindy Hop Federation Archives: Features information on
   Australia, London, Canada; current events; bios on famous dancers;
   movies with swing dancing; book guides; even a list of *Life* magazine
   issues with dance articles.

www.mernyk.org/ross/swing.html
   Ross Mernyk's Swing Dance Steps: Features cheat sheet guides to the
   moves of swing.

www.raper.com/dance/swing/clubs/usaclubs.html
  Raper's Dance Corner: A great list of swing dance clubs and societies across the country, as well as information on music, film, and television events.

http://members.tripod.com/~socalswing
  The Lindy Hop Preservation Society of America: This site includes an etiquette essay, Los Angeles club reviews, calendars, and other dance information.

Band Links

www.406hepcats.bukowski.com
  406 Hepcats: This on-line zine includes an amazing band links page featuring more than 224 groups.

http://members.aol.com/AP21/
  The Swinger's Links: Connections to the best swing band Web sites.

Music Sales

www.amazon.com
  Amazon: Surprisingly good selection of swing CDs.

www.driveentertainment.com
  Drive Entertainment Online: A great place to buy the music of the original swing era, from Bunny Berrigan to Charlie Barnet.

www.hepcatrecords.com
  Hepcat Records: The best source on-line for neoswing music and more.

http://swing-music.com
  Swing-Music: Swing tunes, plus videos, CDs, and books.

Music Sites

www.angelfire.com/pa/Chipperjones10/page6.html
  Chipper's Place: Features mpegs and wav files of music from new swing bands like the Squirrel Nut Zippers, Cherry Poppin' Daddies, and Royal Crown Revue.

www.nfo.net
  The BigBands Database: Features bios of hundreds of bands from the famous (Basie) to the not so famous (the Memo Bernabei Orchestra).

www.bigband-era.com/newsletter
  Swingin' Down the Lane: A Web site dedicated to keeping the big band sound alive.

www.jazzkc.org.links/jazzsocieties.htm
  Kansas City Jazz Ambassador magazine: Includes a comprehensive list of jazz societies around the United States.

http://garywooo1.simplenet.com/bigband.html
  GaryWooo1's Official MIDI Homepage: A nice collection of downloadable standards by such artists as Count Basie, Louis Prima, Duke Ellington, and Tommy Dorsey.

Usenet Groups

Alt.music.swing: A swing scene discussion forum.
Rec.arts.dance: Chat group with postings about swing dancing.

E-mail Lists

www.barflies.net
  Barflies: Royal Crown Revue's discussion list for all things swing.

www.newswing.com
  Swing Foundation: An organization promoting the heritage of swing. It also runs a newsy swing list.

Lingo

www.vex.net/~buff/slang.html
  Twists, Slugs, and Roscoes: A Glossy of Hardboiled Slang: William Denton's lingo list, derived from pulp and detective novels.

www.swingordie.com/slang
  Lee Press-on and the Nails: This band's Web site includes slang, from the jive of Cab Calloway to the lingo of the Rat Pack.

Fan Sites

http://www.angelfire.com/il/SgrDdyBoogie
  SugarDaddy's Rockabilly and Swing: A portal to many wonderful swing and rockabilly links.

http://members.tripod.com/swing_time
>*It's Swing Time:* Not only links but also advice on swing etiquette and recipes for the best cocktails.

www.sarahwilliams.com/swing
>*Get into the Swing:* Features listings of the best swing records, nightspots, swing history, and links to important swing sites.

Fashion Sites

www.bleyer.com
>*Bleyer:* A source for stylish and comfortable spectators, developed by and for Lindy Hoppers.

www.daddyos.com
>*Daddy-O's:* Collectibles inspired by fervent fifties nostalgia, including two-tone wingtips, bowling shirts, crinoline petticoats, and Betty Page Zippo lighters.

www.elpachuco.com
>*El Pachuco Zoot Suits:* A virtual zoot frenzy, this site out of Fullerton, California, offers custom-made elegant suits with all the trimmings.

www.geocities.com/wellesley/2457
>*Marci's Retro Style:* This page features information on hair styling and setting techniques from a bygone era.

www.katstyle.com
>*Katstyle:* Shoes, clothing, and collectibles, including a "white trash belt buckle" and "rearview mirror shrunken head."

www.kstarre.com
>*K Starre Designs:* In addition to dressing Michael Andrew, the lead singer of Swingerhead, Starre boasts a colorful collection of bloomers, ties, and adorable women's dresses.

www.murrayontravel.com/carolnolan
>*Men's Vintage Fashions:* Designer Carol Nolan offers custom-tailored "accurate reproductions of the fashions of the 20s, 30s and 40s."

www.stacyadams.com
>*Stacy Adams Swing:* One of the premier manufacturers of quality spectators; their "Dayton" style is a favorite of Big Bad Voodoo Daddy and Royal Crown Revue members.

www.suavecito.com
   Zoots by Suavecito: This Denver-based zoot suit designer offers sales
   and rentals of zoot suits, swing dresses, and accessories.

www.tumblindice.com
   Tumblin' Dice Creations: Retro-style shirts in leopard, zebra, two-tone,
   and flame designs.

www.zootsuitstore.com
   Zoot Suit Store: The name doesn't lie. This site, presented by Siegel's
   Clothing Superstore, offers scores of zoot suits, in custom fabrics, and
   lots of accessories.

http://www.panix.com/~tonto1/darrow/darrow2.html
www.davenportandco.com
www.geocities.com/~avintagec/
www.rustyzipper.com
www.tastefully-bizarre.com
www.thewasteland.com
www.vintageblues.com
   A virtual mall of on-line vintage clothing stores.

Shopping — General Sites

www.anythingswing.com
   Anything Swing: Selling reproduction clothing (zoot suits, seamed
   stockings), notecards, music, videos, and books.

www.dancestore.com
   Dance Store: Clothes, Bleyer shoes, Frankie Manning videos, and Sears
   thirties and forties fashion books.

www.ebay.com
   eBay: Sit back, put on some swing, and prepare to empty your wallet.
   Thousands of vintage items for sale by auction.

www.thejazzstore.com
   The Jazz Store: A huge selection of books, CDs, posters, and more.

www.savoystyle.com
   SavoyStyle: Featuring everything from Lindy Hop instructional videos
   to T-shirts, books, and shoes. Also includes the Archives of Early Lindy
   Hop, with bios and information on Whitey's Lindy Hoppers.

Movies and Videos

www.flashvideo.com
    Flashback Video: Sales of soundie compilations; one features Jean
    Veloz's *Groovy Movie.*

www.starlightroof.com
    John Cooper's Starlight Roof: Rare and classic videos specializing in
    such genres as swing dancing and Christmas movies.

www.moviesunlimited.com
    Movies Unlimited: Hard-to-find movies, including *Killer Diller* and
    Hellzapoppin'.

RETRO MAGAZINES

Atomic: Living in the Age of Cool. Glossy, well written, and stylish, a great
    new guide to the swing life. $16.00 a year, four issues. 350 Third Avenue,
    Suite 255, New York, NY 10010. 212-448-9877. *www.atomicmag.com*

*Blue Martini Pages: The Who's Who and the What's What of the Swing
    Revolution.* A passionate fanzine. $3.00 per issue. 4877 W. Berkeley
    Road, Phoenix, AZ 85035. 602-415-1992.

Lo-Fi: Easy Living for the Cool Moderns. Covers swing, surf, rockabilly,
    and more. $3.95 per issue. P.O. Box 42, Old Chelsea Station, New York,
    NY 10113-0042. 212-462-3250. *www.nyc-swing.com*

Modern Lounge: Fashion, Cocktails, Music, Cigars. LA's slick new swing
    scene chronicle. $2.95 per issue. 17328 Ventura Boulevard, Suite 164,
    Encino, CA 91316. 818-779-2100. *www.modernlounge.com*

Swivel magazine. Designed like a forties rag, with cool tips on retro
    living. $18.00 a year, six issues. 2695 Broadway, San Diego, CA 92102.
    619-595-0935. *www.swivelmag.com*

SWING ON FILM

They've got great clothes and unbeatable music, but what's with the plot? Swing movies that you'll want to rent just for the storyline are few and far between. That's because many films from the big band era were put together just to showcase the musical and dance talent. "They would often just get four or five groups and throw them in a movie and hope people would want to go see the music part," says Claude Trenier, leader of the early rock 'n' roll group the Treniers, who appeared in a number of movies, including *The Girl Can't Help It*. While most of these movies are readily available on video, some aren't in widespread video release. Check out the Web guide for a short list of companies that sell both hard-to-find classics and compilations of soundies (which were the music videos of their day). So for the nights when you're not out dancing, sit back and get a view of how Hollywood portrays the world of swing.

Ball of Fire (1941, 111 min.)
   In this early forties Howard Hawks comedy, a burlesque dancer (Barbara Stanwyck) moves in with eight professors (including Gary Cooper) to explain the idea of "slang" to them for their new encyclopedia. Sad to say, the movie company, in order to show the movie in the South, cut the scenes showing black trumpeter Roy Eldridge playing with the Krupa band.

The Benny Goodman Story (1955, 116 min.)
   Gene Krupa, singer Martha Tilton, and Lionel Hampton cameo in this drama about the rise to fame of the bandleader (played by a stiff Steve Allen). The story is so-so, but watch this film for the music.

The Big Broadcast (1932, 87 min.)
   A crumbling radio station is saved and rejuvenated by a millionaire who stages an all-star show, featuring Bing Crosby, Cab Calloway, the Boswell Sisters, and the Mills Brothers. Calloway performs "Minnie the Moocher" and "Hot Toddy."

Big Broadcast of 1937 (1936, 102 min.)
   The third installment of the Big Broadcast series, featuring Benny Goodman (in his first film role), Jack Benny, George Burns, and Gracie Allen. The plot's thin: a radio station owner has trouble with sponsors.

The Blues Brothers (1980, 130 min.)
   This John Belushi/Dan Aykroyd classic is about two brothers getting together their old band in an attempt to save the orphanage in which they were raised. Great music, including appearances by Cab Calloway, Aretha Franklin, Ray Charles, and James Brown.

Boardinghouse Blues (1948, 90 min.)
The tenants of a troubled boardinghouse put on a show to save their home in this all-black musical. Moms Mabley and Dusty Fletcher star, with performances by Lucky Millinder's band, Bull Moose Jackson, Una Mae Carlisle, Stump and Stumpy, and more.

Boy! What a Girl (1946, 70 min.)
This mid-forties musical comedy features an almost all-black cast in a story about a group of producers trying to win financial backing for their show. Lots of titillating jitterbugging, actor Tim Moore in drag, and appearances by Gene Krupa, Slam Stewart, and Mary Lou Williams.

Buck Privates (1941, 84 min.)
An Abbott and Costello army comedy featuring dancer Dean Collins and the Andrews Sisters singing "Boogie Woogie Bugle Boy."

Cabin in the Sky (1943, 100 min.)
This Vincente Minnelli–directed musical (his first feature) stars a brilliant black cast including Lena Horne, Louis Armstrong, and Duke Ellington, in a story about angels and devils duking it out for the soul of Little Joe (Eddie "Rochester" Anderson). Although uncomfortably racist, the film includes such gems as Ethel Waters singing "Happiness Is a Thing Called Joe" and Leon James as one of the devil's minions.

The Cotton Club (1984, 127 min.)
Francis Ford Coppola's look at the vibrant nightlife of gangsters and swinging music of Harlem in the early part of the century. Wonderful soundtrack adapted from Ellington and Calloway.

A Day at the Races (1937, 111 min.)
In this Marx Brothers comedy, the slapstick siblings help out a girl who owns a sanitorium and a racehorse. Featuring their typical brand of hilarity and one of the wildest Lindy Hop scenes on film.

DuBarry Was a Lady (1943, 101 min.)
A nightclub owner (Red Skelton) headed for trouble lusts after a beautiful singer (Lucille Ball) in this comedy. Watch for Tommy Dorsey, with drummer Buddy Rich, performing "Well, Git It," plus singers Dick Haymes and Jo Stafford.

The Fabulous Dorseys (1947, 88 min.)
Tepid biography of the brother bandleaders nonetheless features a wonderful jam session with Art Tatum, Charlie Barnet, and Ziggy Elman.

Follow the Boys (1944, 110 min.)
An all-star cast (Marlene Dietrich, Orson Welles, Jeanette MacDonald) rounds out this picture about a man (George Raft) organizing a World

War II–era USO show. Enlivened by performances from the Andrews Sisters, Sophie Tucker, and MacDonald.

The Gene Krupa Story (1959, 101 min.)
Weak biopic, starring Sal Mineo, on the life of the successful jazz drummer covers his drug-possession conviction and fall from grace.

The Girl Can't Help It (1956, 99 min.)
Jayne Mansfield's killer hourglass figure (exaggerated by bullet bras) is one of the attractions in this comedy about a press agent trying to hype the girlfriend of a gangster. Called the best rock 'n' roll movie ever, it's got tons of amazing performances by such artists as Abbey Lincoln, Fats Domino, Julie London, the Platters, Eddie Fontaine, Eddie Cochran, Little Richard, Gene Vincent, and best of all, the Treniers.

The Glenn Miller Story (1954, 116 min.)
A huge hit when it was first released, this convincing biopic stars James Stewart as the patriotic bandleader and includes music from Krupa and Louis Armstrong.

Going Places (1938, 84 min.)
Silly musical about a sporting-goods salesman posing as a jockey nonetheless features Maxine Sullivan and Louis Armstrong doing "Jeepers Creepers."

Groovy Movie (about 1945, short)
This instructional movie is the best place to watch Hollywood-style Lindy dancer Jean Veloz cut a rug.

Hellzapoppin' (1941, 84 min.)
The famous Broadway show is translated by Hollywood, featuring Martha Raye, Ole Olsen, and Chic Johnson. Watch this for its phenomenal Lindy scene, which has never been topped on film.

Hi-De-Ho (1948, 70 min.)
Cab Calloway stars as a bandleader caught between rival gangs.

High Society (1956, 107 min.)
This fifties remake of *The Philadelphia Story* stars Bing Crosby, Grace Kelly (her last film role), Frank Sinatra, and Louis Armstrong, plus renditions of Cole Porter's "True Love," "You're Sensational," and "Did You Evah?"

Hollywood Canteen (1944, 124 min.)
Bette Davis and guest stars such as Joan Crawford, Ida Lupino, Eddie Cantor, and Barbara Stanwyck appear in this comedy that also features Jack Benny and the Andrews Sisters.

Hollywood Hotel (1937, 109 min.)
Benny Goodman and his band, including the famous quartet, perform classic numbers such as "Sing, Sing, Sing." Mel Tormé once said it was a major inspiration. As a youth, he went to see it "no less than five times."

International House (1933, 70 min.)
An odd film with George Burns, Gracie Allen, and Bela Lugosi in a story about a TV experiment bringing a host of strangers to a hotel in Shanghai. Cab Calloway does a classic "Reefer Man."

Jam Session (1947, 77 min.)
Musical about a showgirl (Ann Miller) trying to make it in Hollywood, with music provided by Louis Armstrong, Duke Ellington, Glen Gray, the Pied Pipers, and the Charlie Barnet Orchestra.

Jammin' the Blues (1944, 11 min.)
One of the few respected swing era jazz films, this short includes performances by Lester Young and Harry "Sweets" Edison.

Killer Diller (1948, 73 min.)
Moms Mabley, Nat King Cole, Butterfly McQueen, Andy Kirk, the Congeroo Dancers, and a host of others put on a real show in this vaudeville-style all-black musical.

Miracle of Morgan's Creek (1944, 99 min.)
While not a musical, this film is nevertheless required viewing. Often called the best slapstick comedy ever, this outrageous Preston Sturges feature is about a woman (Betty Hutton) who attends a party, becomes pregnant, and then can't figure out who the dad is.

Mr. Lucky (1943, 100 min.)
Cary Grant plays a Greek gangster type who falls in love with a virtuous woman (Laraine Day). Retro designer Savoia Michele recommends it as "a great flick about ties and one of the best films for clothing."

New Orleans (1947, 89 min.)
Fictionalized account of the birth of jazz, featuring Louis Armstrong, the Woody Herman Orchestra, and Billie Holiday. Holiday, who thought she'd be playing an entertainer, was forced to play a maid; she sings "Do You Know What It Means to Miss New Orleans" with Armstrong and an all-star band.

Ocean's Eleven (1960, 127 min.)
Five Las Vegas casinos. An eleven-man group of scam artists headed by Danny Ocean (Frank Sinatra). One great crime comedy. Catch the Rat Pack in action.

Orchestra Wives (1942, 98 min.)
Glenn Miller is featured in one of swingers' favorite retro movies about
a small-town girl who marries the trumpet player of a traveling band.
Songs include "Serenade in Blue," "At Last," and "I've Got a Girl in
Kalamazoo," and performances by Tex Beneke, the Modernaires, and the
Nicholas Brothers.

Pete Kelly's Blues (1955, 95 min.)
This film re-creates the 1920s jazz age in a story about musicians who
get involved with a gangster. Features Ella Fitzgerald, Janet Leigh, and
Peggy Lee, who was nominated for an Oscar.

Ragtime (1981, 155 min.)
Milos Forman directed E. L. Doctorow's semifictionalized account of
America circa 1906 with an all-star cast, including James Cagney, Debbie
Allen, Mary Steenburgen, Howard E. Rollins Jr., and Elizabeth
McGovern.

Ride 'Em Cowboy (1942, 86 min.)
This Abbott and Costello flick about two hot dog vendors on an Arizona
ranch features Ella Fitzgerald singing "A Tisket a Tasket," plus dancing
from Dean Collins.

Robin and the Seven Hoods (1964, 123 min.)
The Rat Pack (along with Bing Crosby and Peter Falk) is in full force
once again in this story of a gang leader (Frank Sinatra) in Chicago in
1928. Music includes such songs as "My Kind of Town," "Style," and "Mr.
Booze."

Rock Around the Clock (1956, 77 min.)
See this film about the birth of rock 'n' roll simply for the performances
by Bill Haley and His Comets, the Platters, Tony Martinez, and Freddie
Bell and His Bellboys.

A Song Is Born (1948, 113 min.)
This flat remake of *Ball of Fire* stars Danny Kaye and Virginia Mayo as
the male and female leads; the film is buoyed by musical appearances
by Benny Goodman, Louis Armstrong, Lionel Hampton, and Tommy
Dorsey.

Springtime in the Rockies (1942, 91 min.)
A load of frivolity, this film about a feuding Broadway duo stars Betty
Grable and John Payne, with hilarious numbers by Carmen Miranda
(doing "Chattanooga Choo Choo" in Portuguese), bandleader Harry
James, and the wonderful Helen Forrest singing "I Had the Craziest
Dream."

Stage Door Canteen (1943, 132 min.)
This wartime romance between a soldier and a nightclub hostess boasts a staggering number of cameos. Count Basie, Benny Goodman, Kay Kyser, Tallulah Bankhead, Ray Bolger, Helen Hayes, Harpo Marx, Ethel Waters, Katharine Hepburn, Ethel Merman, Paul Muni, and Gypsy Rose Lee all pop up.

Stormy Weather (1943, 77 min.)
Lead actress Lena Horne sings the bluesy title song, Fats Waller does a devilish rendition of "Ain't Misbehavin'," and Cab Calloway and the Nicholas Brothers show up too.

The Strip (1951, 85 min.)
Mickey Rooney stars as a former musician entangled with a group of gangsters trying to help a woman (Sally Forrest) succeed in the movie industry. The film is supported by performances from Louis Armstrong, Earl Hines, and Jack Teagarden.

Sun Valley Serenade (1941, 86 min.)
Figure-skater Sonja Henie stars in this improbable musical comedy as a Norweigan war refugee traveling with her foster parent (John Payne) and the Glenn Miller Orchestra to Sun Valley. Miller performs "Chattanooga Choo Choo" and "In the Mood."

Sweet and Low-Down (1944, 75 min.)
A so-so story of a trombonist who hits the big time in Benny Goodman's Orchestra. Jam sequences featuring Goodman are the highlight.

Swing Kids (1993, 112 min.)
This period film focuses on the struggle of a group of German teenagers (played by Christian Bale, Robert Sean Leonard, and Noah Wyle) who relish American swing music and are persecuted because of it during the Second World War.

Swing Parade of 1946 (1946, 74 min.)
The Three Stooges enliven this icky musical, as does Louis Jordan performing "Caldonia."

Swing Time (1936, 103 min.)
In this winning film, Fred Astaire stars as a dancer who's engaged to a girl in his hometown but falls for Ginger Rogers when he hits New York. It includes such musical gems as "A Fine Romance," "Pick Yourself Up," and "The Way You Look Tonight."

Swingers (1996, 96 min.)
This indie hit comedy is the money. Set in Las Vegas and LA, *Swingers* focuses on the romantic mishaps of a young man living in the retro-

lounge and swing scene. With its fab clothes and lingo, this slick but ultimately heartwarming flick launched the careers of both its stars, Jon Favreau and Vince Vaughn, and the band Big Bad Voodoo Daddy. It climactic swing dance scene, with actress Heather Graham, takes place at the Derby.

Syncopation (1942, 88 min.)
Lame story about the history of jazz starring Jackie Cooper as a trumpet player. Nonetheless, features a swinging jam session with performances by all the regulars: Charlie Barnet, Benny Goodman, Gene Krupa, and Harry James.

Two Girls and a Sailor (1944, 124 min.)
Two sisters (June Allyson and Gloria DeHaven) manage a canteen for GIs and become involved with a sailor (Van Johnson). Features a cameo by Ava Gardner and wonderful music numbers by such stalwarts as Harry James, Lena Horne, and Xavier Cugat.

You Can't Have Everything (1937, 99 min.)
A nice show-biz musical replete with all sorts of backstage comedy and three Louis Prima songs. Stars Don Ameche, Alice Faye, and Gypsy Rose Lee.

Zoot Suit (1981, 103 min.)
A filmed theatrical production, this story of Chicano gang members in the early forties stars Edward James Olmos.

JAZZ MUSEUMS

Want to check out one of Louis Armstrong's trumpets? Gape at a stylin' pair of cat's-eyes rhinestone glasses once worn by Ella Fitzgerald? Or stand near one of trumpeter Harry James's original bandstands? Visit one of the growing number of jazz museums and halls of fame around the country.

Detroit. The Graystone International Hall of Fame Jazz Museum (1521 Broadway, 313-963-3813) displays instruments, memorabilia, and pieces from the great Graystone Ballroom, one of the finest dance palaces of the swing era.

Kansas City. The impressive Kansas City Jazz Museum (1616 East Eighteenth Street, 816-474-8463) not only includes Duke Ellington, Ella Fitzgerald, and Louis Armstrong artifacts, it also provides a great audio tour of jazz music.

New Orleans. Among the treasures at the Louisiana State Museum Jazz Collection (located inside the old U.S. Mint, 400 Esplanade, 800-568-6968) are instruments played by Louis Armstrong, Sidney Bechet, and Bix Beiderbecke.

Orlando. At the Down Beat Jazz Hall of Fame (Universal Studios' City-Walk, 407-224-2189), you can not only check out instruments such as Glenn Miller's first trombone and a pair of Lionel Hampton's vibra-phone mallets but also hear live music at the CityJazz club.

Palm Beach. The new Big Band Hall of Fame Museum in West Palm Beach (812 Fern Street, 561-655-1113) has a trove of swing-era treasures. Here's a short list: Harry James's trumpet, one of Count Basie's captain's caps, a Gene Krupa drum set, a collection of ties worn by bandleaders, and a mirrored ball from the famous Aragon Ballroom in Chicago.

BIBLIOGRAPHY

Benny Goodman and the Swing Era, by James Lincoln Collier (Oxford University Press, 1989)

Beyond Category: The Life and Genius of Duke Ellington, by John Edward Hasse (Simon and Schuster, 1993)

The Big Bands, by George Thomas Simon (Schirmer Books, 1981)

Black Beauty, White Heat: A Pictorial History of Classic Jazz, 1920–1950, by Frank Driggs and Harris Lewine (Da Capo Press, 1996)

The Cotton Club, by Jim Haskins (Random House, 1977)

Dialogues in Swing: Intimate Conversations with the Stars of the Big Band Era, by Fred Hall, edited by Eugene D. Wheeler (Pathfinder Publishing, 1989)

The Duke Ellington Reader, edited by Mark Tucker (Oxford University Press, 1993)

Everyday Fashions of the Forties as Pictured in Sears Catalogues, edited by Joanne Olian (Dover, 1992)

Fit to Be Tied: Vintage Ties of the Forties and Early Fifties, by Rod Dyer and Ron Spark (Abbeville Press, 1987)

Good Morning Blues: The Autobiography of Count Basie, by Count Basie with Albert Murray (Da Capo Press, 1995)

Hamp: An Autobiography, by Lionel Hampton with James Haskins (Amistad, 1993)

The History of Jazz, by Ted Gioia (Oxford University Press, 1997)

Jazz Anecdotes, by Bill Crow (Oxford University Press, 1990)

Jazz Cavalcade: The Inside Story of Jazz, by Dave Dexter Jr. (Criterion, 1946)

Jazz Dance: The Story of American Vernacular Dance, by Marshall Stearns and Jean Stearns (Da Capo Press, 1994)

Jazz Style in Kansas City and the Southwest, by Ross Russell (Da Capo Press, 1997)

Just a Gigolo: The Life and Times of Louis Prima, by Gary Boulard (University of Southwestern Louisiana Press, 1989)

Lady Sings the Blues, by Billie Holiday with William Duffy (Penguin Books, 1995)

Let the Good Times Roll: The Story of Louis Jordan and His Music, by John Chilton (University of Michigan Press, 1994)

Lost Chords: White Musicians and Their Contribution to Jazz 1915–1945, by Richard M. Sudhalter (Oxford University Press, 1999)

MusicHound Jazz: The Essential Album Guide, edited by Steve Holtje and Nancy Ann Lee (Visible Ink Press, 1998)

MusicHound Lounge: The Essential Album Guide to Martini Music and Easy Listening, edited by Steve Knopper (Visible Ink Press, 1998)

MusicHound Swing: The Essential Album Guide, edited by Steve Knopper (Visible Ink Press, 1999)

Music Is My Mistress, by Duke Ellington (Da Capo Press, 1988)

The New Grove Dictionary of Jazz, edited by Barry Kernfeld (St. Martin's Press, 1994)

The Penguin Encyclopedia of Popular Music, edited by Donald Clarke (Penguin Books, 1999)

The Penguin Guide to Jazz on Compact Disc, edited by Richard Cook and Brian Morton (Penguin Books, 1999)

The Rolling Stone *Jazz and Blues Album Guide,* edited by John Swenson (Rolling Stone Press, published by Random House, 1999)

Shoes: Fashion and Fantasy, by Colin McDowell (Rizzoli, 1989)

Swing Changes: Big-Band Jazz in New Deal America, by David W. Stowe (Harvard University Press, 1996)

Swing! The New Retro Renaissance, by V. Vale (V/Search Publications, 1998)

Swingin' at the Savoy: The Memoir of a Jazz Dancer, by Norma Miller with Evette Jensen (Temple University Press, 1996)

Swingin' the Dream: Big Band Jazz and the Rebirth of American Culture, by Lewis A. Erenberg (University of Chicago Press, 1998)

The Way You Wear Your Hat: Frank Sinatra and the Lost Art of Livin', by Bill Zehme (HarperCollins, 1997)

Zoot Suits and Second-Hand Dresses, edited by Angela McRobbie (Unwin Hyman, 1988)

ACKNOWLEDGMENTS

I'm grateful to the countless members of the swing world who offered their time and expertise to help me research and write this book. My thanks go out to Scotty Morris for writing the foreword, Bill Elliott, Eddie Reed, Lionel Hampton, Jonathan Bixby, Steve Lucky and Carmen Getit, Margaret Batiuchok, Petra Mason, Lavay Smith and Chris Siebert, Darrow Cannizzaro, Heidi Richman, Morty Okin, Chris Chavira, Margie Cormier, Paul Kelly, James Hrabak, and Max Young. Dance Manhattan's Teddy Kern opened her heart to me and was constantly available, reading drafts of the dance chapter at the last minute and letting me take Lindy classes at the studio. Similarly, Chuck Haddix, sound recording specialist at the Marr Sound Archives at the University of Missouri, Kansas City, read the chapter on the history of swing and offered helpful suggestions. During a wonderful afternoon at their home in San Francisco, trumpeter Johnny Coppola and his wife, singer Frances Lynne, helped really turn me on to the music. Thanks also to Tophatters' Marie and Ted Lee and the staff of the Metropolitan Museum of Art's Costume Institute.

Thank you to all the swing experts who took the time to fill out my exhaustive survey of the top neoswing albums: Rich Conaty, host of *Swing Time* on New York's WFUV 90.7 FM at Fordham University; Patrick Cullen, DJ of the Atlantic Dance club in Orlando; Melbourne, Florida's DJ Cutter; *Modern Lounge* associate editor David Elsensohn; *Swivel*'s Tammy Francis; Oregon swinger Keith Hazleton; New York DJ Chad "Chops" Kincaid; *Anyswinggoes.com*'s Doug LeClair; Bo Lewis, DJ of the Big Band Dance Party on WNAV 1430 AM, Annapolis, Maryland; *Blue Martini Pages'* editor Lucky Hand; Detroit DJ Sean McDonnell; Dante Murphy, who spins the tunes at Philadelphia's Five Spot; Seattle's Leslie Price of CSL Productions; Nicole Seefeldt, aka DJ Curly, of

KSDJ 90.7 FM, Brookings, South Dakota; New York's "Lo-Fi" Lee Sobel; Denver DJ Tim "Dogboy" Wieser of Ninth Avenue West; *Nocturne.com*'s Karen Wilson; Gregg Wolfe, producer of Minneapolis's *Swanktown Radio* on KBEM 88.5 FM; and Pennsylvania 6-5000 cyberswinger Joe Wood.

A number of friends and colleagues in New York were also instrumental in helping me complete the book. I'm thankful for the invaluable contributions of Perry Turcotte, Anna Holmes, and *Atomic* magazine editor Leslie Rosenberg. Jason Schneider provided the book's stylish illustrations. My friends and family, including Richard Anderson, Lisa Light, Michael Kroll, Caroline Khella, Bill Auerbach, Nadia Murray, and Jeannette Walls were unfailingly supportive. My brother Steve Pener and father, Harry Pener, helped with research. Brad Hurtado, Scott Wooledge, and Fred Bernstein got me through the hectic last week. *Entertainment Weekly*'s Clarissa Cruz first gave my name to Little, Brown, while Alexandria Carrion, Suzanne Regan, Rob Brunner, and Will Lee offered assistance as well. Thanks also to my agent, David Chalfant of IMG.

Finally, there are two people without whom this book would never have happened at all. *Entertainment Weekly*'s assistant managing editor Maggie Murphy first assigned me to write about swing for the weekly in 1998. That story ultimately caught the eye of my sharp and savvy editor, Little, Brown's Michael Liss, a swing dancer himself who, I'm honored to say, is just two degrees of separation away from the original Savoy dancers. (His teacher Margaret Batiuchok was one of the first to meet up with members of Whitey's Lindy Hoppers in the 1980s.) When Michael called me up and asked me if I wanted to write a book on swing, little did I know what an enriching and captivating experience it would turn out to be.